PRAISE FOR
ELLIOTT SMITH AND THE BIG NOTHING

"Nugent does a fine job of getting to the heart of Smith's craft and seems to truly understand the pop culture moment in which he flourished."

—*New York Press*

"Smith's heartsick fans will be grateful for this effort."

—*New York Times Book Review*

"[Nugent is] a competent writer, with a knack for comical insight and concise description that fits well with Smith's own songwriting."

—*The Wire*

"[Nugent] did his research and left few stones unturned in telling Smith's relatively short and very sad story."

—*Chicago Sun-Times*

"Nugent is an author driven by a passion to understand a hero (or antihero), and his book is fascinating for its depth of reporting and detail."

—*Willamette Week*

"[This] book serves as a fitting tribute to a complex, much-missed entertainer."

—*Gotham*

"The book's enduring strength lies in its passionate analysis of [Smith's] music, lyrics and, most revelatory, recording methods."

—*Pavement*

"[Nugent] o⟨...⟩ ⟨...⟩r, layperson-friendly way.

—*MSNBC.com*

"Nugent displays an affectionate understanding of his subject."
—*Blender*

"[Nugent] is quite confident in his grasp of Smith's psyche."
—*Seattle Weekly*

"Open[s] a window of insight into our reluctant hero [Elliott Smith]."
—*Austin Chronicle*

"The author understands the magnificently thick atmosphere of Smith's music intimately, and submerges us in it."
—*Salon.com*

"Nugent manages to gather enough of [Smith's] spirit to provide a clear picture of his talent and impact without overstating his case."
—*CNN.com*

"The connection Smith forged with his fans continues after his death and is sure to increase . . . with Nugent's biography."
—*Portland Oregonian*

"[Nugent] breaks through the mystique behind Smith's songs."
—*Paste*

"Nugent has done a solid job of research and reporting in this worthwhile biography, a book clearly written by an admirer of his subject, but one who doesn't let his admiration get in the way of describing a life that had its good times and bad."
—*Glorious Noise*

"Elliott Smith was on the verge of true celebrity . . . You'll never hear him sing live or even bump into him in a mall somewhere. This book is all you have, and it's worth reading. It's as close to him as you'll ever get."
—*Curled Up with a Good Book*

Elliott Smith

AND THE BIG NOTHING

Benjamin Nugent

DA CAPO PRESS
A Member of the Perseus Books Group

Cataloging-in-Publication data for this book is available from the Library of
Congress.

First Da Capo Press edition 2004
First Da Capo Press paperback edition 2005
ISBN-13 978-0-306-81447-1 (pbk.)
ISBN-10 0-306-81447-1 (pbk.)

Published by Da Capo Press
A Member of the Perseus Books Group
http://www.dacapopress.com

Da Capo Press books are available at special discounts for bulk purchases in
the U.S. by corporations, institutions, and other organizations. For more information, please contact the Special Markets Department at the Perseus
Books Group, 11 Cambridge Center, Cambridge, MA 02142, or call (800)
255–1514 or (617) 252–5298, or e-mail special.markets@perseusbooks.com.

3 4 5 6 7 8 9—08 07 06

IN MEMORY OF

AK, CR,

IN RETROSPECT SWEET KIDS

CONTENTS

ACKNOWLEDGMENTS

Alexandra Van Buren, Amy Williams, and Ben Schafer were essential. I was stunned they let me focus on Smith's life and work even after his death became a news story.

A stranger to Elliott Smith's kin, I found them reasonable and polite. For information I turned to Smith's friends and acquaintances; Marc Swanson was especially valuable for persuading others to talk and for setting straight many of my errors, as was Bill Santen for being the first of Smith's colleagues to trust me. David McConnell, Dorien Garry, JJ Gonson, EV Day, Rob Schnapf, Pete Krebs, Andrew Morgan and everyone else quoted herein made the book much better than it otherwise would have been and enabled me to avoid anonymous sources.

Gabriel Snyder led me to Alec Bemis, who led me to two crucial interviews. My sister Annie Baker duped Hampshire College security forces so that I could look at freshman photos. Jessica Flashman, Rachel Maude Reilich, Laura Stupsker and the Icehouse provided places to crash. Props to Matthew Elblonk.

I am forever indebted to Mel Flashman and my parents, Conn Nugent and Linda Baker.

INTRODUCTION

$\mathcal{E}$LLIOTT SMITH SITS hunched in a wooden chair on a stage in Portland, Oregon, in February 1999. He lists forward over his acoustic guitar to edge his mouth close to the mic, wearing the thin, conspiratorial smile of a person accustomed to talking to himself. His fingers pluck at the strings professionally, but his voice is quiet and he barely looks up between songs, so it's easy to believe he's singing alone. After the applause that follows each song, the hometown crowd falls into a clean silence—nobody reacts to the music, nobody moves, and nobody talks. The crowd doesn't want to hear him perform, it seems, so much as it wants to overhear him.

This is a singer whose solo career started out as a private affair, a series of songs he wrote largely under the stairwell of an old house in this city with no intention of making them public. Except for his father, Gary, and a scattering of old friends, the audience doesn't know this. But Smith's records and his concerts retain the feeling of internal dialogue and everybody picks up on it. Only when he acknowledges requests does Smith shatter the illusion that he's singing alone.

"How was New York?" somebody asks; he moved there from Portland almost two years ago, and now he's spending more and more time in Los Angeles. "Okay," says Smith, "I didn't like it better there than I did here." This is taken as a ringing endorsement of Portland—more applause. Later on, after a particularly long ovation, he stokes the local pride: "It's really fun to play here." Elliott Smith, by Elliott Smith standards, is really working the crowd this time. He's dressed like a punk, with white patches on his knees and a wool cap pulled over his limp black hair, but it's the quietest punk rock show I've seen. Smith sings like he's contemplating secrets, and he is.

-Ð-

Three years later, I'll ask Lucinda Williams what advice she'd give a novice songwriter. She answers without hesitation: You have to look into the darker side of life. Smith's music exemplifies this idea; his life had good and bad in it like anybody else's, but he exercised a gift for writing about melancholy. He wasn't the stricken cartoon depressive people thought he was; he was a wit, a philosopher, and a workhorse. But he was also an Orpheus, happy to explore the depths. It's often said shortly after the death of a musician that there was nothing romantic about his problems, but Smith embroidered songs around scraps of turbulent emotional experience until the problems were romantic. That was the bond between his music and his life.

The means by which that life ended have been "undetermined" since the LAPD decided in January 2004 that it acted hastily in calling the events of October 21, 2003, an apparent suicide. So far, nobody's been charged with murder. There is no open-and-shut case for suicide or for homicide, but there is evidence that suggests some possible answers.

Some readers, no doubt, hope for a book about Smith's death, and some Elliott Smith fans surely will be offended by any discussion of his personal problems. It might be possible to fill a book with reminiscences of Smith giving money to the homeless and doing the moonwalk, but that would be as deceptive as writing a book that described only his sad moments. If I were to write exclusively about Smith smoking crack and weeping in taxi cabs it would be the Gossip Page version of his life; but the sanitized character sometimes put forth by people who liked Smith is a Personals version: "Good at Ms. Pac-Man, great sense of humor, loves to dance and talk Kierkegaard." Neither provides much insight into how he came up with his songs, how he developed his empathy for the downtrodden, or how he acquired the wisdom evident in his lyrics.

Besides, with some artists, a certain amount of bad behavior is excused by the strength of the work that dwells and feeds on that behavior. For those of us who didn't quarrel with Smith personally, no self-destructiveness or self-deceit on his part could drain the fund of goodwill built up by his records. I'm a typical Elliott Smith fan, meaning that I fell in love with his music at a time when I wanted to fashion a noose out of my vintage t-shirt collection. In my first summer after college I broke up with my girlfriend, got into car accidents, and entered data into a computer at a bookstore; Smith's first album, *Roman Candle*, became the only object, inanimate or otherwise, that understood me.

While the role Smith played for so many people like me was companion in misery, Smith recoiled from articles that suggested he might be a poster boy for depression, arguing that the sadness in his words was necessary for making the happiness meaningful. In one sense this was an argument belied by action—Smith's behavior and conversation often suggested he *was* more genuinely sad than most rock musicians. But he had a valid point in that his themes were different from those of misery's usual representatives in rock. Robert Smith of The Cure, Trent Reznor of Nine Inch Nails, and Kurt Cobain all aimed their curses outward—at lovers, government conspiracies, and complacent masses—as often as they aimed them inward. In Elliott Smith's songs the harsh light of his scrutiny shines almost exclusively inward, onto his most personal troubles. The happy moments come when the narrator finds he is liked and understood despite what that light has thrown into relief—when the self-doubt recedes and allows sweeter emotions to take root.

Smith was no egomaniac; he criticized and doubted himself to the point of excess, and self-doubt was one of his undoings as a man and one of his great distinctions as a songwriter. His narrators often feel contempt for their own impulses. From "There was a grown man dying from fright," the first words of "Division Day," to "I think I'm gonna make the same mistake twice," a refrain in "Punch and Judy," Smith fixates on character flaws. When you match up his life with his music, or consult his close friends, quoted in these pages, it becomes clear that sometimes he sings about himself.

In 1991, the year Smith moved from Amherst, Massachusetts, where he attended Hampshire College, back to Portland, Oregon, where he'd been an honor student at Lincoln High School, grunge was about to enter its heyday. A chunk of the nation's youth would soon cling to the pronouncements of Kurt Cobain, who was given to the inflammatory and the dramatic: "Rape me," "God is gay, burn the flag," "I wish I could eat your cancer when you turn black." Cobain became, to his own amazement and consternation, a messianic figure for his millions of teenage and twenty-something fans. He publicly declared Portland a candidate for The Next Seattle, and the city was awash in loud rock bands. Smith was in one of them, Heatmiser, and unsatisfied with the music he was making. "I've been recording stuff on my own since I was in high school. By the time I was in a band, I lived in a part of the world where it was all grunge music," he once told *Rolling Stone*. "Which I liked, but it seemed like, why would anybody wanna hear this right now?"

He left behind grunge for four-track voice and guitar recordings, and wrote songs that aimed, in his own words, "to show what it's like to be a person." That may seem a hokey mission statement at first blush, but Smith's songs were indeed concerned with the emotional fluctuations of everyday life, the ones brought on by average loneliness, decadence, apathy, poverty, love. His lyrics didn't have to take the listener inside tantrums, the way Nirvana's or Pearl Jam's or Bikini Kill's lyrics did. Bands like Belle and Sebastian, Bright Eyes, and The Strokes followed Smith in that direction, his albums having represented rock's first steps toward reinventing itself once the well of grunge had run dry.

There was a hole in popular music of the late '90s where rock's songwriters should have been. From 1995 to 2000, when most of Smith's music was released, it was the best of times for Tricky, Wyclef Jean, Orbital, The Backstreet Boys, and, at the very end of the decade, the burgeoning New York dance-rock scene. Meanwhile, the audience for pop music decided pop could lose the people with guitars who delivered songs they'd written themselves from a seated position. After Kurt Cobain's suicide in 1994, alternative-rock records stopped selling like they had when he was alive. The alt bands that survived, like Silverchair and Bush, stuck to the volume level and bellowing quotient of their predecessors but dispensed with the wordplay and folk overtones that set Cobain apart from Scott Weiland, the sensitive belter of Stone Temple Pilots. The indie rock world from which Nirvana had sprung was growing disillusioned with singer-songwriters too. Pavement broke up almost precisely at the end of the century. Other comparatively high-profile indie bands of the time, like The Make-Up, played rock-star caricatures on stage and on their CDs, retaliating against the fake earnestness of big-money alt-rock by being fakes. Still others floated off into experimental music largely because, as a delighted Thurston Moore observed, it was one genre guaranteed never to become popular, immune to dilution by major labels and hungry imitators.

Most of the bands that helped Smith carry the torch for songwriting once he hit it big in 1998 didn't find widespread recognition, but there were a few notable exceptions: The Magnetic Fields, a vehicle for Stephin Merritt, Smith's rival as a lyricist and melody writer, and Belle and Sebastian, who followed in Smith's footsteps more closely than any other band of the time period, achieved a degree of fame a year or two after he did. Belle and Sebastian's frontman, Stuart Murdoch, laid down his intentions in "Get Me Away from Here I'm Dying," off *If You're Feeling Sinister*: "Nobody writes them like they used to/So it may as well be me." If Smith had written a manifesto, that assertion would have been near the top. Smith had started writing catchy, traditional folk-rock songs with explicitly personal rather than sociopolitical content when grunge was at its peak commercially and artistically; when grunge died, it turned out Smith had chanced upon a key to rock's revival.

That leaves the questions of what forces in Smith's life made him the songwriter he was, and where he picked up a moral philosophy that sometimes bordered on the Puritanical. Something compelled him to depart from the loud rock of Heatmiser and take up a folk-rock sound, with a vocal style so different from his previous one that it's hard to identify the two styles as belonging to the same singer. Something made him sink into a troubled period toward the end of his life. The same characters, events, and ideas that shaped his songs shaped the trajectory of his thirty-four years.

One of the unfortunate aftereffects of a premature death is the haze of convenient oversimplification that settles over the victim. To much of the press, Smith quite understandably looked like a simple case of an artist too sensitive to function in the hard world, let alone in the wasteland of Los Angeles. Some journalists did ample detective work on his death but nobody had much time to take a close look at the life that preceded it. Fans Photoshop'd the word "Hero" over his picture and propped it up against the Solutions store wall in Los Angeles (previously photographed for the cover of *Figure 8*).

Neither the sensitive-martyr nor the hero tributes get Smith right. The Smith that materializes in interviews with people who loved him is a tough man, the kind that cracks his friends up at a bar even as they worry about his problems. And he often wrote songs from the perspective of an anti-hero, a character who leads by negative example. There was a trace in that narrator of Johnny Boy from Martin Scorsese's *Mean Streets*, the delinquent street kid who courted death by racking up debt to small-time mobsters. The extremity of Johnny Boy's behavior awakened those around him to their own subtler self-destruction and self-deceit. When he died, he wasn't a martyr; he had provoked destruction for no good reason and he knew it. But the effect he had on people who observed him was a kind of salvation. They saw he was a version of them, and with that epiphany came a shot at grace.

Smith probably wouldn't have cared for the idea of a book being written about him. It would have offended his humility and his desire to fashion his own identity. His position would have been that he was just an artist trying to get through life and make music. One of the most concise summaries I've encountered of Smith's view of himself came to me from his friend, the sculptor E. V. Day:

"We bonded talking about being an artist, talking about the loneliness, the solitude, talking about who has control, and why it's important to make work. We talked with wonder and conflict about what we do. He had the ability to be very funny, but he also had the sadness, and his ironies made him a dynamic person. He always wanted to be truthful and real; he wasn't a phony. He was a very pure artist. And when you live with that kind of purity, it's really hard to deal with the rest of the world. Because you're not playing on the same field. . . . It's sort of about acknowledging that you're so lonely in this individuality that in a way there is no payoff. You're just trying to do more of what you do and stay alive."

This is the story of an artist who just wanted to do what he did and stay alive, and there's nothing simple about that. First he did a lot of good work, and suffered, and survived. Then he was rewarded for his work, and he numbed himself, worked less, and did not survive. This book will provide clues to how it happened. Smith threw himself into the labor of self-expression to the point that he came to need it. Maybe this book will illuminate for a seventeen-year-old taking guitar lessons what it means to live that way.

One

AN INSTRUMENTAL: "STAIRWAY TO HEAVEN"

STEVEN PAUL SMITH was born at 12:59 a.m. on August 6, 1969, at Clarkson Hospital in Omaha. The hospital is about fifteen blocks west of the Mutual of Omaha building and one block east of Saddle Creek Road, which arcs through the prosperous neighborhood that spawned the founders of the indie rock label Saddle Creek Records.

Steven Smith's parents, a twenty-four-year-old medical student named Gary Mac Smith and his twenty-five-year-old wife, Bunny Smith, née Bunny Kay Berryman, lived nearby on 41st Street, according to his birth certificate. The apartment complex still stands, and if it stood in a place with greater extremes of wealth and poverty than those of the tidy neighborhood surrounding the Nebraska Medical Center campus, it would flirt with squalor. But in its current context, with students carrying their backpacks home from class and nearby vegetarian dining, the building looks merely humble and uncomfortable, like a cut-rate roadside motel. It's shaped like a C, with a tiny courtyard of grass bisected by a cement path filling in the middle. The apartments are small, conjoined brick bungalows. It's hard to imagine they allow an optimum level of privacy. They certainly wouldn't allow a young couple with a newborn optimum space. But it was a one-minute walk from where Gary took classes. The hospital where baby Steven was born was essentially part of the campus.

This must have been a trying time for the Smiths, he a native Nebraskan, she a Texan. They would part ways soon after the baby arrived, and Bunny would move with her son back to the state where she was born. The couple had married in Dallas in 1966, when Gary was already living in the little apartment on 41st Street. When Steven was one-and-a-half, in 1970, Bunny filed for divorce and was granted custody of their only child, while Gary, who had just earned his MD from the University of Nebraska College of Medicine, was granted visitation rights and asked to pay child support. He would go on to become a psychiatrist in Portland, Oregon, where he lives today.

Portland would be the place Steven Smith went when his family life in Texas didn't work out, and where he became a professional musician. But Texas was a well from which Smith drew material, the place where he experienced life outside the liberal cities and college towns where he spent the rest of his days. He had a tattoo in the shape of the state on his arm, and while he might have scoffed at that tattoo's significance, he pondered the Texan side of his family and his Texan childhood until the last.

Bunny's family had roots in Texas. She was born in Beaumont near the Gulf coast to a family of musicians eluded by commercial success—everybody played something and everybody had a day job. Smith told *Under the Radar* magazine that his maternal grandfather installed signs for a living. Bunny's parents still live close enough to Dallas to attend local Elliott Smith tributes; they showed up at one hosted by a local record store.

To see the environment that molded Smith's childhood one must travel nearly 600 miles south of Omaha to the metroplex of Dallas–Fort Worth. It's a sprawling fusion of two Southern business cities that has come to resemble urban Southern California with its sailor knots of freeways and armies of strip malls and chain restaurants. The western-wear boot and hat shops don't become a feature of the landscape until you leave city limits, but it's still Texas—there are preachers all over the radio, and folks in the area hear more country music than anything else. There's the drawl and the Southern courtesy in everyday talk at shops and bars, along with traffic jams that are Angeleno in their scale and bitterness. Texas-sized American flags are visible from the freeway that snakes through the city center.

-ᴓ-

It's March 2004, a rainy day in Dallas, and heading south from downtown, first on the 35 and then on the 67, the drive to Duncanville takes about twenty minutes. A beige wooden sign welcomes me to town, and shortly thereafter I pass churches representing a full range of protestant denominations. The first church-ordained message that confronts me is spelled out on the marquee sign for a branch of the Church of Christ: "READ THE BIBLE IT WILL SCARE THE HELL OUT OF YOU."

This is where Smith spent his boyhood, in Duncanville, De Soto, and Cedar Hill, adjacent towns off the 67 freeway south of downtown Dallas. These are streets full of ranch houses and malls, streets that occasionally erupt in an explosion of passion for either Christianity or football. By the side of Camp Wisdom Road, one of the main thoroughfares, there's a new megachurch roughly the size of an airport terminal. Churches abound, and they occupy relatively new buildings, as do local residences. Away from the larger streets is straight-up blue-collar and middle-class suburbia: one-story houses packed tight into envelopes of green. Some of the houses and lawns are spic-and-span, but some clapboards sport patches of rotten wood and some lawns patches of weeds, like soft spots on an apple. It's spring and there are purple blossoms everywhere.

A quarter of Duncanville's 36,000 residents are black, a fifth Hispanic—substantially larger proportions of both minority groups than in the United States population at large. The local used-CD shop has a lone copy of Smith's fourth solo album, *XO*, but it has a whole section devoted to local hip-hop. It's the kind of suburban landscape often portrayed as housing unbroken fields of white families, but a lot of the people walking around local malls aren't white. Duncanville is also diverse economically, in a more obvious way than one might expect: In a mall parking lot, a homeless-looking guy approaches me to beg through the open window of my car.

Drive west on Camp Wisdom past the megachurch and a series of strip malls, and eventually you will see a football stadium towering on your left. It's about the size of the football stadium owned by almost any amply endowed small Northeastern liberal arts college. A sign affixed to it consists of a circular drawing of a raging panther's head and red letters reading "Panther Stadium." This is a facility of Duncanville High School, and from even a slight distance it dwarfs the flat but expansive school complex. Aside from the larger churches, it's the most imposing structure for miles, and the sign's fang-filled maw seems as heartfelt a declaration of collective identity as the industrial-sized cross that bisects the front of the new megachurch. It's a martial exhortation, and so is the slogan that appears occasionally on signs by the road: "Duncanville: City of Champions."

In 1973, a month before Steven Smith turned four, Bunny Smith became Bunny Welch when she married Charles Hughes Welch, Jr., a native of Longview, Texas. The marriage was presided over by an elder of the Reorganized Church of Jesus Christ of Latter-day Saints. That sect, which shortened its name to Community of Christ in 2001, is the second-largest denomination of the Latter-day Saint movement founded by Joseph Smith in the nineteenth century, the Church of Jesus Christ of Latter-day Saints being the largest at 11 million strong (according to its own estimate). Community of Christ members read the Book of Mormon along with the Bible but don't generally call themselves Mormons because of the term's association with the Church of Jesus Christ of Latter-day Saints and because they believe the term was not originally associated with the church. Community of Christ claims about 250,000 members, and its headquarters are in Missouri, not Utah. The elder's ministration of Bunny's second marriage suggests that she and Charles Welch were Reorganized Church followers at the time. But Steve Pickering and Mark Merritt, friends of Steven Smith's from junior high, distinctly remember Steven, Bunny, and Charlie attending a local Methodist church—it was Merritt's church and the Welches started attending it when Smith was in junior high.

The differences between the Mormon church and Community of Christ date back to the death of Joseph Smith, when one contingent, led by Brigham Young, settled around Utah's Salt Lake, and another, the Reorganized Church, named Joseph Smith's son Joseph Smith III its new ordained leader and remained in the Midwest. Community of Christ's world headquarters are in Independence, Missouri, the place Joseph Smith proclaimed was the center of Zion, God's idyllic kingdom on earth. For over a hundred years the church was run by Joseph Smith's patrilineal descendents. The Reorganized Church never accepted the nineteenth-century century Utah Mormon practice of polygamy, and it came to reject secret temple rites and the baptism of the dead, two of the Mormons' most distinctive and controversial practices. In the mid-'80s, the Reorganized Church authorized ordination of women as elders, which the Church of Jesus Christ of Latter-day Saints still does not do. The church's decision to change its name a few years ago is generally thought to reflect a desire among prominent members to no longer define itself in relation to the Mormon church and to move closer to mainstream Protestantism. Community of Christ's official literature, as one might expect, is less conservative than that of the Church of Jesus Christ of Latter-day Saints. It allows that "there is no official church creed that must be followed by all members." The church also supports the organization Call for Renewal, which is run by an evangelical Christian whose stances are left of center on poverty and environmental issues. Relatively liberal as it may be, Community of Christ is clear on the subject of judgment: "Our eternal destiny is determined by God according to divine wisdom and love and according to our response to God's call to us. God's judgment is just and is based on the kind of people we have become in relation to the potential of our lives."

The threat of divine judgment never completely left Smith alone in adulthood, as he explained to *Spin*: "Mainly church just made me really scared of hell. It still just scares the shit out of me. If you grew up being threatened with that, it's really hard to be like, 'Oh, it probably doesn't exist.' Even if everyone you meet tells you there's no place like that . . . I would have to go to hell on a technicality—because there's some things you're not supposed to do that I can't seem not to do."

One of his friends from adulthood, Marc Swanson, remembers the same concerns. "He wasn't religious, I don't think, but he believed in an afterlife. I know he was scared of going to hell and he was pretty serious about that." On the other hand, Swanson remembers that Smith "didn't like many organized things, or hierarchical things," so he'd have probably chafed against a traditional religious practice.

The house the Welch/Smith family gave as its official residence at the time of Bunny's second marriage sits on Duncanville's East Center Street, a quiet, curving street that could belong to any American suburb; it could have produced Dennis the Menace as easily as it did Elliott Smith. Brick, with a small cement porch sporting white columns a much larger version of which you might expect to see on a Southern plantation house, its side door opens onto a medium-sized, fenced-in backyard. There's nothing at all unusual or fancy about it, but it looks like a much more comfortable place to raise a child than the apartment Gary and Bunny lived in when Smith was born. It's also not far from Lakeside Park, the neighborhood where Smith lived during junior high. If there were moves between the time the Welches moved to town and Smith's beginning junior high, the family landed close to where they started.

Donna Barton, whose Duncanville family was friendly with Smith's family and (at least, in Barton's recollection) used Charles Welch as their insurance agent, remembers Steve, as he was then known, as a shy boy. Three years her senior, he stood by and watched quietly during an Easter-egg hunt, too cool to participate.

Smith won a local competition for a piano composition in elementary school—likely Central Elementary on East Freeman Street—but life as a rock musician started in sixth grade at Duncanville's William H. Byrd Junior High (now William H. Byrd Middle School) on Wheatland Road. Steve played clarinet in the school band with Julie Doyle, who is now a member of the Dallas indie rock ensemble The Polyphonic Spree, known for their exuberant live show and uniform of white robes.

"He dressed like most average guys in junior high— conservative," writes Doyle, who grew up entirely in Duncanville, in an e-mail. "He was on the football team. Average hairstyle. There were only a handful of kids who were considered punk rockers or stylish dressers."

The enduring friends Smith met at Byrd were Mark Merritt, Steve Pickering, and Kevin Denbow. They were the kids he played music with, the closest thing he'd ever have to a band in Texas. It started in sixth grade, when Mark Merritt and Steve Smith struck up a conversation in the lunch line. "We sat down and there was this shoot-the-shit discussion about guitar and music," says Merritt. "We discovered we both played a little bit and after that both of us started hanging out."

Soon, they convened to play guitar on a regular basis. "He'd been playing long enough to know the same amount of chords I did," says Merritt, who'd started playing at eight and whose father had been giving him informal lessons for a couple of years. "The only [guitar] I had at that point was my dad's Gibson classical, and eventually Gary [Smith] got him a Martin Sigma acoustic guitar, and acoustic pickups and a Peavey Backstage amplifier." Sigma is a cheaper division of Martin, the premiere brand in acoustic folk guitars. A Peavey Backstage is a small, modestly priced amp, and pickups are the devices that electrify an acoustic guitar in order to generate volume and texture. "I showed up at his house one time, and he was like, 'Look what my dad got me.' That would have to be not too long after we first met, I would have to say '81, in sixth grade. That was the guitar I remember him owning; from time to time he would borrow one of mine." If Smith owned a guitar before the gift from Gary, Merritt doesn't remember it. Smith's equipment wasn't top of the line, but it was better than Merritt's.

"Shortly after we met was when he had his guitar and his Peavey amp," remembers Merritt, "and I got hold of this piece-of-shit electric guitar and spent ten dollars of my allowance on an amp. I would bring over this shit guitar and this shit amp, and we were thirteen years old, and we put my cheap-ass little amp on top of his Peavey and we thought we had our first stack. It was pretty cool. My amp was made out of plastic, but we thought it was so cool to stack one on top of the other—it was like two feet tall and it gained a little more prominence if you put it on a chair in the acoustics of the garage—and play our little tunes. We just thought it was such hot shit."

There were no originals at this point, only exercises and covers. "Both of us being young and somewhat naïve to the whole process, we were still kind of teaching ourselves how to play—we started experimenting with finger styles and we were fooling around with open chord tunings, like experimenting with how high you could tune a high E string before it snapped. We would try Pink Floyd tunes, and Beatles tunes, and finger-picking and open chords. We would teach ourselves everything from 'Amazing Grace' to 'Puff the Magic Dragon.'"

The same school year Smith befriended Merritt, he found another musician and comic in Steve Pickering. "We met in English class in sixth grade," says Pickering. "I sat behind him and we were both trying to be the funny guy in class. The teacher would call on him and hand the paper back to him and he'd say something funny and it was my challenge to say something funny back. In sixth grade, humor was mostly insult humor.

"I just wound up at his house on a Saturday. I was riding around that neighborhood on my bicycle, and I asked another kid riding his bicycle where his house was and knocked on the door," Pickering recalls. By seventh grade, Pickering, who like Smith played clarinet in the school's band (Merritt was a trombonist), had joined Merritt and Smith as a pianist, although by Pickering's reckoning Smith played piano better than he did despite Pickering's five years of lessons. What impressed Pickering most was the day Smith sat at the piano in the Welch living room and picked out a Dan Fogelberg song he'd heard on the radio.

Their social lives were not entirely limited to playing music indoors. It's a wholesome, unadventurous existence Pickering remembers sharing with Smith in Duncanville: "Everybody had a basketball hoop in their driveway; it was your dad's obligation to install a hoop. We would ride our bikes around the neighborhood, ride to the library, ride to the 7-Eleven to play video games. The 7-Eleven had Ms. Pac-Man. I remember he was a lot better at basketball than I was, but he wasn't a vicious competitor. He'd win about 75 percent of the time. I was friends with another guy in the clarinet section, and the three of us would tear around the neighborhood on our bikes. Occasionally we would go up to the bowling alley."

But Smith was not average in the way he approached music. According to Pickering, "In sixth grade it wasn't a huge part of what we did, but it was in the summer between sixth and seventh grade that I noticed that he was musically inclined beyond other people I knew."

Smith cast his junior-high experience in bleaker terms. He recalled a scrappy, redneck upbringing much grittier than what Merritt and Pickering remember of the childhood they shared. "I got into a lot of fights in Dallas and was just sort of a hostile person," he said in a 2003 interview with *Under the Radar* magazine. "I'd get into fights about once a week or two. I don't think I ever really picked a fight, but I would totally fly off the handle if somebody said word one. You had to be like that or you'd get more shit. But I didn't have to be as much like that as I was. I was pissed off about other things—at home—so if anybody said anything at school, I'd just [shakes his head] . . . And I didn't even win most of the fights. I wasn't that big, but sometimes it's the little guys who've been beat on enough who figure out how to hurt somebody, even though they're not going to win. You have to fight harder and faster."

As far as Doyle recalls, Smith wasn't one of the little guys who was picked on. While he grew into a diminutive, five-foot-nine man, he wasn't small enough by junior-high standards for it to be a stand-out characteristic: "I have no memories of him being bullied," writes Doyle. "Steve was a big guy in those days."

Merritt and Pickering don't remember him as particularly big or small for his size; it was only later that he would come to be smaller than most boys. Nor do they remember him getting into fights with any kind of regularity at Byrd or during his one semester at Duncanville High; the two of them remember just one bout. "I didn't see it personally," says Pickering. "I remember that he had to go the principal's office, which was a big deal at the time. The kid he got in a fight with was a substantially larger kid. I wouldn't have called him a bully, but I remember thinking, 'Wow, I would not have fought that guy.' He was a big stocky guy. While they were waiting to see the principal they worked out whatever difference they had."

The differences between Smith's memories of Duncanville and those of his Texan friends suggest that Duncanville acquired a special symbolic quality for Smith after he left for Portland. He would sing in "Southern Belle" of a "southern town/where all you can do is grit your teeth." It was a Southern town that represented for Smith an attitude to define himself against—one of traditional, redneck masculinity. Much of his day-to-day life there might have been standard-issue suburban leisure time, and it might have been a place where he was able to work at his music the way most kids in garage bands do. But elements of a rougher existence found their way to the forefront of Smith's descriptions of Texas.

Smith had an older, female friend who drove a muscle car with a grim reaper painted on the hood. In Pickering's recollection, she wasn't so much Smith's girlfriend as an older student at Duncanville who took the small group of freshman boys under her wing. "It was a big, fat-ass muscle car," says Pickering. "She played clarinet and he played the clarinet. It would have been summer '83, at marching band rehearsal," that she and Smith met, he says. "She wasn't a metal head. She did buy us tickets to go see The Police in the fall of '83 at Reunion Arena. She invited Steve and he invited me. It was the *Synchronicity* tour. Steve was into it; he knew a bunch of Police songs—he knew all the words to 'Roxanne.' That was the first concert I can remember him deliberately going to with people of our age group. The girl with the car had to get [tickets] for us, because our parents wouldn't let us camp out all night in front of the Ticketmaster. We were in the first balcony and it was a huge-production arena rock show." Smith told *Under the Radar* magazine about a separate occasion when he got drunk and played pool at a neighbor's house; neither Merritt nor Pickering remembers this.

The girl both Merritt and Pickering remember Smith getting involved with was a Byrd student named Kim. "She was in junior-high band. I considered her to be one of the more popular kids in her grade," says Pickering. "When you're dating a guy in junior high, you're hanging out with his friends more than you probably want to, but she put up with us and was nice to us. I remember calling Steve once and saying, 'There's this new movie out called *The Outsiders*,' and he said, 'I already saw it with my girlfriend.' That was probably the kind of thing they did together. He would have been in eighth grade, she would have been in seventh. That would be the first girl I remember him being interested in for a period of time."

Smith described his Duncanville self as a reluctant but rather successful jock. "I had to play sports in junior high in Texas because everybody in Texas has to," he told *Under the Radar*. "I played football. I played defensive guard of all things. I was not any bigger and I was always very average. I was always a little on the small side in height and weight. First I was a wide receiver, which is great in junior high when nobody can throw the football. . . . You hit kind of hard for about the first ten plays, then the rest of the game you're just kind of running out there and bumping up against the cornerback. I just became aggravated by people who were bigger than me and threatening me and saying some of the things that junior-high kids say. You know, when you're down there like inches away from somebody's head and some guy is going, 'I'm going to fuck you up!' So the play starts and I'd just sort of dart out and cut him off at the knees and that was that. They'd always put the big guys by me because I was the small guy on the defensive line, but I got my guy every time because I was smaller and quicker and I guess angrier in general or something. I just can't believe I played so much sports. I can tell you it doesn't build character by itself. Except maybe building the character to not play sports because you were forced to." Pickering confirms that football didn't seem to be important to Smith. "I recall him playing football, but I don't remember it being something he was into."

David McConnell, who would be Smith's musical collaborator on his last album, *From a Basement on the Hill*, recalls that Smith told him he experienced physical abuse as a child, and that Smith said he also suspected he might have been abused sexually, but couldn't remember any incident clearly enough to say for sure. The theme of searching in oneself for some distant memory would become a theme in Smith's lyrics, and the abuse memories are one more instance of Smith's recollections of boyhood being darker than Smith's childhood friends' impressions of him.

Smith's stories about his musical taste during his formative years also diverge from the accounts of his friends. Smith often joked about how much he had liked Kiss and their makeup. "I saw that Kiss reference in interviews and laughed at it," says Pickering. "I don't remember him being into Kiss in junior high. It was classic rock—The Beatles, *Sgt. Pepper's* and The White Album, The Who, Led Zeppelin, Pink Floyd, Rush. He came over to my house and played what sounded like a classical piece on acoustic guitar and he explained to me it was a traditional folk song that Peter, Paul & Mary had recorded. I remember in eighth or ninth grade he owned a Jackson Browne record, and his tastes started expanding somewhat. He was branching out and getting into a lot more and different stuff—by eighth and ninth grade it was The Clash and U2. I don't know how he heard of them, but one of the songs he learned on guitar was 'Should I Stay or Should I Go,' which is in a pretty different musical category from The Beatles, so I think even then his tastes were expanding exponentially. He was always the one saying, 'Hey, you should check these guys out.' He always had a broader musical knowledge base than I did."

Smith was inclined toward musical leadership by the time he ordained his friend Mark Merritt a bassist. "The way I got voted a bass player is he'd went out and gotten himself a Gibson SG [electric guitar] and a couple of stomp boxes [effects pedals] and he was really getting heavy into the electric world, and the discussion came up that maybe we should think about starting a band. We were like, 'Maybe we need a bass player and a drummer and somebody who can sing.' And he was like, 'Somebody should start playing the bass.' He had better gear and was better than I was, so I went out and got a bass, and he introduced me to Rush. He was like, 'Dude, here's something to shoot for.' He was responsible for making me the Rush head I was as a teenager; my goal became to play every Rush tune known to man."

It was also Smith who pushed the group into its first attempts at public performance, Merritt remembers. He was a miniature

Jimmy Page figure, calling the shots and assuming the center of attention as lead guitarist. "One time when it was Pickering, Steve, and myself, and another guy playing drums, there was a contest being held at one of the churches. Steve said, 'We ought to do something,' and I'm like, 'I'm game.' And I was wondering about song selection, because it was at a church." Smith took the reins and chose the tunes. "We were the very last act and we played two songs: Steve played guitar and I played 'bass' on a crappy electric guitar, on four strings with the treble turned off." On this particular gig, Pickering was on keyboard. "The first song was 'Tequila.' It was a rousing success—among our parents, at least. Everybody knew that one. And that was my first public performance in a band." The second song, which drew a response Merritt doesn't recall as quite so enthusiastic, was "the instrumental of a long version of 'Stairway to Heaven.' None of us were brave enough to actually sing.

"We were probably in the seventh or eighth grade because [Steve] had gotten the Gibson SG at that point. He knew every guitar part to 'Stairway,' right down to the solo. He was almost fanatical about playing these songs, even at fourteen years old. He was a really fucking good musician and he had a great ear. Out of all of us he was the first to learn a specific song. 'Stairway' or Rush, he was the first to play it."

In Merritt's and Pickering's recollections, Bunny Welch, who worked as a teacher, was a supportive mother and an aid to her son's progress in music. "I thought he got along with her really well," says Pickering. "She was really nice to us. You have three or four thirteen-year-old boys running through your house cranking up amps and she was remarkably tolerant."

"When they moved to a different house," says Merritt, Bunny "moved a piano to his bedroom."

That house was on a larger piece of property on the border of Duncanville and the adjacent suburb of Cedar Hill. Smith didn't live there very long: The move took place when he was in junior high, and one semester into high school Smith went to live with his father and his stepmother, Marta Greenwald, a social worker, in Portland. In later interviews, Smith would cite family problems in Dallas as the reason he moved, but he was oblique about his reasons when he spoke to friends at the time.

"He caught me by surprise," says Pickering. "He didn't dwell on it for months ahead, he didn't have conversations where he said, 'I gotta get out of this town.' Just in the winter of '83 I remember him saying, 'So after Christmas I'm moving to Portland.' I just remember being shocked because I do not remember him indicating in any way that he was desperate to move and had to get out. I couldn't conceive of picking up and moving to a new town where none of your friends lived. I asked him why and he said, 'Well, I want to go up and live in Portland with my dad.'"

"It was pretty obvious that he and his step dad didn't get along," Pickering says. "I just attributed that, at the time, to that natural inherent resentment a lot of kids have toward their stepparents. The 'you're not my dad' thing. Charlie did come off as an authority figure. Charlie would be like, 'No you can't go out and play this weekend, you have to stay and mow the yard.' I remember it being a bone of contention more than it should be, and Steve just being 'grrr' about it. I think about that time I remember Steve becoming an anti-authoritarian. That was probably how a lot of kids felt about their stepparents. . . . I remember a couple of conversations where he specifically was angry at Charlie but it was nothing at the time I construed as exceptional." Any issues between them seemed like "natural teenage resentment. . . . I don't remember Steve ever saying, 'I can't stand him, because he's not my dad.'"

But Smith was clear on the point that leaving Dallas for Portland left him, in his own words, "really worried about my mom." He would talk about his troubled relationship with Charlie to friends into the last years of his life. David McConnell, who knew Smith during a troubled time in his adulthood, recalls Smith's complaints. "He had a lot of animosity toward his stepdad. I think he felt pretty hurt by him. The way he described it, he wasn't a very good dad."

Smith's mother and stepfather would be recurring figures in the songs Smith would go on to write. His most direct treatment of his life in Duncanville, and perhaps his most blatantly autobiographical work, is "Some Song," performed live at his earliest solo acoustic performances and released on a compilation by one of his record labels, Olympia, Washington's Kill Rock Stars, in 1997. One of the lines drops an important place name: "You went down to look at old Dallas town/where you must be sick just to hang around."

The place where Duncanville kids looking for an urban education would have likely gone in the early '80s is Deep Ellum. Now it's equal parts hipsters, tourists, and frat boys at night, but at the time it was a place where it could be dangerous to hang out. There were skinheads back then, and the neighborhood still retained the aroma of the wrong side of the tracks, which it had been until recently. It was and continues to be a place highly familiar to any Dallas police officer. If young Steve Smith met up with punk rock before he moved to Portland, Deep Ellum is likely where it happened. In many ways, it would have been the part of Dallas best able to prepare Smith for the bohemian music scene Portland had to offer. It had an active street life, dimly lit rock clubs, and a hint of danger.

He also may have discovered edgier music at Bill's Records. Dallas is not a city of many independent-minded record stores, but one opened when Smith was twelve, shortly before he left the city for good. Bill's Records is still owned by Bill Wisener after twenty-two years of operation. Located in northern Dallas, across town from Duncanville, it was a place a boy could find some sign of musical life beyond the arena rock that dominated the '80s.

Pickering says that everyone from Duncanville referred to where they lived as "Dallas," even though kids from Duncanville almost never actually had the opportunity to hang out anywhere in Dallas proper. So when Smith refers to "Dallas town" in "Some Song," he's probably talking about the town where he grew up rather than referring to the city as distinct from his suburban neighborhood. The subject of the song is a kid's internal suffering and his tormented relationship to peers and family. The whole story, the whole plaint, is framed by a skeptical comment about the person relating it.

The first words are "It's a junkie dream, makes you so up-tight/Yeah it's Halloween, tonight and every night." The portrayal of this character grows even more critical a couple lines later: "You're a symphony, man, with one fucking note." The song then goes on to tell the story of this single-note character, to describe his "junkie dream." As it turns out, Halloween every night means a constant return to childhood, and that recurring vision is described in detail. In the chorus, the song slips into the perspective of the person having the "junkie dream": "Help me kill my time/ 'cause I'll never be fine."

This ambiguous figure—the troubled complainant deserving of both scolding and understanding—populates a good half of the songs Elliott Smith wrote. And ambiguity characterizes his attitude toward where he grew up and toward himself. He didn't show much affection for Texas when he got older, but he knew he couldn't leave it behind completely.

In the Kill Rock Stars version of "Some Song," Smith sings, "How they beat you up week after week/and when you grow up you're going to be a freak." The "they" could be most easily understood as other kids in school. But in live versions of that song—and there are at least two recorded instances of this—he sang, "Charlie beat you up week after week." Of course, Smith took pains to explain that his songs shouldn't be interpreted as diary entries, and "Some Song" shouldn't be understood as a factual report. When *Spin* asked Smith if his stepfather "had a violent side," he wouldn't answer on the record. "He's had a tough time in his life and has moved forward in a lot of ways. We didn't get along when I was a kid," Smith allowed, adding that he didn't want to "dredge that all up" with Charlie, whom he never mentioned by name.

Steven was already able to write songs in Texas. "He was always dabbling in something," says Merritt, "even if it was just little instrumental numbers he would write up. The first time I remember witnessing him try to write a song was when he and I went to South Padre Island way down in south Texas on a family vacation, right next to the border with Mexico. We went there the summer before he left to go to Portland. It was a weird set of circumstances: My family was planning on going to South Padre Island for a week, and they said, 'Hey, it'd be cool to bring Steve. Have a buddy, bring the guitars.' We went down there and did the beach thing. We came back after that, and then a week later I went to the same place with his family, and once again we took the guitars and spent another week. And it was during the second vacation, with his family, when he said, 'Hey, let's write a song,' and we tried it. He was really kind of getting into it. We were fishing around for chord schemes. We sat down with the full intent of writing a song. I remember him being real intent about it, really fascinated by the process of how to write a song, and by that time he had delved into a wide range of tastes, and during that time we were talking about lyrics such as Pink Floyd's. That's when he really started paying attention to lyrics: Were they writing about something that they knew, or were they writing some cheesy-ass love songs for kicks? He'd write some ideas down and scratch that out and say, 'That doesn't make sense.' But he kept at it—and he was fourteen.

"He definitely took the reins of the songwriting session. I was there to help discover chord structures and I was there to play what he told me to play. I remember being like, 'I have no idea what I'm doing, but he does.'"

Two

CONDOR AVENUE

When Smith moved to his father's house the following winter he didn't cut himself off from his old life. He came back to Texas for prolonged visits a number of times. "After Steve moved to Portland," says Pickering, "I came up and visited him twice—in March '84 over spring break, and then again in summer of '86. Bunny and Charlie continued to live in Duncanville for the next couple years. In the summer of '84, Bunny had visitation. In the summer of '85 [Steve] came back into town as well."

The move from Dallas to Portland was a huge shift in terrain. Steven was suddenly living with a different family in a city that would earn the nickname Little Beirut for its anti-war demonstrations, a small metropolis teeming with independent-minded rock bands, clubs, record stores, and book stores.

"My dad lived up there," he later said of the move in *Under the Radar*. "I saw him every year for like a week or two. So I knew who he was. It wasn't really like I moved out into nowhere, but it was a difficult move. It took some getting used to. I didn't sleep at all for about the first six months I lived there. At that time the situation at my mother's home was very fresh in my mind. I was very worried about my mother. But everything turned out okay."

Housing records in Portland show that Gary Smith and Marta Greenwald, who lived with their daughter, Rachel Smith, owned a three-story colonial house with a big yard near Division Street and Hawthorne Boulevard in southeast Portland. A wide gable protrudes from the top story and there is a deep, wraparound porch. Across the street is an Episcopal church with a large circular glass window that is black from the outside and looks as if it could have inspired the reference to "the cathedral with the glass stained black" in Smith's "Speed Trials." There are industrial-sized roses blooming beside some of the houses on the block. Condor Avenue, the street that would provide the name for Smith's first great song, was a bus ride away in southwest Portland.

On a May afternoon in 2004, a teenage punk rock couple shuffles home from school carrying backpacks and skateboards. Downtown is a few minutes away by bus, and Hawthorne Boulevard, home to a lot of the record stores and coffee shops that have made southeast Portland a popular destination for recent college grads at loose ends, is a short walk away. It's unclear how much time Smith spent there; his girlfriend from his senior year of high school, Shannon Wight, recalls that by the time she knew Smith his family lived in southwest Portland.

Pickering visited Smith in his pleasant new circumstances twice. "He obviously liked it up there. In '86 when I visited he had friends there, and it was his town. He obviously had found a place where he had a social network. As I've watched and read the interviews over the years—I remember a guy who was upbeat and reasonably outgoing, smart and funny and talented; I don't remember him being unusually sad or depressed or anything like that. Just from playing basketball or riding our bikes, listening to *Sgt. Pepper's* or The White Album, I did not get the impression he was depressed or had more than the usual level of sadness.

"The first time I visited him in Portland was spring '84 in March, and I don't recall him looking significantly different at the time. . . . My next trip in the summer of '86 I did meet a bunch of his friends. I don't remember their names, but I did hang out with five or six of his friends. He'd been there for three months the first time I went up. Mostly what I was impressed with is he would take the bus everywhere—if he wanted to go to downtown, if he wanted to go to Clackamas Town Center.* I remember thinking that was amazing, because in Duncanville there was no bus. His hair might have been a little bit longer, but I still recognized him as the same guy. . . . I remember a girl he spent some time with in my visit up there"—at this point it wouldn't have been Shannon Wight—"and it was him and her and me tagging along. I don't remember anyone calling him Elliott until college. I called him Steve and he did not correct me on that, and everyone in July of '86 up there called him Steve."

The oft-repeated tale that Smith changed his name at fourteen from Steve to Elliott is false. "He was always Steve Smith," writes Julie Doyle. "It was news to anyone he'd gone to early school with." He was Steve Smith all through high school.

Pickering was able to track Smith's musical progress in Portland. He was now in what was by high-school standards a real band: Stranger Than Fiction, with fellow teenagers Tony Lash, Jason Hornick, and Garrick Duckler. There were actual recordings. "I have two Stranger Than Fiction tapes—he was hanging out with those guys at the time—which I brought back to Texas and listened to excessively," he says. "But he was still Steve at that point as far as I knew. He ran me off a dub and slapped a label on it. I remember coming back in '86 with a really well produced Stranger Than Fiction cassette and being amazed at the sound quality of it. And I do have an earlier cassette. I think that must have been when he came back summer of '84 or '85. That was more with a drum machine. One of the things I remember being impressed by the most was a guy playing upright bass. The drums sounded really good. I remember him coming back in summer of '85 or summer of '86. Mark Merritt had come into a drum set somehow, and I remember Steve, he could play the drums. That's

---

*A mall in southeast Portland.

when I realized this guy could play anything, it was just not difficult for him."

Smith started some of his best work during high school in Portland. "Condor Ave.," the second song on *Roman Candle*, Smith's
first album, "was definitely written in high school—or begun,"
writes JJ Gonson, Smith's girlfriend in the early '90s, in an e-mail.
"'Kiwi Maddog 20/20' was not only written, but also recorded,
then. He took the old tape and reworked it, but just a little bit.
The title comes from a bottle he and our housemate, Chris Her-
ring, polished off one night." It was "bought for the color—like
antifreeze—and choked down on a dare."

Early in his senior year at Lincoln High School in southwest
Portland, Smith went to a meeting for prospective applicants to
Hampshire College. At the meeting he found an acquaintance from
Lincoln: Shannon Wight. They started dating, and after she got an
early-decision acceptance to Hampshire, he decided to apply—he
hadn't gotten around to applying anywhere else, says Wight, and
he wanted to follow her. She sensed that this might be "a terrible
idea" as far as their relationship was concerned. In her Hampshire
College freshman photo, Wight looks like an all-American girl,
perfectly unremarkable in appearance. She has long straight brown
hair, a dark sweater and no visible streak of rebelliousness.

Smith's relationship with Wight didn't survive long once they
got to college, but it was there that he met some of the people who
became central characters in the rest of his life. Hampshire was
the first place where he could present himself as a person set
against the upbringing he felt had been thrust upon him in Texas:
a sensitive, feminist musician of philosophical bent named Elliott
Smith. Steve Smith—the boy on a bike in the Dallas suburbs who
wore the clothes his parents bought him and lived on classic
rock—ceased to be a person you could meet and shake hands
with. He became a specter haunting Elliott Smith, cropping up
over and over again in song.

Three

ELLIOTT

STEVE SMITH WAS christened Elliott Smith shortly after he and Shannon Wight landed at Hampshire College, in Amherst, Massachusetts—a good time to change names, it seemed to Wight. They came up with the name Elliott Stillwater-Rotter as a joke, which Smith shared with other students occasionally. Wight and Smith broke up soon afterward, but "Elliott" Smith was permanent.

Elliott is spelled with two *t*'s, like a surname, because Wight was inspired by the middle name of her previous boyfriend. When she mentioned this to Smith later on, she recalls, he was surprised, although she remembers telling him where she came up with the spelling at the time. Smith later explained his name change by saying that Steve sounded too "jockish" or "sporty" for him and Steven "too bookish," and indeed that may have been what made him keep "Elliot." It's another instance of Smith slightly adjusting or spinning his early personal history, probably by accident. Others would speculate that perhaps the name came from Elliott Avenue, which was near Smith's high-school home in southeast Portland. But originally the catchy, delicate appellation *Elliott Smith* had nothing to do with Smith's hometown or his character. He never changed his name legally.

Elliott Smith turned out to have a puritanical streak. At Hampshire in the late '80s, second-wave feminist scholars like Catherine MacKinnon and Andrea Dworkin were frequently under discussion. Smith was later quoted in interviews as looking back on this time in his intellectual development as a detour. "I was reading all this heavy-duty feminist theory—Catherine MacKinnon, in particular. I really took it to heart, and it just kind of drained all my energy away," he told a reporter for *Spin*. "I didn't want to do anything. If you're a straight, white man, she made it seem impossible to live your life without constantly doing something shitty, whether you knew it or not. So I was convinced that I was just constantly making an ass out of myself and bothering someone just by being me. So I narrowed my future down to 'fireman,' because my occupation would be useful, without a doubt. Someone really has to put out fires, while it's not particularly essential for me to play songs. It's important that somebody should play songs to people, but I don't know, I got all turned around by reading all this stuff, and I failed to notice that apparently the point of it was more to spit it back out in a paper than to take it all to heart [chuckles]."

Smith seems not to have befriended many other straight men in college, choosing several gay men as his closest friends. First there was Neil Gust, who Smith credited with persuading him to drop the fireman plan for a life on the stage. "Neil is telling me, 'We are going to form a band.' I was like, 'Yeah, right. That's probably one of the most sexist areas I could possibly wander into,'" he told *Spin*. "'I'm gonna jump up on stage and pretend like everybody ought to pay attention to me? I'd feel like a fucking peacock.' And he was like, 'Man, you're talking yourself out of all the things that you really want to do.' And I was like, 'Yeah!' Eventually I caved in and I'm glad."

MacKinnon's stance was that the First Amendment, with its protection of free speech, and the Fourteenth Amendment, with its promise of equal rights to all races and ethnicities, were on a collision course. And she didn't much question which had to give way. Certain forms of misogynistic expression, MacKinnon argued, specifically pornography, were damaging to women—therefore, they should be made illegal.

It's perhaps not a philosophy that jibes well with a career in naked self-expression, saying as it does that free speech is a problematic pillar on which to found a society. It's easy to see why a career in a less personally expressive occupation—like firefighting—would seem an elegant solution to the dilemma of someone like Smith, who believed that by dint of his race and gender he could accidentally do harm to others.

It wasn't just MacKinnon contributing to Smith's budding sense of guilt. Portions of Hampshire's student body were loyal to the identity politics that characterized the intellectual life of the late '80s. On February 23, 1988, Smith's sophomore year, members of Students of Under-Represented Cultures (SOURCe) took over a quad on campus called Dakin House. The action took place while much of the administration, faculty, and student body was engaged in one of the college's "all-community meetings." According to Hampshire's student newspaper, *Permanent Press,* the meeting was "cut short at 4:00 when SOURCe representatives announced they would appreciate a show of support at Dakin Quad. The RCC quickly emptied and students reassembled outside the site of the SOURCe occupation. Food and sleeping bags were provided by various members of the community. . . . A 9:00 p.m. vigil was planned and groups of students fanned out to inform the community."

Among SOURCe's demands were "institutionalized funding for SOURCe," a "search for a full-time salaried staff person for SOURCe," and that "the living room of Dakin Master's House be dedicated as a permanent cultural space for students of color." SOURCe issued a statement to the "Hampshire Community." It opened, "We, as students of color, experience Hampshire as a racist institution," and further explained, "the demands we have requested are essential for the continued well-being of all the members of this community. Multicultural diversity, the learning about all peoples, should be desired by everyone. It is beneficial to everyone." The administration met with SOURCe and complied with most of their demands.

Hampshire in the late '80s was a place where, for some, a "culture" was something that could take possession of a living room, and that was entitled to a living room in which it could properly flourish. The danger of racism is something that one can perpetuate without knowing it because it doesn't depend on any concrete action on the part of single individuals. To quote Smith on his own youthful understanding of MacKinnon and multiculturalism, if you were a "straight white man," it could be "impossible to live your life without constantly doing something shitty, whether you knew it or not." In this way of thinking, a club in which the performers and audience are largely white might be thought of as a white "cultural space," just as the living room at Dakin was supposed to be a "Third World" cultural space. In this context, Smith's fears about the sociopolitical dimensions of being a musician—in his own words, a "peacock on stage"—begin to make more sense. To a lot of nineteen-year-olds studying liberal arts at a time when "PC" was still a cresting wave and not yet the butt of jokes, the logic of SOURCe might carry water.

Smith spent his first Hampshire years in a student-housing complex known as Enfield, down a gentle slope from the library and the center of campus. Partially obscured by trees, Enfield is composed of grim yellow-to-beige rectangular buildings that generally house two "mods," households shared by students. Although conditions are fairly wretched in the muddy season that follows winter in rural Massachusetts, the Hampshire campus offers a stark, clear view of Mount Monadnock. In October it's an orange-and-crimson monolith, good compensation for living in hideous architecture.

In one of the final interviews of his life, with *Under the Radar* magazine, Smith recalled the odd jobs he worked during college to help make ends meet, such as taking care of dogs that were used in laboratory experiments. "He had to clean the kennels," says Myles Kennedy, Jr., who heard Smith tell stories about the job when he worked as his tour manager in the year 2000. "The dogs didn't ever like [the cleaning], and every time he went to work he was almost dog bait, getting them out of the kennels. It sounded pretty horrendous."

Smith later said that he found the student body at Hampshire by and large "annoying," but he did establish a few good relationships there. His college friend Carl Germann remembers the first version of Heatmiser, which consisted of Gust and Smith on acoustic guitars, performing at the coffee shop on campus, with a shy Smith hiding behind his hair. When he lived off campus, Smith lived with Gust and other Hampshire students—he was no recluse, nor did he have a social life apart from Hampshire students with the local townies.

Carl Germann, who graduated from Hampshire one semester earlier than Smith in 1991, had befriended Smith through Gust, who was then a social force in his own right, at least on the Hampshire campus. Germann remembers Smith as a musical collaborator of Gust's from freshman year on, and by far the shyer, more retiring of the pair. Both Gust and Smith had long hair at the time, but Smith's was dyed orange, in Germann's recollection, with brown roots. Gust was the striking figure, with straight brown hair and a long, thin face, "almost like a Jesus kind of look." At first Smith, Gust, Germann, and two women, Mary Jane Weatherbee and Mandy Daramin, lived together in Enfield's Mod 51. "We considered ourselves the coolest kids in the whole school," laughs Germann. For all the talk about Smith being a perpetual outsider, Hampshire was one place where he stood squarely amongst the in-crowd. Because "Neil was good looking," and "they were in a band," Germann recalls, social acceptance was not a problem for the clique. They were known as the kids in Mod 51, and they would show up at parties in groups.

In the late '80s, Massachusetts had a thriving rock scene, albeit one centered more around Boston than Amherst. The Pixies, composed partially of onetime UMass Amherst students, were big at

Hampshire, as were Dinosaur Jr., whose frontman, J Mascis, was an Amherst kid, and whose bass player, Lou Barlow—a future buddy of Smith's—grew up in nearby Westfield. The rest of the world may have been more interested in Debbie Gibson, but in the Massachusetts college world alternative rock was already king. Gust, for example, was listening to some of the more prominent international alternative-rock bands of the day: The BoDeans, REM, and The Godfathers.

While short on rock groups and rock venues in comparison with Boston, ninety miles to the east, the Pioneer Valley was a reasonably hospitable environment for a budding musician. Amherst was a small, quiet town where the only nightlife to speak of was centered around a few bars where University of Massachusetts frat boys gathered in Cossack-like hordes on weekend nights. But downtown one could find faint but distinct signs of rock-and-roll life. There was a clothing and knickknacks store called Faces that contained a record shop, at one point known as For the Record, which eventually became its own store. There and at the great but now vanquished Main Street Records in downtown Northampton, Smith pawed through records and CDs (the latter still a novelty) and looked at flyers with Gust, admiring or mocking band names, deciding which shows they wanted to see, and distributing flyers for his own shows.

Smith was open-minded about the pop of the day, says Germann, and all kinds of music played in the two houses into which the Mod 51 kids migrated midway through college. "Mary Jane was a punk rock kid: She had platinum blond hair. I was sort of a trendy, whatever was trendy I liked; I'd bounce from one thing to the next. For a while there Mandy and I went through a love of pop music, Top 40 pop music, and Elliott sort of got into that. Neil hated it. Janet Jackson and stuff like that made his ears bleed. There are a few songs of that era that make me think of Mandy and Elliott, 1990 pop-song one-hit wonders we all loved because they were so bad they were good. Elliott would listen to that, he didn't mind. We'd listen to crappy pop

music and he'd sort of get into it a little bit. I did challenge Elliott and Neil once to write a song like that, like Janet Jackson.
'It's so bad it's good. Can you do this?' They were like, 'We
could do that. It'd be very simple. But we don't want to.' They
took their music very seriously, Neil especially. Neil knew what
he wanted to do, and he wanted to be a musician. Elliott never
really planned it out. I don't think he was quite as serious about
it, at least to us."

But he was serious enough about it that the songwriting he
did during that time was a private process. During one summer
he and Germann lived together, he played riffs from Television
songs in plain sight but would retreat to his own room for real
composition.

Besides being the better-looking, more assertively ambitious
musician, who was Neil Gust to Elliott Smith at this time during
their lives? What made it such an enduring friendship?

The friendship between Smith and Gust went beyond Heatmiser—it was Gust who appeared on the cover of *Roman Candle,*
Smith's first solo album, and it was Gust who took the photograph of Smith for the cover of *Either/Or.* Gust's post-Heatmiser
band, No. 2, toured with Smith even when Smith moved to New
York and Gust remained in Portland.

Gust had a confidence that Smith lacked. Smith's high-school
band, Stranger Than Fiction, had never played live, preferring to
limit itself to four-track recordings. Gust seemed to be the more
prominent singer and songwriter in their Hampshire days. But
when Heatmiser's actual recording career began, Smith seems to
have received equal billing in the band, most prominently in the
band photo on the flap of its first album, *Dead Air.* Of all the
songs on *Dead Air,* however, the standout is Gust's "Can't Be
Touched." Gust's vocals are stronger than Smith's and blend better with the band. While Smith may have been recording great
songs on his four-track in high school, in Heatmiser he was initially the less promising of the two musicians. It would be unfair
to say Smith rode Gust's coattails, but he followed his lead and

was able to become a successful indie rock musician in Portland largely because of Gust's help.

The *Frog Book*, the freshman photo book for Smith's class at Hampshire, provides ample evidence of the contrast between Smith and Gust at the time. Smith's hair is a wilder, shaggier version of the coif sported by Sean Penn's Jeff Spicoli character in *Fast Times at Ridgemont High*. Dyed a lighter color but with the brown roots heavily grown out, Smith's bangs obscure his eyes almost completely; he looks like an amiable sheep dog. Gust, by contrast, looks like he could play the head of the poetry club on *Beverly Hills, 90210*. His long hair is swept back from his forehead into a graceful, leonine mane; his face is perfectly sculpted and his expression is gentle and proud. If anyone in the '87 Hampshire College *Frog Book* looks ready to become the next Michael Stipe, it's him.

After freshman year, Smith left the dorms and started to live in houses off-campus with friends. "We had three people in my apartment and three people in theirs, three men and three women," says Germann, whose apartment was in a house on North Street in Northampton, a block from the house Smith and Gust lived in on Cherry Street. "And it ended up being very split: Neil and Mandy and I were all gay; Amy, Mary Jane, and Elliott were straight. So there was this sort of awareness. And it was as we were coming out. I was out, and Mandy was slowly coming out, and Neil was slowly coming out. It was very PC, very Northampton, very Hampshire College. It was this awareness of who you are as a gay person or a straight person and a man or a woman. And that was a lot of what we talked about—his [Elliott's] identity as a straight white man. And he sort of had an issue with that, with falling into that category of straight white man, and not wanting to be part of that category. I think that's sort of why he studied what he studied. Elliott talking about being a fireman—he wanted to go beyond being a straight white guy, he wanted to help people, he wanted to save people, to transcend that label."

But he still dated women. Smith and Wight broke up soon after their arrival at Hampshire, but Smith briefly dated Mandy Daramin, Germann recalls, before briefly getting back together with Wight early in their senior year. Most of his social life revolved around the Mod 51 group, but Wight made an appearance on their radar when she showed up as Elliott's girlfriend at their Thanksgiving dinner in 1990—the last Thanksgiving of college.

Germann's memory matches Smith's own assessment of his refusal or inability to detach himself emotionally from the fashionable theories of the time. "It was such a time of identity politics. It was so prevalent and what we were studying was just so about that. I think that he sort of went back to how he was raised, and thought about the men in his life, and then sort of thought about where did he follow in their footsteps and where did he go off, and took what he was learning and reacted and very seriously internalized and thought about it. We'd talk about how he needed to go beyond that identity and where could he go from there. It's not like, '[If] you were a gay white man that'd be great.' It's not like you want to go through life thinking in those terms. You just want to trek on through. Mandy as well talked about that, and Amy, our other roommate, would talk about the fact that they don't wake up every day thinking about how they're women— you don't have to think about it. But Elliott thought about it; he thought about everything. Everything was a very internal struggle, in terms of that."

Smith's collegiate brow-furrowing might seem like an irrelevant set piece in the story, except that one of Smith's distinctions as a lyricist, in his early days, was his Puritanism. And Smith knew the theory he studied in college was a kind of Puritanism, or as he later put it in interviews, somehow "right-wing." The characters in Elliott Smith songs are constantly doing harm to other people not out of malice but out of selfishness and licentiousness. The outlook Smith adopted at Hampshire, in which the path of righteousness was narrowed to a tiny range of options and career choices, was an extreme he soon shied away from. But it was also the opposite of an attitude he inveighs against over and over again on his albums, most explicitly in "Ballad of the Big Nothing": "You can do what you want to, whatever you want to" is the refrain of that song, and it's meant as an ironic retort to those very sentiments.

Smith said in a 2003 interview that he didn't feel especially comfortable hanging out with other straight men while in college: "I was around twenty or nineteen and a lot of straight guys were . . . you know, just having kinds of conversations that I couldn't relate to. You know, just like very high school."

Germann's breakdown of Smith's circle of friends at Hampshire backs up that recollection to some extent. After the Mod 51 clique left the mods, Smith was one of the few straight guys in his social group, along with Constantine Roumel, who Smith later hung out with in New York City. His name seems a likely inspiration for the Constantina character who lives in a place that sounds like the downtown Manhattan neighborhood of Alphabet City (then a decrepit place where people bought heroin) in the song "Alphabet Town" off Smith's self-titled album.

The traces of depression in Smith's life at this point, as far as Germann noticed, went only a shade beyond the standard emotional moodiness common to college students. "He had stomach problems. And there would be an entire day when he would be in bed, and not come out. He would have some moments when he was melancholy and everybody would be hanging out and he'd just decide, 'All right, I'm done with this,' and go read or play guitar or something like that. He would spend a lot of time in his room in the summer I lived with him, and there'd be times he'd just go and play music by himself for hours and then he'd come out and be totally fine and the life of the party."

E. V. Day, the sculptor, who had a class with Smith at Hampshire but did not become a close friend until ten years later, had only the vaguest impressions of Smith as someone who might have depressive tendencies. "It wasn't just like, 'This is a depressed person who's not cool to hang around with.' It wasn't that, it was a certain 'zing' you get from somebody."

Smith was not, despite his eventual acquisition of admiring female fans through his music, a magnet for Hampshire College women, says Germann. "No, he had the long hair hanging in his face. He seemed very quiet. Once you got to know him he was really very charming and funny, but I think that for the most part he was a long-haired guy that hung out with this group of people he lived with. Neil at that time was the charmer. [He had the] chiseled face. He was the one people would look at, particularly if they were performing."

Smith's brand of humor wasn't generally loud or broad, but it showed itself more than just occasionally. Germann recalls a running joke wherein Smith attempted to spend an entire day speaking in clichés. He lasted about an hour. Even with Smith's capacity for humor, Day found him intimidating. "He had a small physique with a very tough-looking face, but he just sort of exuded this sort of unease that—he reminded me of Pig Pen. You know, he had the aura cloud of mud and dirt around him—it's like that it was almost comical, but he wasn't messier than anyone else per se." It was more like a thunder cloud than the Peanuts character's grime cloud, she recalls. She was afraid of the vibes she got from him. "He wasn't that clean but he wasn't dirty, he was grungy—but he really had it, unlike anyone else, and he was sort of petite, and exuded this thing, and he was very soft-spoken, but it was almost like there was a sort of a thunder cloud over him all the time. I was sort of intimidated and afraid of him, I was afraid to talk to him or be alone with him. It wasn't fear for my life or anything, it was just a kind of energy."

Much of Smith's public persona was already in place: the slightly foreboding presence matched with a gentle disposition, humor, and self-deprecation. He was already the Elliott Smith his fans would recognize.

During the later years at Hampshire, Smith lived mostly in a house on Cherry Street, several blocks from downtown Northampton. The neighborhood looks as if it could be in one of the subtly bohemian areas in Cambridge or Jamaica Plain: In old wooden houses, imperfectly maintained, groups of young people and families live side by side, sometimes under the same roof. The Bridge Street graveyard sits a stone's throw away. This was the home base for Smith and his friends.

Besides Gust, the closest friend Smith met at Hampshire was Marc Swanson, though the two didn't become close until after graduation.

Swanson grew up in Merrimack, New Hampshire, a small town gradually being enveloped by suburbia, the son of a high-school teacher. Born within a week of each other, Swanson and Smith spent their childhoods in similar circumstances, living in areas where middle-class suburbia ran headlong into working-class rural culture, although background wasn't at the root of their bond. As Swanson puts it, "We didn't really talk about that, [but] it seemed like all our close friends were pretty much from the same socioeconomic situation. It seemed Neil and Joanna [Bolme, Smith's future girlfriend] and me, all the friends from Hampshire, I think we all grew up in pretty quasi-suburban places and were probably for all intents and purposes lower middle class, but not where we grew up. I had free lunches at school because we had no money, but we had a house. We didn't live in a trailer and we didn't live in a really shitty house and we didn't live in an apartment, and I never considered myself poor."

Swanson grew up in an environment that was fiercely libertarian. New Hampshire has a "hands off" approach to taxes and to zoning and hunting regulations. If you want to start a farm there that mostly sells used cars, Swanson explained to me, New Hampshire doesn't mind. Today he's an artist in Greenpoint, Brooklyn, making sculptures and installations that are often reminiscent of the customs of his home state. He had a gallery show in 2003 titled "Live Free or Die," and he's perhaps best known for his sequined antlers. When I met him at his apartment, there was an employee named Devotion (Swanson called him "D") sitting on his living-room floor applying silvery material to what looked like a plastic horse's head. *Vice* magazine called Swanson "simultaneously Ted Nugent and Liberace."

After dropping out of the Art Institute of Boston (he finished art school later), Swanson hung out in Boston with some of the tougher elements of the punk rock crowd, but found himself gravitating toward Hampshire College, a two-hour drive to the west. He was gay and artistic, and in '80s Boston he didn't find as much overlap between punks and artists and gays as he would have liked. "In the age I grew up in, in the punk rock world being an artist meant you were a pretentious academic. And you were in with the man. I was embarrassed to tell people when I was in Boston that I wanted to be an artist. I basically hung out there with skinheads and whatever, whatever was going on. The art-school kids, they were artfags, they had this whole other thing. They were in this institution to become institutionalized." (It's clear from the way he says this that his perspective has shifted since then.) But at Hampshire he discovered kids who liked punk rock and art and critical theory and weren't afraid to talk to about it. First he befriended Gust. "I didn't really know Elliott that well at Hampshire; he was really introverted and quiet there. And I think honestly he kind of made me nervous. He was part of our group of people but it was a pretty big group of people. He was very serious, and it was alternative school and everyone kind of had their own thing, but it seemed like Elliott had more things to be dealing with. There we didn't really talk about a whole lot of stuff, like I probably made him nervous and he made me nervous. Me and Neil bonded cause we were both gay guys so that was our thing."

At a party at Swanson's house, one of the last the group that came together at Hampshire would celebrate before dispersing to faraway cities, Gust finally came out to Smith. "It was this big, sort of momentous thing," Swanson remembers. "Neil and Elliott were gone forever. All of us were there—Mandy, Carl, all hanging out. They disappeared for a while and came back teary-eyed."

Gust and Smith would be friends, on and off, for longer than Smith dated any of his girlfriends.

The friendships that would stay with Smith for a decade and a half had been put into place. His career started after college, in Portland, where he would meet two long-term girlfriends, JJ Gonson and Joanna Bolme, and acquire the advisers that are the mainstays of a professional musician's existence. But he discovered his milieu, his corner of bohemia, at Hampshire. It was a group of liberal, to some extent college-educated, young people, who by and large liked punk rock, grew up in modest homes, and didn't shy away from academic ways of thinking. As bands, relationships, living situations, and problems emerged and fell by the wayside, this group would remain a constant in Smith's life.

Four

ROMAN CANDLE

WHEN YOU STEP off a plane in Portland during the winter, you feel as if your nose has been pressed into a wet towel. This is the signature smell of the city, a mustiness attributed to continuous rainfall and an outlying formation of paper mills. Between September and May, there is usually either a whisper of perspiration in the air or a blinding downpour. Portlanders don't carry umbrellas; they pack raincoats. If you were young and in a band in Portland in the 1990s, you were likely wearing highwater jeans and a hoodie beneath your raincoat, topping the ensemble with a mesh trucker hat. (This look was discovered by New York fashion designers around seven years after its appearance in Portland.)

The Lutz was to musical Portland in the mid-'90s what Odeon was to literary Manhattan in the 1980s, and the discrepancies between the two are instructive. The Lutz runs on cheap beer, and while it might be acceptable to drink hard liquor there, it's not the kind of place you order a glass of wine. It has a television that's usually tuned to *The Simpsons,* minimal natural light, neon beer signs in the windows, and blood-red pleather booths. Unlike other Portland hangouts, like Montage and Satyricon, there's nothing in the décor to betray the eccentricity of its clientele to the outside world. The jukebox plays Ween al-

45

bums—"Baby Bitch" is a popular selection—but also plenty of heavy metal. There's nothing to distinguish The Lutz from the hundreds of blue-collar bars like it all over the city—until you notice the hoodies and high-waters.

Portland's rock musicians were both overwhelmed by and resistant to the commercially successful grunge pouring out of Seattle in the early '90s, and sought to set themselves apart from both big-time alternative rock and club music by disavowing glitz and bourgeois comfort. Somebody's house was a legitimate place not just for an evening on the town but for a show, and most houses were rented by a rapidly shifting cast of young people. Some were '50s split-levels, some rambling, wooden, and pre-war, with room for at least six. The residents rarely stayed the same from year to year, but the houses' names often did. In addition to places like the Power House or the Dustbin, where bands played in the basement or the living room, there was Heatmiser House, named for Smith's first and only serious band in Portland.

Portland streets divide the city into quadrants: northeast, southeast, northwest, and southwest.

Northwest boasts the biggest houses, the most lyrically tree-shaded lanes, and a generous cut of the designer boutiques. Northwest 23rd Street is the epicenter of local gourmet shopping, and subdivisions of homes that would not be out of place in the Hollywood Hills offer views of the district.

Southwest Portland comprises most of downtown, a small collection of modest skyscrapers that includes The Portland Building, a profoundly non-intimidating, orange-fringed example of early postmodern architecture cruelly maligned by critics and locals as "proof that Kmart has an architecture department." Portland's larger rock clubs, like Berbati's Pan, are in the western portions of the city, but the scrappier eastern quarters are where local musicians live and fraternize.

Northeast Portland is home to a large fraction of the city's non-white residents. Portland is primarily a white and white-collar town, but in "northeast," working-class neighborhoods house mostly blacks and Hispanics, as well as a sizable Vietnamese Town. It's a place where, for most of the '90s, you could easily find a room for two hundred dollars a month.

Southeast Portland, a mix of working- and middle-class neighborhoods, is only marginally more expensive. Most of its bars and rock clubs are a short TriMet bus ride from Hawthorne Boulevard, which is ridden with breakfast cafés like the Cup & Saucer and shops selling used records, vintage clothing, and drug paraphernalia. In the late '90s, it wasn't uncommon to spot excitable indie rock kids smoking cigarettes in front of places like the Cup & Saucer, muttering to one other that Elliott Smith was sitting inside.

The visual melancholia that pervades Portland found its corresponding sound in Smith's early recordings. With the exceptions of its parks and streaks of stylish commerce, Portland is a gray city, with a dearth of sunlight and grandiose architecture. People move there for jobs or because it's unpretentious, uncongested, liberal, and coated in oversized evergreens and roses. It's a short drive from the coast, Mount Hood, and towering forests—pretty but rarely striking.

Smith and Gust moved to southeast Portland shortly after their Hampshire graduation, renting a house in the rose garden–filled neighborhood of Ladd's Addition. Smith was still writing solo songs, but now Heatmiser was a professional focus. Tony Lash, their new drummer, had been Smith's high-school drummer in Stranger Than Fiction, and he'd developed a formidable ear for recording. They found a bass player in Brandt Peterson, who Smith later described as older, more punk, and more confrontational than the other members of the band. Things moved quickly: A little over a year after they landed in Portland, Marc Swanson recalls, they mailed him a cassette with an album's worth of recordings.

Heatmiser had the good luck to arrive in Portland at the same time as a few similarly minded bands who would put the city on the map. One of the bands starting up was Motorgoat, a collaboration between two California transplants: bassist, keyboardist, and guitarist Sam Coomes and his wife, drummer Janet Weiss. There was also Calamity Jane, a rough all-female punk band with a bass player named Joanna Bolme; Crackerbash, a loud three-piece ensemble led by Sean Croghan; and Hazel, a loose, catchy punk band led by multi-instrumentalist Pete Krebs. Krebs had dropped out of college to start life as a musician in Portland after a bout of protracted illness in the late '80s, but he remembers the early '90s as his halcyon years, a little Northwestern golden age overshadowed by the Seattle grunge phenomenon.

"Back then in the Portland indie scene, there was a crop of bands that came out all at the same time that were tight friends," remembers Krebs, now a soft-spoken professional musician with wire-rimmed glasses and two full sleeves of tattoos, still living in Portland. "Everybody kind of knew everybody. It was a pretty extraordinary time because they were bands that had interesting things to say and cool sounds. So there were bands starting up of people who came from the same place, who grew up listening to cool music and just ended up in Portland at the same time. Everybody was in their early twenties, mid-twenties; it was this harmonic convergence that kind of happens all the time in different towns. In Portland it happened then, and it's probably happened three times since. There was a strong sense of community there for about eight months. And then everybody started, like, 'Holy shit—you're touring where, you're playing with who?' You know, Calamity Jane touring with Nirvana for 20,000 people in Brazil or wherever it was*, you're like—'What?'"

Heatmiser may not have received any international touring offers from Nirvana, but they did get signed to a reputable indie label that helped them build a fan base, grunge kid by grunge kid. Frontier Records, founded by Lisa Fancher in 1980 and based in

---

*Calamity Jane opened for Nirvana in a stadium in Buenos Aires. They were booed offstage.

Sun Valley, California, grew up with the Southern California hard-core scene and evolved with California punk. One of its earliest releases was *Group Sex* by the Circle Jerks, a band fronted by Keith Morris, the original singer for seminal LA punk band Black Flag. The label went on to embrace goth bands like Christian Death and eclectic rock bands like American Music Club. In the late '80s they made their first major Northwestern acquisition by signing Seattle's Young Fresh Fellows, the poppy, geeky forerunners of Barenaked Ladies. Along the way Frontier released the first album by Suicidal Tendencies, who went on to find fame on MTV. Heatmiser released three albums on the label: two LPs, *Dead Air* (1993) and *Cop and Speeder* (1994), and the EP *Yellow No. 5* (1994).

Frontier has made public two documents left over from Heatmiser's tenure that suggest there was a generally harmonious relationship between the band and its office-bound handlers. One is a note from Smith in the handwriting familiar to readers of the lyric sheets to *Roman Candle*, *Elliott Smith*, and *Figure 8*. It has cutie-pie Japanese cartoon characters printed on it, and an upbeat message: "Hello, here's the tape and, well, some penguins and sharks—luv, Elliott." A postcard the band sent from Ohio (it's stamped with the logo of the Rock and Roll Hall of Fame) is even sunnier. Addressed to "Our Friends @ Frontier," it sends greetings from Gust ("Hi. We're getting a lot of free drinks. Bet you wish you were with us. Ha Ha Ha. Love, Neil"), Lash ("P.U.!"), a possibly sarcastic Peterson ("We've made so many lovely new friends, and Indianapolis was great! Miss you, Brandt"), and Smith ("You can play 'Smells Like Teen Spirit' here on the jukebox. Lost my train of thought. Love, Elliott").

"They were really excited when Frontier approached them and they were doing really well in Portland," Swanson recalls. "People really gave Heatmiser a chance," says Bill Santen, a musician playing around Portland in the '90s with a revolving cast of supporting musicians under the name Birddog. Built to Spill's Doug Martsch, he remembers, became such a fan that he wore a Heatmiser t-shirt when he came to town.

After Smith became nationally well-known, early Heatmiser songs became an in-joke for a lot of Elliott Smith fans who considered them vastly inferior to his solo work. But the band was part of a rock scene that blazed trails, largely as a result of Gust's forthrightness about being gay in his lyrics. Portland would eventually become home to a lot of explicitly gay-themed punk bands, some of which described their music as "queercore." But in the early '90s—Heatmiser's first record, *Dead Air*, was released in 1993—it was novel to hear gay love songs set to punk rock.

"I really liked Portland compared to San Francisco because there was this whole scene up there where everyone was just into indie rock bands," says Swanson, who'd moved to San Francisco. "It didn't matter if they were gay or straight or whatever, which was a really big deal to me at that time. Whereas San Francisco had a gay thing but nobody went to see rock bands . . . it definitely wasn't the same thing as Portland, where it was this whole contingent of the gay indie rock kids, which was a real revelation to me. . . . All of a sudden Neil and Elliott had all these friends who were also playing in bands who were gay guys."

On *Dead Air*, Smith sang lead vocals on eight songs and Gust on six. Some of the strongest songs on the album are Gust's, because they seem best served by the feel of the band. Gust's voice strains less than Smith's to be heard above the tank brigade of the guitars. And in the context of Heatmiser, Gust's expressions of gay-white-guy angst are often more interesting than Smith's lyrics. Before queercore officially existed, it must have been refreshing to hear, over Fugazi–Minor Threat riffs, references to picking suits from men's magazines ("Candyland") and romantic plaints like "I don't know what's genuine/so I go back and forth with him" ("Can't Be Touched").

But it wasn't that novelty that attracted all of the band's fans. There was a jock component at the shows, and it perplexed Smith; he remarked later that he felt like he was playing to kids who would have beat him up in high school, and that the tough punk personality he adopted for that band was a posture.

But Swanson remembers a Smith who clearly felt the rage in the music he was singing. "Elliott was a toughie. He was the lead guy on a lot of those songs and . . . I just remember him being so 'raaah!' He was pissed and it was obvious. And it was strong, it was there, his songwriting was really good, but he was obviously in it. I remember that one "Wake.*" I remember it being super powerful and the kids in Portland just going crazy." Smith had gotten a tattoo: the state of Texas, a reminder of a place where, as he described it, he'd endured hardships and acted like a tough kid.

While Heatmiser was acquiring its local following of fist-pumping kids, privately Smith and Gust had stuck to their arty Hampshire ways. As Swanson remembers, "He and Neil had posters of art work in the house. They had Jasper Johns [posters] and stuff, they didn't have the Renoirs they got from their parents."

About a year after they left Amherst for Portland, they sent Marc Swanson a tape recording of some of the songs that would end up on the first album, *Dead Air*. It had the sound of a disciplined band, with precise rhythms and clear melodies, despite the onslaught of electric-guitar power chords. It was nothing like the Elliott Smith sound the world would come to know.

It was during this period, as Swanson came up from San Francisco to visit Gust, that Smith's shyness finally cracked, and the two became confidantes. "I remember one day while I was there I was like, 'Can we go have lunch together?' And he was like, 'Really?'" says Swanson. "And I was like, 'Well, Neil's not up for it and we can go have lunch together.' Things like that with Elliott were kind of a big deal; that meant we were *friends*."

At this point, Smith was obliged to take the kinds of jobs that frequently turn budding rock stars into law-school applicants. He later recalled that he once got a bad sunburn installing solar

---

*The first song on Heatmiser's 1994 EP *Yellow No. 5*.

paneling—and bad sunburns are tough to come by in Portland. He was a skinny young man. The former Portland promoter Todd Patrick remembers Smith saying that in the early '90s building contractors would give him illegal construction tasks that involved his ability to squirm into small spaces.

"We were playing a lot, but it's not like we were making any money," says Pete Krebs. The two musicians hated their day jobs and were looking for a way to make money faster. "Finally it dawned on us we could be making twenty bucks an hour instead of ten bucks an hour [splitting the money with the carpenter who subcontracted to them], and so he and I got all the equipment to do drywall work and started doing sheet-rocking together as a little company. . . . We did a good eight or ten projects like that. . . . That was during the winter time and I remember it was always fucking freezing. . . . We drywalled, mudded, did all the plaster work on this houseboat up in Ridgefield, Washington, this tiny town on a river. It was the middle of winter and we'd drive up I–5 and get off at Ridgefield and drive though the fields to this little town, across the railroad tracks to where there was this community of houseboats, and we'd haul these big boxes of plaster shit out on these docks. It took us like twenty minutes to walk to it. It was freezing; it was right there on the river and it was just shitty work. It was a houseboat so everything was always moving. We had this portable propane heater that looks like a jet engine with flames coming out the back; that was the only way to heat this thing up, so it was super dangerous. So we did all this work, and got paid, didn't do a very good job, and everybody hated it. About three or four weeks later there was some kind of storm, and it wrecked this houseboat. The houseboat sank or floated away or something. We were both happy about that and bummed out at the same time. Served him right, fucking rich guy."

As much as Smith may have hated day jobs, the assumption in Portland at that time, says Krebs, was that nobody would ever make any money off their music. Nirvana and Sonic Youth may have shown it was possible, but nobody considered it a likely possibility for the members of the Portland indie coterie Krebs and Smith were part of. "You were really into music so you played in a band and everybody had a shitty day job, or two. If you had a bunch of Portland people around a table in 1991 or 1992, and said, 'Well, this is going to happen to you: You're going to be on a major label. You're going to have a major drug addiction, which you'll pull out of. You're going to be on the Academy Awards. And you're going to move to Chicago and become part of this culturally significant art rock scene. And you're going to be a bar musician. And you're going to buy a house,'—nobody would have believed that. It wasn't even in the category of stuff you thought about. You played in bands because you grew up listening to cool bands and it was just natural."

Heatmiser's manager was JJ Gonson, who has made a career as a photographer and a manager since she abandoned her plans to be a musician as a young woman. By the time Krebs and Smith were working construction jobs together, she and Smith were dating, and soon Smith sublet his room in the house he shared with Gust and moved in with Gonson on Southeast Taylor Street. It turned out to be a life-altering decision—it was in that house that Smith started to put down the songs that started his solo career, leading him in a direction radically different from Heatmiser.

"The Taylor Street house was an old Victorian style, and it had a deeply set staircase with deep acoustics," writes Gonson in an e-mail. "Elliott did a lot of his writing and rehearsing in that staircase. He worked on those songs for a long time before he put them on tape, some of them for years. He recorded in the basement, which was not a pretty place. Lots of people had moved through that house, and the basement was piled high with abandoned stuff, so he sort of carved out a little niche, set up a stool and a mic stand, and meticulously recorded the whole thing, going back and punching in tiny changes, sometimes a single word or chord. The wonderful breathy sound on *Roman Candle* is largely due to the quality of the mic, or lack of it. It was a little Radio Shack thing— the kind you used to get bundled with a tape recorder. It had very little power and was very noisy. He also sang quietly, perhaps so as not to be heard by all the people always coming and going upstairs, so you can hear every breath and string squeak. The little powered studio monitors he used we got at Artichoke [Music, a store on Hawthorne Street]. The owner restored old bicycles as a hobby and I traded him an ancient, and very knackered, Schwinn I had found in an abandoned warehouse (doing a promo shoot for some bad metal band) for them. We had no money to get them. I don't know what he would have done otherwise."

It was recorded on an eccentric instrument probably no more expensive than the first guitar Gary Smith bought Steven in junior high. "The Le Domino is a tiny acoustic guitar, I think probably made in the '50s," writes Gonson. "We saw it at Artichoke Music and fell in love with it. It is black with tiny domino decals on the frets and around the sound hole. More importantly, Elliott loved the sound. So, I bought it and he played it for a long time, recorded all of *Roman Candle* on it and used it for his solo shows and even his first solo tour, before it started to get worn out. I still have it."

At first, Smith just played the tape to his friends. Krebs remembers the first time he heard it. The two of them were working at "this warehouse being converted into small loft spaces for business and artists and whatnot. Elliott and I were doing shit work, on top of scaffolds, scraping ceilings and shit like that. So at seven-thirty, eight in the morning I'd come by his house and pick him up or he'd pick me up, and we'd drive downtown and we'd work for a couple hours, drink coffee and talk about music, and then we'd split for a couple hours and go to record stores and go back and work some more. It was a drag. It was a dead-end shitty job, but that's where we got to know one another, and that's when I first heard his music. He was like, 'Yeah, I recorded some of my own stuff, you know?' He had a little cassette, and it was a lot of the stuff that ended up on *Roman Candle*, this cassette. It was me and him fifty feet in the air on a scaffold listening to *Roman Candle* before it came out." Krebs knew how good it was, and from the way he looks back on this time in his life it's clear he mourns for it.

Gonson nurtured Heatmiser even as she helped plant the seeds for the solo career that would eventually help derail Heatmiser and take Smith places far beyond the Portland rock scene. If it wasn't for Gonson, in fact, Elliott Smith's solo work might have stayed stowed away on a series of tapes lying around Portland attics. According to her, Smith didn't intend to put the songs on an album.

Two of the songs on *Roman Candle* stand out as being concerned with Smith's childhood. "'Roman Candle' was the song about Charlie. And '[No-Name] #4' is as much about Bunny as his songs are about any one with thing," writes Gonson. Both of those songs were written with a level of frankness Smith might not have permitted himself if he was recording an album with release in mind. "Cavity Search [Records] had just recently started up, and [the owners] Christopher and Denny were friends of ours, and had made a Heatmiser single. I just used to hang out there sometimes, and this time I happened to have a cassette of what Elliott was doing and put it in. I was Heatmiser's manager, so I used to carry stuff around and play it for whoever would listen—it was a habit that carried over to his stuff, though I wasn't his solo manager (we were too close for that; he didn't have one until later). They were stunned and said, 'We want to release this—just the way it is.' It wasn't even a demo, not even that official, just friends hanging out together one afternoon. Elliott didn't even believe it until they had pestered him about it for a while. He never meant for his solo stuff to be heard or released. I don't think he ever would have considered playing it for anyone at any kind of label and probably was a bit horrified that I had. (I don't remember, but I was certainly never a shy manager, and sometimes it was a sticky point between us.) Those songs were just something he needed to get out of his system that he didn't think there was a place for in Heatmiser, who were (as one reviewer so pointedly put it) 'Chugga Chugga Boy Rock.' Heatmiser were *amazing*, don't get me wrong, but their whole thing was very guitar-heavy and intense. Elliott had all these songs all piled up in his head, and nowhere to use them, so he put them on cassette. I think he did things he wouldn't have done had he thought they might be heard in a real way—like the soaring vocal on the song we wrote together ['No Name #1,' working title 'Saint-Like']—which made Neil laugh the first time he heard it. A good thing, no doubt, that he could be uninhibited by his own lack of expectation. . . . I don't think he would have written so candidly about his childhood if he had thought Bunny might ever hear it, either. It surprised him completely when people responded positively to what he was doing. It was much later that he brought that energy, or lack of it, to Heatmiser, in songs like 'Half Right.' Too late, sadly."

Roman Candle stands alone among Smith's releases for its unusual attention to physical description in the lyrics. A year later, on his first full-length album, *Elliott Smith*, he would find a new poetic resource in drug metaphors. The song "Roman Candle" uses incandescence as a metaphor for repressed anger, as Smith expresses feelings toward Charlie Welch that mirror the feelings of many children toward stepfathers: "He could be cool and cruel to you and me/knew we'd put up with anything." But a number of the songs thereafter, such as "No Name # 4," are short stories; they ride on narrative, character, and description as much as on Smith's distinctive finger-picking, not yet fully formed. The character that Gonson suggests partly represents Bunny Welch is described thus: "For a change she got out before he hurt her bad. . . /The car was cold and smelled like old cigarettes and pine."

"Condor Ave." would hold up throughout his career as one of Smith's top-tier compositions. Starting with is first line, "She took the Oldsmobile out past Condor Avenue," it stuck to the vernacular of workaday Portland. Condor Avenue is a not-particularly-striking road in southwest Portland. Unlike the aggressively streetwise New Yorkese employed by the Velvet Underground and the New York Dolls, Smith's is a muted, civil, almost Midwestern tone in its reluctance to move past concrete description: "You're in the Oldsmobile and driving by the moon/headlights burning bright ahead of you." At the same time, gasps of incivility burst through: "Now I'm leaving you alone/you can do whatever the hell you want to." The sentiment and the delivery are a blend of country and punk. The reticence of the small town competes with the frankness and toughness of the big city; the combination is deeply Portland.

Together, "Condor Ave." and "No Name #4" are the most fiction-like of Smith's songs and they both involve troubled women in cars. The first appears to be a girlfriend who meets some bleak fate in an Oldsmobile. As she drives, the narrator tries to reach out to her and despairs at the impossibility of communication: "I'm lying here, blowing smoke from a cigarette/smoke signal signs that you'll never get." While the narrator and his beloved seem to be doomed by a failure to speak to and hold on to each other, the narrator encounters a man who shares his entrapment: A drinker, "bottle clenched between his teeth/looks like he's buried in the sand at the beach."

In this last description, Smith effectively deploys substance abuse as a metaphor for other forms of self-destructive behavior, and the metaphor is a handy one for several reasons. For one, a songwriter taking substance abuse as his literal subject (even if love is the figurative one) can easily steer clear of the Celine Dion clichés of contemporary Top 40 music, the language of hearts, embraces, great divides. And he participates in a hipper tradition, that of Hank Williams, Johnny Cash, and Kurt Cobain—their addiction laments, disavowals of vice, and caustic self-portraits. Whereas self-destruction in love is usually a series of verbal transactions—lying, cutting yourself off, arguing—self-destruction with drugs and alcohol is a physical process—clenching the bottle between your teeth, putting a spike into your vein. A storyteller need only make the concrete actions vivid to get his meaning across. That's a powerful tool in a lyricist's hands. The emotional danger doesn't have to be compared to physical danger, as it is in the central metaphor of "Roman Candle"; in substance-abuse stories, the emotional danger springs from concrete action.

The cover of *Roman Candle* features a photograph taken by Gonson. It shows Neil Gust and Amy Dalsimer, a friend from

Hampshire, walking through an open-air market in Manhattan during an early Heatmiser tour. But the point wasn't to put his friends on the cover rather than himself, even though it seems like a deliberate gesture of self-deprecation. "He really liked the way that picture looked as a 'piece of art,'" writes Gonson in an e-mail, and Smith asked Gonson to dig it up when it came time to select a cover image. In any case, the image reflects the content of the songs: They're snapshots of apparently mundane but meaningful moments from characters' lives.

The first known Elliott Smith solo show took place at Umbra Penumbra, a now-defunct café near downtown Portland, in September 1994. Smith played a set there that was entirely solo and acoustic but still preserved some of the hardness of the Heatmiser sound. One song that never appeared on an album, "Big Decision," involved verses delivered with the machine-gun speed of an auctioneer. But by and large the songwriting process Smith had developed by 1994 was one conducive to contemplative, rather than combative, music.

"He was so good because he was constantly tinkering," says Pete Krebs about Smith's songwriting. "He wouldn't sit there with a guitar and work it out, he would get a title and walk around at night, when he lived in the Heatmiser house and that neighborhood. . . . He said, 'I'd just get these songs in my head and I'd just concentrate and work through where they went, and by the time I got back from my walk I'd have a song.' It'd be more than a melody. He would arrange it and come up with a lot of information that way."

Through 1994, Heatmiser, and not solo work, was Smith's primary non-construction occupation. But even before his solo career started in earnest, he expressed doubts about his place in Heatmiser to Krebs. "It was before the solo thing, really. . . . Heatmiser was the thing [Smith was known for]. Everybody kind of agreed with Elliott [about Heatmiser], and I don't mean this as a slight to Neil or anything like that, but it seemed like his songs just kind of got lost in the wash. . . . Heatmiser rocked; I really liked Heatmiser. They were just really big and rocked really hard and we played with them a lot. There was a vibe to that band that was really incessant. You just really got into it. . . . Elliott just didn't deal very well with the democratic process that's necessary for a band. Elliott kind of needed a back-up band. It's not that he didn't like playing in a rock band, but I think he felt really confined by it. Being on the road, touring, maybe playing music that he felt like he had compromised on a little bit. I remember talking to him about [how] his tunes just kind of got steamrolled, the subtleties got steamrolled. And he just really didn't like it. . . . Because Elliott . . . knew a lot about recording and microphones and he was really fascinated by that stuff, I think he really quickly identified what he wanted and how he wanted it and how he wanted to pursue the music he was playing. He and Neil were friends from way back so it seemed natural that they would have a band together. I don't think he liked being in a rock band. It wasn't an egotistical thing, he was just much better off as a solo artist."

In 1994, Smith and Krebs put out a split 45-inch on the tiny local label Slo-Mo. Krebs's contribution was the song "Shytown." Smith's was "No Confidence Man." It was recorded in one day, Krebs remembers, at a house then shared by Janet Weiss and Sam Coomes. "Our friend Moira [Doogan] . . . was like, 'Hey, I'm starting this little label, do you want to do a 45?'" says Krebs. "And so we went to Sam and Janet's house when they were still together, over there off of Hawthorne on 37th—Janet still owns that house—and there's a little setup and we just did it in an afternoon. Elliott did all the engineering and I found all the weird noises. We both had these tunes and there's a bunch of forks and knives and spoons hanging from a fishing line. It was an actual instrument they had in their recording [studio] . . . and I was just like, 'We should put that on there.' And Elliott had these dumb masks: a bear mask and a weird bat mask. There's black-and-white shots of us with guitars wearing these masks. We took the pictures outside of Janet's basement. We laughed a lot—we both have the same sense of humor—it was just kind of this dumb sense of humor. He had that old Domino guitar."

Smith's social life at the time was fairly typical for a Portland musician. In addition to doing construction with Krebs, he also worked as a painter with Ralf Youtz, drummer for both the original, temporary line-up of Built to Spill and the short-lived Doug Martsch–Calvin Johnson collaboration The Halo Benders. Todd Patrick—the Portland promoter whose club, 17 Nautical Miles, expired with a party in which a guest punched a hole through the wall into the Hallmark store next door—remembers Smith showing up for karaoke night at the Galaxy Lounge and hanging out at The Lutz.

But his social reputation was unusual in two regards. "He was regarded as an eccentric guy, a very standoffish person, just painfully shy," Patrick says. "But he also wore his emotions on his sleeve. . . . Because . . . he would successfully communicate his feelings and stuff like that, people would get to know him, they'd know how he was feeling. He was a shy human being who was also capable of being very nice and very moral and not cold and not a dick. . . . People kind of felt sorry for him, they kind of looked after him—unlike some other famous people in a small town like Portland. You get a little famous in Portland or any town of that size and anyone who's not famous is going to be resentful. They're going to say that your fame is undeserved and that you're a snob now and this and that. Other people who have achieved a similar level of fame—various things were said about all those other people, but not Elliott Smith. Maybe it's just because his whole painfully shy reputation covered any snottiness he may have betrayed towards people and no one ever took it personally when he'd snub them. But I think he was generally a decent guy who tried to be nice to everybody. Except for the fact that [people] thought he was really fucked up. People thought he was personally weird. Although I would say that among the people that knew him a little better than the average fan, there was a sense that he wasn't as fucked up as he was made out to be."

During this period, Smith got the second of his two tattoos, the one of Ferdinand the Bull on display in the cover photograph of *Either/Or*. The character was invented by author Munro Leaf for a 1936 children's book, *The Story of Ferdinand*, featuring the illustrations of Robert Lawson. Lawson's cover image of a bull sniffing a flower was copied for Smith's tattoo. In the story, Ferdinand was a strong bull with a peaceful disposition. Picked by a fluke to enter the ring with a matador, he refuses to fight. Instead of going on to fame and fortune, he decides to return to his old pasture where he loves to smell the flowers. Smith told an interviewer that he got the tattoo both because he wanted an image of a bull on his arm and because he felt some kind of solidarity with Ferdinand the Bull, a character who was regarded as a failure because he was unwilling to do the things expected of his kind. Smith said that he, like Ferdinand, wanted to work "outside the system."

"When I first met him I didn't get it," says E. V. Day, "and then I totally got it. It's like . . . he's this big bull who doesn't want to fight and would rather sit down and smell the flowers and wishes he wasn't this big bull. He's small but he's so big in his art and in his music. His music is orchestral and so this little man, this little beautiful man made this huge romantic music, and so his bigness, I think, is about the talent inside of him, the vision inside of him. I think he realized he was a big person in a lot of ways: his morals, his ideals, and a lot of things he could never live up to, the expectations he could never live up to inside of himself. I think it's funny to think of him as this large bull too. That's maybe the third element, which is the humor, which is survival. We'd talk about humor as survival from emotional agony, conflict, stuff like that."

That's not the kind of thing Smith was talking about when he actually had the tattoo punched into his arm. "I was around for Ferdinand," JJ Gonson writes in an e-mail. "He'd already got Texas. Ferdinand was done by the wife of a tattoo artist friend of ours. . . . They had a new shop; she was learning and it was one of her first jobs and took a very long time. I never quite understood why he did it. He had this truly perverse fascination with bullfighting, which he had actually never seen, and probably would have been put off by had he [seen it]. It was completely out of character for him. Somehow he had missed the point of the children's story, which I'm not even sure he had ever read and which is about pacifism. Ironically, that would have reflected his actual character (I remember conversations about passive resistance) more accurately."

-Ɵ

When Cavity Search quietly released *Roman Candle* in 1994, the reception was mixed, unusually so for an album nobody had heard of. "With Elliott you think about him being universally liked in a certain world," says Swanson, "but I tried to cram that record down people's throats when *Roman Candle* came out, and so many people were like, 'Whatever, it sounds like Simon and Garfunkel, not my thing, really boring, all the songs sound the same. . . .' I could never get anybody to listen to it, and then I figured out this really funny recipe: The time to get someone was to get them as soon as they broke up with someone. . . . I'd be like, 'You should listen to this,' and it'd be the same person I'd given it to six months earlier who said it was boring and sounded like Simon and Garfunkel, and they would come back to me, like, 'Your friend's amazing.'"

JJ Gonson had opened a Pandora's box by playing Elliott's self-recorded tape for her friends at Cavity Search. The Northwest got its first taste of how distinctive Smith's work could be when it was deeply personal and unaccompanied by a punk rock band. Still, nobody had any idea how good a guitar player and poet he was. That discovery would provoke the decline and fall of Elliott Smith, indie rock musician with a miserable day job, and the rise of Elliott Smith, big genius.

Five

NEEDLE IN THE HAY

Bill Santen graduated high school a year early in Lexington, Kentucky. He was a thin, deer-eyed kid, classically good looking. He could play guitar and he surprised people who knew his proper Southern family with his determination to be a musician. Before he could drink, he headed to LA and then to Portland, and began to play acoustic guitar in bars.

About a year later, he was a heroin addict standing in front of a house Elliott Smith shared with Sean Croghan of Crackerbash in northeast Portland, asking if he might borrow a hundred dollars. He'd called first, but Smith wasn't exactly in the mode for entertaining company. "Elliott came out in his flannels," Santen recalls. Smith took his friend upstairs and gave him what amounted to a career-counseling session. "Elliott mudded and drywalled his own walls," says Santen, and he showed Santen how to do it, talking as he worked. When they walked out together, Smith gave Santen a wad of bills amounting to one hundred dollars.

Later, when they were touring together in 1997, Santen put one hundred dollars on the table of a room they shared. "[Elliott] said, 'I knew what you were probably going to spend this on, but it was time somebody took a chance on you.'" Looking back on his Portland days, Santen, who now lives in Kentucky and no longer has a drug problem, says Smith's kindness helped straighten him out.

The loan wasn't the first act of generosity Smith had bestowed upon Santen. The two met sharing an acoustic solo bill at the Egyptian Room on Division and Southeast 37th. Now one of Portland's most popular lesbian discos, back then "it was pretty much a strip bar," says Santen. "We were doing it once a week and looking for different people to come play." Santen wrote Smith a letter saying he liked playing with him. A couple weeks later, "he called up out of the blue and said he was going up to Seattle with Mary Lou Lord," and invited Santen to share the bill at RKCNDY (pronounced "Rock Candy"), "a pretty stupid LA-style club by the Space Needle. . . . Everyone was coming for Mary Lou; nobody knew who he was."

Mary Lou Lord was by that time on Kill Rock Stars, the Olympia, Washington, label then synonymous with the feminist punk "riot grrrl" movement. The label's main attraction was the three-quarters-female Bikini Kill, a loud, anthemic, political band with song titles like "Reject All American" and "Distinct Complicity." But Lord, a native of Salem, Massachusetts, came from an entirely different underground: the T subway system in Boston. Having acquired a local reputation as a busker with an acoustic guitar, she stumbled across fame in the punk rock universe by falling into a romantic relationship with Kurt Cobain shortly before he settled down with Courtney Love, when Nirvana played Boston in the early '90s. Lord had cut an EP for Kill Rock Stars featuring seven folk ballads and one rock song, "Lights Are Changing." "Lights Are Changing" was a departure from her busker mode—it contained drums, bass, and electric guitar—and it was a split from the regnant indie rock sound of the day in that it was unabashedly a '60s song. The melody and the chiming guitars recalled The Byrds and early electric Bob Dylan, as did the lyrics, which were not as concerned with social controversies as with old-fashioned relationship themes.

The Smith–Lord alliance was revealing in a number of important ways. Smith was still the co-frontman of Heatmiser, and by accounts he gave later on, staying in the band only as a favor to

Neil Gust. "Neil never asked me to do that—it was just my trip," he would later say of his determination to stick with the project. Heatmiser was, in Smith's words, "trying to be Fugazi." It would be an understatement to say they were grunge as opposed to folk-rock—they were about as far from folk-rock as you could go and still have verses and choruses. For a Heatmiser member to be traveling up to Seattle to open for a neo-folkie was, if not an act of remonstration, an act of broadmindedness. For Smith to perform with a folk-rock act at RKCNDY must have seemed fey in a distinctly un-Heatmiser way.

Lord had discovered Smith because she was dating Slim Moon, the founder and owner of Kill Rock Stars. Not long after the release of *Roman Candle* on Cavity Search, she was deep in conversation backstage at a show featuring Moon and his band Witchy Poo, when Moon came and told her to come to see the guy performing. She hadn't listened for long before she decided the "little punk kid" on stage was "the quintessential songwriter of our generation besides Kurt Cobain," as she later put it in an interview with Harvard's radio station.

Lord introduced herself to Smith, who already knew who she was, and invited him to tour with her. Moon signed Smith to Kill Rock Stars and put out his second, self-titled album in 1995. While it was recorded in much the same way as *Roman Candle*, at home, it was promoted heavily, with posters of Smith appearing in record-store windows all over the Northwest. By the time Santen got to know him, his solo career was well under way through a Kill Rock Stars showcase at the LA club Jabberjaw, where Smith had met his longtime manager, Margaret Mittleman, and his longtime producer, Mittleman's husband Rob Schnapf.

Heatmiser was hardly a critically acclaimed platform from which to launch Smith's solo work into a position of indie rock prestige, no matter how many Portland kids came to the shows. "I think most people who had good taste thought Heatmiser sucked," says Todd Patrick. "They didn't like them at all; they were a 'grunge band.' Which is funny because if you listen to *Mic*

City Sons [their last album], they were going in a completely different direction. That band was not regarded very well. I think it's almost surprising how much he [Smith] was accepted there by artistic people who had good music taste, critical snobs like yourself and I."

Smith's task was to win over critical snobs as a touring musician, and in the beginning his solo tours were as uncomfortable as the next punk rocker's. Patrick first met Smith in 1995 when Patrick was a twenty-year-old indie rock fanatic in Texas. He and his girlfriend of the time drove ten miles from their Austin home to Lubbock to see a bill in which Smith opened for The Softies, by a skateboard ramp. The two acts—The Softies being a quiet, largely acoustic indie pop duo consisting of Rose Melberg and Jen Sbragia, at that point based in Portland—were traveling with their guitars in a Geo, and as Patrick recalls things were not going smoothly. "They got kicked off their slot by Possum Dixon* at some bar in Austin. I tried, with this guy who owned a record store, to book them at a show"—Patrick's first effort as a promoter. "It didn't work."

But Patrick could offer Smith and The Softies shelter, and he found the obscure solo artist both kind and eccentric. "They stayed with us for four days, The Softies and Elliott. I got to know The Softies pretty well and I got to know what a unique guy Elliott Smith was—us and The Softies went out and bought some beer, and he spent the entire time in our apartment on our computer. We had an Internet connection, which was sort of unique. I guess he had never been on the Internet, and he spent the entire time in our apartment logging on. He didn't leave, and he was very standoffish and he was constantly calling somebody. When he left he was really nice to us . . . he gave us copies of every record he'd made, his first single, a cassette, everything he had. . . .

---

*Possum Dixon was an LA indie band that tasted the beginnings of national attention in the mid-'90s with their album *Star Maps* and then returned to obscurity.

It was sort of incongruous that he'd been this really weird stand-offish guy the whole time but he was so sweet."

Patrick followed Smith and The Softies to their next gig, at Rice University in Houston, and on to the one after that in Louisiana. After they parted ways, Patrick remembers, Smith left the tour early, possibly weary of life in the Geo that carried all three musicians from show to show. "The Softies told us that he had told them he was on all these amazing pain killers, opiates." In retrospect, it was an early sign of problems to come, but it didn't look like an overly serious one at the time. It was around this time that Smith met Dorien Garry, a doorkeeper at the club Maxwell's in Hoboken, New Jersey. She was only eighteen, but they hit it off and he crashed at her place. She would come to be one of his good friends, and she remembers him as being admirably good-humored considering nobody had come to see him play.

In fact, Marc Swanson remembers the earliest days of Smith's solo career as one of the best times to be Smith's friend. "When we really started to spend time by ourselves was when he started to play by himself. He would come to San Francisco, and I'd just meet him at the club; the first couple albums it was like I'd go meet him, he'd go throw his guitar in a cab, and we'd go to my house or a bar and hang out. He didn't know a lot of people in San Francisco, and it got to be where there was an endless stream of people waiting to talk to him. So I think of that as a really nice utopian time with him, because that was even before the old Hampshire students were showing up, or anybody was, when Elliott would come to town."

When Swanson hung out with Smith during those times in San Francisco, there was a strong note of youthful earnestness in the conversations. "I remember him telling me, and we used to argue about it years after that, that he thought visual art was a better medium to—I don't know about express yourself, but more pure, more respectful, and he said he tried to write songs like someone would paint. I would often argue with him, 'No, no, no, music's way better because you have this whole other element with this other group of people and you can work with melody as well as poetry.' [He thought] the art world was kind of safe from this sort of mass media consumption and people were more pure about what they were doing. It wasn't that he was an elitist about it, but we would jockey back and forth over whether it was better to make visual art or better to make music—which kind of shows our age . . . to think about one creative pursuit being better than the other. Now I just think it's kind of silly. We were twenty-four, twenty-five, maybe twenty-six."

The sculptor E. V. Day, who befriended Smith later in New York, remembers Smith's affection for the art world. "He loved art and had such respect for artists. And he really felt like artists were the best, like the top geniuses. Because it was pure expression—in music it's filtered and it's produced and it's packaged and all these changes are made to your final product. And we would argue about all those different things." Like Swanson, Day is successful. Some of her more famous works include exploding dresses, red tatters suggestive of flesh suspended in mid-air. She's stretched thongs into a shape resembling fighter planes and arrayed them, dangling from the ceiling, into a fleet aimed at G-spot bull's eyes painted on a museum's walls.

Of all the new connections Smith was making on tour, the most important may have been Mittleman. Once they'd formed their relationship, they'd stick together as he changed record labels (from Kill Rock Stars to Virgin to DreamWorks), moved around the country (Portland to New York to Los Angeles), went from being a member of a band with a solo project on the side to a crossover success story, and weathered break-ups with Joanna Bolme and other girlfriends. Her husband, Rob Schnapf, worked on five of Smith's albums with his partner Tom Rothrock (if you include Heatmiser's *Mic City Sons*). Smith would invite himself over to Mittleman and Schnapf's house in LA, Schnapf later recalled, just to play croquet in their yard. When they parted ways in early 2001, Smith went through one of the hardest years of his life.

Mittleman came into management after a long journey through disparate sectors of the music business. Working in music publishing at the powerhouse BMG in the early '90s, she went to the Sunset Junction street fair in Silverlake and saw a performance by a young Beck Hansen. She gave him her card, he got her a demo, and eventually she persuaded BMG to give him a publishing deal. Rob Schnapf and Tom Rothrock recorded Beck's hit "Loser" shortly thereafter, and put it out as a 12-inch vinyl single on their label Bong Load. Mittleman had proved she could find and break talent with the best of them. Two years later, she and Schnapf first saw Smith's Jabberjaw show, where he had the crowd move outside to watch him play because of the extraordinary heat. She was moved by how silent he rendered the crowd.

But just as Smith's career was shaping up from a business perspective, a strange thing was happening to his reputation: His second, self-titled album, which Kill Rock Stars released in 1995, made people think he was a junkie. The first song, "Needle in the Hay," seemed the most obvious bundle of references, including mention of "marks," and meeting up with "the man." Another song, "The White Lady Loves You More," looked only slightly subtler: "Keep your things in a place meant to hide"; "Need a metal man just to pick up your feet." Adding to the druggie ambience, the chorus of "St. Ides Heaven" featured Smith and Rebecca Gates (of the Portland band The Spinanes) singing "High on amphetamines/the moon is a light bulb breaking." The cover of the album, a photograph by JJ Gonson that showed cut-out figures tumbling from a building like suicides, seemed like a portrait of the death-cheating soul that had written the songs. But Smith was no heroin addict.

Not long after the release of *Elliott Smith*, Santen had a candid conversation about the drug with Smith. "He had a show in Boise with The Softies. And I was back in Portland and I was a mess and nobody knew, and I was like, 'Elliott Smith, everyone knows he's a junkie, and I'll offer him a ride to Boise.' And when we were up there I told him I was a mess, and he told me he'd never done it. I was pretty shocked by that. But not really—once you get in that kind of trouble you can tell if someone's been through it or not."

On another occasion, says Santen, "we were driving back from Boise and I was having a talk with him, saying, 'I don't want to go back to Portland, I don't know what to do, I'm in a mess with everything.' We were talking about how heroin had taken over the city. I was talking about swimming across the Columbia River to get some heroin, and he was like, 'I'd swim across that river for a piece of carrot cake.' We spent the next two hours going around looking for carrot cake, after we were having this really heavy moment in the car."

You can hardly blame listeners for thinking Smith had a heroin problem. It's hard to figure out what else might have inspired a song like "Needle in the Hay." Smith said it was a "fuck you" song, to "everybody." But the song doesn't seem to be about somebody who's been wronged and wants to tell everybody to fuck off. One hears both anger and humiliation as the narrator describes falling out of a bus at 6th and Powell (an innocuous downtown Portland location) and wandering aimlessly, shutting himself off, copping dope "so I can be quiet whenever I want." In a semi-autobiographical read, such as Gonson suggests for "Roman Candle," it is about trying to locate a hidden source of pain or misunderstanding. The "needle in the hay" could be just as much a metaphor for the painful places in Smith's psyche as a metaphor for heroin—a needle in a hay stack is a sharp object concealed from sight that irritates from within, like a bullet that stays lodged in the body years after a gunfight. The song is perhaps less concerned with the experience of being a junkie than with Smith's latent potential for self-destruction, his buried, unwanted impulses.

One of the most telling statements about Smith's songs came from Luke Wood, the label executive who worked with Smith at DreamWorks, shortly after Smith's death, in a tribute hosted by the LA-based radio station KCRW. "I've never seen anyone better with metaphor in pop music than Elliott Smith, because he would talk about the layers of his lyrics in a very articulate planned-out way, and there'd be a metaphor for something else that was a metaphor for something else and by the end of the song he would hint at you about what it was really about," Wood said. "And that's partly, I think, why the mythology behind Elliott and some of his personal issues is much larger than reality, because he used addiction or sadness or depression as metaphors for relationships or as metaphors for how you get through life."

The most important metaphor on the self-titled album is substance abuse. And Smith made it clear in an interview with the Mississippi-based zine *Spongey Monkey* that it was indeed a metaphor: "I just wasn't in as bright of a mood when I was making it up," he said. "The first one was more about people, that was the angle of it. The second one, I wasn't hanging out with people as much. Sometimes people are like, 'Oh, the second one is all about drugs and stuff,' and it's not about drugs. It's a different angle or topical way of talking about things. Like dependency and mixed feelings about your attachment. It's good for you on the one hand, and on the other hand it's not really what you need."

"Southern Belle," another song from *Elliott Smith*, sounds in some ways like a folk song; it even has bluegrass touches. But the song starts with a droning guitar chord, and Smith maintains that drone and uses it to great effect. Like "Venus in Furs" or "All Tomorrow's Parties" off *The Velvet Underground and Nico*, the heart of the song is the way the melody deviates from and returns to that drone. While at first "Southern Belle" branches out into acoustic bluegrass punk, the coda owes much to the Velvets. A second guitar track comes in to emphasize the drone note against the ongoing melody of the other guitar. It's a more emphatic version of the pattern Smith established earlier in the song, with the drone doubled across two guitar parts. But for most of the song, there's only the single acoustic guitar, carrying the drone on the higher strings and the melody on the lower strings. It's a solo acoustic execution of one of the Velvets' signature concepts.

Smith's ability to play two parts at once on the acoustic guitar made it possible for him to graft the Velvets' style onto a song that had the energy and bitterness of early Dylan protest songs. He rectified the feeling of lethargy that accompanies most songs built around a drone by surrounding his drone with activity and maintaining a rhythm without heavier instrumentation that might have weighed the song down. The result is a song with both the sinister quality of the Velvets and the righteous energy of folk music, perfect for capturing the narrator's disdain for the pernicious "you" he addresses.

The lyrics are classic Smith in their mix of drug innuendo and scolding. "How come you're not ashamed of what you are?" the narrator asks, before lamenting the fact that "you're the one she got." On the other hand, the narrator allows "I live in a southern town/where all you can do is grit your teeth," which in the context of the more explicit drug references scattered throughout the rest of the album suggests the effects of amphetamines. The narrator's contradiction corresponds to the mixture of Velvets-style rock and bluegrass in the music. And the tension between the two sentiments and styles is one Smith uses to his advantage over and over again. The strain between them runs from "Needle in the Hay" through "Speed Trials"; his self-titled album and *Either/Or* share that strain as a defining characteristic.

On one tour in 1997, Santen would travel with Smith across the country to Atlanta, where Pete Krebs met Smith to take over Birddog's slot on the way back to Portland. It was an enjoyable experience for Krebs: "Most of the time when we got together we would just have beers and crack jokes, so it wasn't songwriters' summit or anything like that. He was just a really funny guy. Maybe it was because we had a really similar sense of humor, but I just thought he was a fucking scream." Krebs's pictures from this tour include a series in which Smith does the moonwalk against the backdrop of a fittingly lunar Western landscape. "Elliott was a real good moonwalker, and we were at a rest stop in the desert in front of one of the Indian moccasin shops, with the desert mountains behind us."

"He called me up and he was like, 'You want to do this tour? I need to make a hundred dollars a show,'" Krebs remembers. "That was a really interesting experience because before that tour, Elliott and I were kind of—we came from the same place. In my mind we were equal, not necessarily in artistic ability, because I always thought he was leaps better than me, but I just figured, 'We're friends, we come from the same place.' But that was the first time I noticed an inequality, in a way. Elliott was beginning to get special treatment for what he was able to do—and rightfully so. People were definitely cognizant of what he had going on. In a way I think that in retrospect it was kind of naïve of me to have gone into it with that frame of mind. I flew down, like, 'Oh yeah, me and Elliott are going to go on tour together,' and I think he had the same thing. He was just like, 'Oh yeah, it'll be fun, tour with friends.' He was always really good about playing with friends and helping out people. So we did this tour, but it was like touring with a star all of a sudden. The tour manager guy was hired to focus on Elliott. I don't know who hired him—Margaret Mittleman was involved at that point. It was the first time I went, 'Whoa, people outside of town really know who this guy is.' He was much bigger outside of Portland for a while than he was here, it seemed to me. Because you had that exotic, 'he's not from here' kind of thing, 'brilliant genius from Podunk, Oregon, comes to New York City' thing happening for him. It was really striking the way people would interview him and the way people would treat him. I kind of got to see that firsthand. It's the situation where you've got a close friend or someone that you know really well and you don't see them for a while and you hang out with them and something has changed in their life. They have a lot more recognition or money or there's some inequality that happened, but you didn't notice, or now things have changed. So you just sort of sit there and go, 'Whoa, this is really different.' That's what that tour was like. It was really fun hanging out, and I think Elliott wanted things to be the way they always were, but all of a sudden he was thrust into this limelight being like this savant, this genius. People saying, 'This is the greatest thing I've ever heard in my life.' And this was before a lot of the big shit happened. After it was over I was just like, 'Wow, that was a really strange experience.'"

Smith had his share of low-budget punk rock touring, both with Heatmiser and on his own, and this was travel de luxe. For a lot of indie rock bands, simply being able to sleep in hotels instead of on acquaintances' floors is a magnificent accomplishment. "Margaret [Mittleman] had him really busy. He was constantly doing interviews and stuff, radio spots, and he had this handler guy—not that he needed it—smoothing out all the rough edges. It was a different kind of touring. It was like, 'Wow, this is what it's like when someone is smoothing out the rough edges,' because you're used to going on the road and starving. He drove us everywhere. We were always on time, we always ate, we always had a place to stay. It was amazing. I'd never toured like that before. I'd been eating shitty and sleeping in nasty places for ten years."

Krebs saw a new side of the music business, and he was also seeing a grim new side of Smith. It wasn't because of heroin, that mythic destroyer of lives on tour; it was because of Smith *threatening* to do heroin. "Elliott was just kind of a drunk at that point. Maybe he messed around a little bit and took pills or whatever, but at that point [1997] he was always just kind of threatening to become a junkie. We'd go to the show and we'd hang out, and at some point Elliott would have enough drinks that he kind of started to do the 'poor me' thing: 'You know, the world is just really hard for me, and there's a side of me I don't know if I'm going to be able to control,' and dark allusions to needles, and it created this dynamic where people just sort of felt like, 'Oh, here's this brilliant guy and I have to save him from this really bad choice.' And that was a dynamic I saw played out a lot, increasingly so, as he got more and more into his head. . . . I'm certainly not trying to dis him or anything like that. He'd eat a peanut-butter-and-jelly sandwich during the day [only], so he would start to drink and then it'd be like, 'I dunno man, I'm just like, just feel really horrible.' And you'd be like, 'Well, what's wrong?' And there's like twenty minutes trying to get him to say what's wrong, and he'd say what's wrong, and then you'd spend the rest of the night trying to make Elliott feel better. For the first couple weeks of it it's fine, you'd be like, 'This guy is brilliant, he's my good friend, he's hilarious, I love him, I love being with this guy'—'C'mon man, life is good, it's really not that bad.' But then after a while it just got to be a drag because you'd start to see it as this recurring theater production or something where Elliott was getting the response he really needed. Elliott got the response of people saying, 'O god, isn't it horrible that you might like destroy yourself? How can I save you?'

"It was just like dark threats, of, 'I have this thing that I really feel like I can't control. And I'm keeping it at bay, but I want you to know I might not be able to do this.' From what I understand—after that tour we didn't see each other as frequently—that started to manifest itself as 'I don't know if I'm going to be alive much longer.'"

Smith, the author of the self-titled record with the abundance of heroin references, was still thinking about the drug but not doing it. But talking about how there was a part of him susceptible to heroin's temptations was alienating in and of itself in much the same way an actual heroin habit could be. Smith's preoccupation with heroin frightened people and irritated real friends with its monotony.

Smith was fun to be around when he didn't lapse into self-pity. He was happy early on in the same tour with Krebs because he had just met Amity—a woman after whom he would name a song on his album *XO*. He was happy through much of the Southeast. In Kentucky, Smith and Krebs begged their driver to lend them the car so they could go out on the town. The driver conceded, and they drove the green Ford Taurus out to a college bar and ran into a young girl who was considering joining the Army. Krebs and Smith spent the night talking her out of it, which was their idea of a good time. "But as the tour progressed, especially as we got closer to Texas, he kind of got more and more dark, because he had this thing about being in Dallas," says Krebs. "We played Dallas together and he did not want to be there. He was like, 'Oh yeah, I have bad memories of my childhood.'"

Even more striking than the contrast between Smith's recollections of his Dallas childhood and his friends' recollection of that childhood is that Smith's memory of Dallas was so negative he found it traumatic even to be near his hometown. The bitter memories he carried of childhood figured only slightly or not at all in Mark Merritt and Steve Pickering's memories of Steve Smith. Shortly after his traumatizing childhood there, he spent time visiting Bunny and Charlie at the house he'd lived in. It's remarkable that years later, after Bunny and Charlie no longer lived in Dallas, he should have had such an aversion to the place. It was as if the real Dallas had become the same as the harrowing literary construct of "Dallas town" that appeared in some of his greatest songs. In "You Gotta Move" on *Mic City Sons* he sings of a Dallas "where the sky burns bright white"; and, of course, in "Some Song" it's a place "you must be sick just to hang around." Dallas seems to have been Smith's metaphor for a set of problems, but it was either a metaphor so powerful that it changed Smith's own perceptions of the real place, or during his years in Portland and Amherst Smith had come to look back on his Dallas childhood as a period far worse than he thought it was when he was living it.

Dallas and heroin were two of the most prominent ogres in Smith's songs, and both his incomplete memory of his own boyhood and his educated guesses about the inner life of a heroin addict were to some extent products of his imagination. They inspired great songs and tortured him personally; he was deeply sensitive to images stuck in his head that posed no concrete threat to his well-being. What haunted Smith were dangerous corners of his mind, corners that he peeked into when he wrote his songs but that were better left alone if he had any intention of living a happy life. Smith preferred to think about them and explore them in art rather than think of them as baggage to get rid of.

Krebs thinks that as much as Smith might have thought about doing heroin, he never saw heroin as an end, a route to death. He saw it as a dramatic episode in his life. "The thing about Elliott in his drug use is that I felt like it was somehow in his plan to get strung out, to get really far out there. I always felt like the whole heroin thing, he nodded to it, no pun intended. He had it in his mind that that was going to be part of the picture."

It also helped get him attention both on a personal level, drawing concern from friends, and in the public sphere, creating a recognizable public image of Smith as somebody who wrote about drug addiction. "He was getting some mileage out of people freaking out when he would talk about it, so he liked that. I really feel like the plan was, 'I'm going to get really fucked up and come back from that.' I never thought that he would intentionally kill himself or OD intentionally; if he died it would be an accidental OD. He had plenty of opportunities to kill himself when he got really depressed; I always just felt like he would have done it. I heard he tried a couple of times and they were half-hearted attempts and something happened. With the heroin thing I just thought that that was part of the plan, I thought he was going to do his thing and then he was going to come back. That was the big picture, and he would overcome his demons or have some depth of experience he could draw from artistically or somehow satisfy some romantic vision he wanted to be like. But I don't think his romantic vision was finally tragic. I think he liked being a tragic character but he wanted to be around to see the results of that characterization."

Marc Swanson thinks the Smith songs that dealt with drugs were generally a blend of autobiographical and non-autobiographical material. Literal, simple interpretations were rarely the best ones. "I think in a way a lot of times Elliott's songs were about bigger things, more than people realize, but they also could help to be self-portraits in a way because I think most good artists are taking themselves and their interaction with the world and reinterpreting through the light of what they make. I think you would get a lot of different answers from people about what different songs are about, because often if you got deep into a certain subject he might say, 'Well that's what that song was about.' And I don't know if it was ultimately *just* about that. There was always this running thing of which girlfriend it [a song] was about, depending on when he wrote the song, whether he was going out with JJ or Joanna. I think there are some autobiographical items in them all the time. But I would never take 'St. Ides Heaven,' [to be] about walking around high on speed or something." (The chorus of "St. Ides Heavan" begins, "High on amphetamines/The Moon is a light bulb breaking.") "Who knows, maybe, but I wouldn't assume that it happened a couple nights before."

Heroin wouldn't become an issue for Smith until Los Angeles—alcohol was his first problem substance. He was a good social drinker—he liked to have deep conversations in bars. "A lot of what me and Elliott did is sit in bars until four in the morning or however late they were open," says Swanson, "and just talk."

On tour in the mid-'90s, Santen remembers Smith as more focused geek than rampaging musician. After he hooked up with Mittleman, he traveled to shows in the backseat of a Lincoln Continental or the Taurus. "He was so together. When we were [on tour] he bought a tape machine and he read that manual diagram by diagram just studying that thing," says Santen. "He was so disciplined, recording and reading. It was pretty inspiring."

As if challenging himself to increasing heights of nerdiness, Smith alternated between recording-equipment manuals and science fiction. "He was pretty hard to travel with," says Santen.

"To begin with, the tour manager didn't stop; he'd drive four or five hours without stopping. The first thing [Elliott] did on tour was buy *2001: A Space Odyssey*, so most of the time driving he would just read and I'd be crawling out of my skin." Smith brought exactly one tape with him on tour, and listened to it over and over again: a Velvet Underground album. "It was one of those reissues, with two versions of 'Mr. Rain.' It starts with 'We're Going to Have a Real Good Time Together' [*Another View* (Verve, 1986)]."

But it wasn't that Smith was anti-social. He was by all accounts a funny guy who cared deeply about how people perceived him and even had ambition and a sense of direction. "He'd kind of wake up at night," says Santen. "I asked him a lot of questions. I knew he knew where he was going. It was fun asking him stuff about life and his experiences playing music and places he'd been. He had the outlook, 'You know what, just do what you're doing, don't send music off to record labels, don't do any of that crap.' He taught me how to be simple about things. The way that he recorded is the way I record now. Simple as can be."

And Santen found Smith to be an excellent confidante, even though their relationship never approached the kind of closeness Smith seemed to experience with close friends like Sean Croghan or Neil Gust. "Whenever we'd do something in Portland that wasn't music, I'd just call him and we'd meet at Dots. That was right across the street from me. I don't know if I'd ever had another guy like that. It wasn't like we were best friends by any means. He was just an acquaintance I could call up and be like, 'Let's get a beer.' I can't imagine doing that now with anybody. And it's weird because we weren't really that good of friends."

Dots Café, on Southeast Clinton Street, is a quintessential Portland establishment, from its vaguely retro-'50s name to its abundance of beer and pool tables and its dim lighting. It's a place where you could order a vegan sandwich with a can of beer and then play several rounds of pool with a cigarette trapped between your teeth. Entrees didn't cost more than six bucks. The place embodied some of the qualities that distinguished Portland in the '90s from other "left coast" cities like San Francisco. On one hand it had vegan options, an album by X on the stereo, and cave-dark pseudo-Victorian wallpaper; on the other it had cheese fries and smoking and Budweiser in a can, a location-specific fusion of cosmopolitan and blue-collar aesthetics.

As much as this seems to mirror the music Smith made in Portland, with its blend of comforting, folky guitar and punk rock darkness and minimalism, Smith seemed to have his sights set on a different part of the world. "He talked about New York like it was Oz. When he found out I'd never been there, that was all he talked about," says Santen. "He talked about how much I'd love it and all the great things you could do there. I don't think he cared much about Portland. . . . One of the things he told me is that he hated Portland because everybody played music and everybody did the same thing. He wanted to move to New York City so he could meet people who made movies and were artists and did different stuff."

As Smith started to yearn for life beyond Portland's music scene, the music world was starting to turn away from the Northwest in general. The early '90s, in the United States, had been a time when Northwestern grunge established itself as a force on the album charts along with the pop R&B ballads of Whitney Houston and the ascending genre of hip-hop, still only a decade old in the consciousness of most Americans. The press of the time was full of the concurrent rise of "rap and grunge," but the latter grew stale while the former—focused in New York and Los Angeles—took over. By 1996 hip-hop was achieving an unprecedented degree of acceptance in the upper-middle-brow kingdom of *The New Yorker* and the *New York Times*, largely as a result of The Fugees' breakthrough album *The Score*. It was a turning point not just for hip-hop but for rock as well. Accustomed to being the only acceptable pop-music option among the smarter-than-average set, rock lost ground to hip-hop among Americans with brainy inclinations. Groups like The Roots were claiming college students and artistic teenagers who would have formerly gravitated toward alternative rock. In cities like New York and London, began to look as if rock were on the way out. Despite the commercial success of Oasis and some of their Britpop brethren, hip-hop and techno dominated among young people who considered themselves connoisseurs of music. As *The New Yorker* put it in a 1996 profile of the doomed child alt-rock star Ben Kweller, "alternative" now meant mainstream. And by the logic alt-rock had itself installed in the psyches of teenagers on both sides of the Atlantic, that meant it was hopelessly out of style.

But Portland was sealed off, somewhat, from these trends, which were financially catastrophic to anybody who hoped to make a living with an acoustic guitar. While Portland had something of a rave scene, hip-hop groups remained barely visible even as hip-hop came to dominate radio and album charts elsewhere in the western world. For one thing, Portland was a predominantly white city, and the prospect of Oregonian rappers retained, in America's pre-Eminem innocence, an aura of absurdity. When hip-hop bigwigs like Jeru the Damaja came through Portland, they sometimes found themselves disappointed by the mellowness and passivity of the crowds. It was not a dancing town, outside of a small swing-dance scene. In Seattle, there were optimistic mutterings that a local hip-hop scene was poised for greatness, but never in Portland. And while Portland did have dance clubs, its ethos of non-stylishness and informality—call it the raincoat aesthetic—made the city barren ground for the seeds of a real techno movement. The Portland rave scene, though represented in a few serious record stores for DJs, worshipped Detroit house and never came into a sound of its own.

As all these movements slid past Portland, the local indie rock scene clung stubbornly to its position of prominence. The Northwest had already lost its claim to being world headquarters for rock 'n' roll, but it remained rock 'n' roll territory. At shows by techno acts of the moment like Spring Heel Jack, attendance was mediocre, while at shows for veteran acts like The Scofflaws there'd still be enough (fully grown) skinheads in attendance for there to be large, regular brawls on the floor.

As Smith's solo efforts got more and more serious and elaborate, indie rock turned further away from the kind of music he made. When *Roman Candle* was released in 1994, Liz Phair had just a year earlier been a hot new thing for her minimal ennui opus *Exile in Guyville*, and footage from Nirvana's *MTV Unplugged* concert was played regularly in the wake of Kurt Cobain's suicide. Both Phair and the acoustic version of Nirvana shared Smith's personal tone and stripped-down approach to rock and folk. But when Smith got famous in 1997 and 1998, he was an anomaly, a holdout for guitar rock when nobody cool was playing a guitar. What was cool was every variety of "post-rock": fusions of electronic music and hip-hop, like Massive Attack, or intricately layered groove music like Stereolab or Tortoise.

The increasingly isolationist climate of mid-to-late-'90s indie rock would nurture Smith's solo career even as that very career became one of the influences that lead indie rock bands out of seclusion, back into the embrace of major record labels and back into public scrutiny.

Six

EITHER/OR

WHILE HEATMISER HAD represented a collaboration of apparently equal partners as far back as *Dead Air*, the band's sound had been such that Gust's songs, not Smith's, were the standout tracks. The strongest tune on *Dead Air* is Gust's "Can't Be Touched," with its swaying rhythm and power chords, the melody carried along by the iron tone of Gust's singing. On *Mic City Sons*, the best tracks are mostly Smith's. Gust still weighs in with impressive songs ("Low-Flying Jets" and "Rest My Head Against the Wall") but the highlights are Smith's "Plainclothes Man" and "Get Lucky."

"Plainclothes Man" was more like the Elliott Smith solo work to come than any of the songs on his self-titled album. On *Mic City Sons*, Smith, Schnapf, and Rothrock figured out a way to wed the intimacy of Smith's solo work to bigger production, and Smith would follow that path on a few songs on *Either/Or* but especially when he was reunited with Schnapf and Rothrock on *XO*. "Plainclothes Man" looks in retrospect like the blueprint for the last two Smith albums: the familiar double-tracked vocals over acoustic guitar and then, gradually, the intrusion of electric guitar, drums, and keyboard. "Get Lucky," the album's first track, wouldn't be out of place on *Figure 8*. The guitar has classic rock swagger, but the vocals still have the soft, breathy tone of *Roman Candle*.

The Smith songs are still dramatically different from the Gust songs on *Mic City Sons*, but the production had changed to bring out some of the best traits in Smith's songwriting and singing. Smith had become the most famous member of the band, because his self-titled album was garnering a reputation. Dorien Garry remembers that in 1995, Smith became a client of Girlie Action, then a tiny, brand-new PR firm with a handful of employees. Garry had recently been hired as a junior publicist there and her job included handling minor press for Smith—zines of the day like *Ben Is Dead*—while the agency's co-founder, Felice Ecker, handled the larger media outlets.

On the other hand, Heatmiser seemed bound for its own fame and glory. The band had signed a deal with Virgin Records for *Mic City Sons* to be released on its alt-rock division, Caroline. It was a deal with a couple distinctive features: One, according to Smith, was that the label retained the rights to release any solo albums by any member of the group if the band split. The other was that it provided the band with enough money and freedom to stock up on studio equipment and record the album in a house (Heatmiser House) by themselves. The result was that Smith came to disagree with Lash about how they should produce parts of the album, producers Rob Schnapf and Tom Rothrock were brought in to help them find their way, and the band decided to break up—but Virgin retained the right to release future Elliott Smith records.

For now Smith was touring nationally with the self-titled album and then *Either/Or*, his second and last Kill Rock Stars album, sometimes accompanied by Mittleman. He was a musician's musician, on the radars of only the most serious of connoisseurs. In the winter after the 1995 release of *Elliott Smith*, he shared a bill with another obscure figure at the Manhattan club Fez: Stephin Merritt, playing with his band The Magnetic Fields.

One of the musicians who came to that gig was Mike Doughty, the singer of Soul Coughing, a band that had just hit its stride as a breakout act from an avant-garde Manhattan rock scene centered around the Knitting Factory in Tribeca. After two albums on indie label Slash Records, they put out their first Warner Brothers release, *Irresistible Bliss*, in 1996, and their last, *El Oso*, in 1998, before calling it quits in 2000, around the same time Smith moved to LA. In their major-label days, they cut a couple songs that received some national airplay, such as "Super Bon Bon." The mix of genres—funk, hip-hop, jazz, no-wave— had nothing in common with Smith's music, but the two singers shared an attentiveness to words and a loathing of cliché. Doughty was developing a solo acoustic act (his manager termed it "Sebadoughty," for its resemblance to Lou Barlow's indie rock band Sebadoh) that came to resemble Smith's music far more than anything he'd done with his band.

It was the first of many times Doughty went to an Elliott Smith show. "[Smith and The Magnetic Fields] were both not particularly notable to anybody at the time, but my A&R guy took me and he totally snobbed out on me for my never having heard of either one of them," he says. "It had to have been early in the week, not very crowded, and clearly with an incompetent sound guy because both acts spent the evening scowling at the guy. . . . Stephin Merritt was so in angry-Stephin-Merritt mode, about the sound guy, about the subway that rumbles past that venue, about the shittiness of the crowd, he was just basically glaring. Whereas Elliott was just looking woeful, he was openly looking like Charles Bronson out at the sound guy. . . . And it was incredible. I went and got the records of both acts, and it was *Elliott Smith*, and after that I went to every gig Elliott did in New York. If I was in New York and he was in New York, I was there."

Doughty's A&R man at Slash Records, Randy Kay, took him to hang out with Smith and Mittleman after one show. "I guess after the fifth or sixth time I saw him, we met him after the show at the camp theme bar next door to Brownie's, and we hung out, and we talked about drummers, and the old Sam Cooke records and the drum sounds on them and how basic they were. . . . I said, 'Well, have you thought about making a record with Mitchell

Froom? [And he said], 'No, I haven't heard of him.' . . . 'Oh, he's really great, and blah blah blah,' and Margaret Mittleman was just freaking out. When I said 'Mitchell Froom,' she was just completely aghast at the idea. She just totally got her back up, it was like super visible." Froom is a frequently unconventional producer whose credits include Suzanne Vega and Los Lobos as well as weirder projects like Cibo Matto and the soundtrack for the cult movie *Café Flesh*. Of course, Smith ultimately picked Mittleman's husband, Rob Schnapf, and his partner, Tom Rothrock, as his producers. "I remember him speaking almost apologetically about having someone from BMG hanging out, as was the custom of the time," says Doughty, referring to the indie-cred issues of the mid-'90s that dogged musicians who in other periods might not have cared at all.

Mittleman proved highly effective at negotiating contracts and making Smith money, and her skills were in dire need—Smith wanted to get out of a record deal. (It was unclear why Smith didn't want to stay on Virgin after the break-up of Heatmiser, but he didn't.) "There wasn't a bidding war," he told the English zine *Comes with a Smile*. "I didn't want there to be one. They get really ugly and people's feelings get hurt. No, I was in a band that broke up and we were on Virgin and they had a claim to me after that. So DreamWorks bought me out of that. I couldn't stay on the label I was on either way."

Smith's "couldn't" might be understood to mean "couldn't" in an emotional sense, except that it's hard to imagine Kill Rock Stars could come up with the cash to buy Smith out of a deal with a major label like Virgin. Andy Factor, Heatmiser's A&R man, gave Smith no reason to complain, by both Smith's account and Santen's: Smith described Factor as a "friend" in an interview, and Santen's account indicates he wasn't just looking for brownie points: "His A&R guy at Virgin [Factor] was wild about him, he loved Elliott Smith."

Swanson confirms Smith's desire to leave the label: "I remember he talked quite a bit about how he didn't want to be on Virgin, how he wanted to switch. I think after that he started to feel really uncomfortable about complaining about his situation at all to anyone—maybe he could to another musician on his level but not to a friend who was a struggling artist."

Santen recalls Smith's story of what exactly went down when Heatmiser announced their break-up to Andy Factor: "Him and Tony [Lash], they weren't getting along, [Elliott] didn't like the way the record sounded, and the A&R [guy] came into town to say, 'Let's hear the record.' And they sat down and had a meeting with him [and said], 'We broke up.' And he said, 'Okay, Plan B.' Just skipped a step. [Smith's] point of view was, 'Fuck these guys, they want my soul,' but the other point of view is that there wasn't anyone else interested at the time and they fucking loved him, and I think he decided he didn't want anybody who had anything to do with [Heatmiser]."

"I remember asking him, 'Could it be then that [Virgin] puts out your records?'" recalls Dorien Garry. But Smith remained uncomfortable with the situation, not because of anything Virgin had done wrong, but because of the way he had come to be signed to the label. "He fought really hard," says Garry.

On the solo side, there were still modest tours with the likes of Mary Lou Lord. In the mid-'90s, Lord recalled in a Harvard radio interview, they both applied to perform at the music industry's most important conference for indie rock bands: South by Southwest in Austin, a festival where hundreds of bands showcase themselves over the tequila-amplified buzz of journalists, radio programmers, and label executives. They were both rejected, Lord said. On tour, they were headed through Texas anyway, so they conspired to show up at the festival. It was St. Patrick's Day, and they set up on the street with Mary Lou Lord's amp and played in front of a Kinko's. A few drinks later, they were dedicating Irish songs to Shane MacGowan of The Pogues, and Slim Moon and Calvin Johnson showed up. Neither Johnson's Olympia-based K Records nor Moon's Olympia-based

Kill Rock Stars had showcases at South by Southwest, as ambitious indie labels generally do, so the site became an impromptu outsider outpost.

Years later, when things started to go seriously awry for Smith in LA, one of the things his friends from this period missed most was his playful side. "He had the best kind of sideways conspiratorial glance," says Ramona Clifton, who got to know Smith by introducing him to Lou Barlow at a show. "He'd be talking and make a little joke, and he'd look at you like, 'Did you catch the joke?' And he would do this little sideways grin. He always seemed sort of slightly awkward, not a dancer type of guy, but then he would just slide across the floor, straight moonwalk. He would do it onstage every once in a while with Heatmiser."

Even this early on, a relatively healthy time in Smith's life when drug use and drinking didn't get in his way and his career was ascendant, there was the apparent contradiction in his character that would stay with him: Smith and Lord had a good time on tour, even as Smith often appeared shy and closed-off to people who weren't close to him. As Swanson puts it, "Elliott was hilarious; he was one of the funniest people I ever knew. When we hung out, most of the time we had a really good time. When I think about Elliott I think about him laughing. We would often get into these stupid characters, we'd goof around for hours on end, like he'd be the mad scientist and I or someone else would be Igor. And we'd play those characters out endlessly. And you'd tell him a joke and he'd tell the same joke over and over again and just be in stitches about it and tell it to everybody he'd be in contact with. It was definitely this running thing with him . . . saving up the new jokes you heard for Elliott, and the funniest ones, always in the typical Elliott way, were really funny without being mean to anybody."

On the other hand, says Swanson, "There's also the other half of that guy that was crying a lot, too. To be honest, not to say this in a mean way, but I probably shouldn't say it: By the time we were thinking about us living together, I didn't know if I wanted to live with him. He was a tough person . . . to be friends with. He was very sad and had a lot of demons and problems to deal with."

Before you got to Smith's sadness, you had to penetrate a lot of layers—layers of sweetness and shyness if you were an acquaintance, and layers of good humor, intellect, and esprit de corps if you were a friend. His songs were personal, and they offered clues to his concerns. But they were clues, not roadmaps, and he rejected the idea that people could assume they had the roadmap to his psyche because of psychology or twelve-step-program talks or because he had a business relationship with them.

"It's almost like the sadness came on stronger when he started to do better. This is obviously just a theory on my part too, but I was always really nervous for him because it seemed like the better he was doing, the more he had to justify to other people that he wasn't doing well," says Swanson. "This idea that him being successful as a musician was hurting all of his other musician friends. It started to happen more and more, where it was like, 'One, I can't sing; I can't do anything. But I'm also really sad.' In one way, if you're sad, and then you have everything that's supposed to make your life good and you're still sad—is that Kurt Cobain, is that what happened to him? If you've got the whole world at your feet and you're still sad, what do you strive for after that? And Elliott's sadness was deep and very sad. You could tell. I'm not going to go into specific conversations about that stuff, but I remember understanding that the sadness was probably a kind of sadness I had never even felt before, even though I had had pretty sad times in my life. And I think, in general, just like a lot of people, Elliott, to be frank, started to drink a lot and self-medicate through a lot of these things that had happened to him in the past or whatever it was making him sad. I think it was probably things that had happened in the past, and that he needed to deal with it. But the idea of therapy or anything like that, or when people would try to do the interventions and get him help

. . . I think the writing was on the wall that he needed some out-side help. But I think that's tough to do with a fiercely intelligent person."

In this time, the mid-'90s, one of the better periods in Smith's life, it was hard to worry about him while his career was so clearly picking up steam. Lou Barlow was one of indie rock's most popular artists, and he first saw Smith play on a Kill Rock Stars tour on his birthday, July 17, in 1996. "He was playing to a pretty large room, kind of sparsely attended, and the seats were maybe half full," recalls Ramona Clifton, a friend of Barlow's. "There were maybe fifty people there or something. We started playing and Lou and I couldn't move. We were rooted to the spot. I remember Lou saying after a song or two, 'Fuck. He's re-ally good.'"

Soon, Smith was on the road with Sebadoh, a band with one of the biggest draws in indie rock and fans disposed to like Smith's contemplative, lyrics-centered guitar music. After the July 17 show, says Clifton, "Elliott was just walking around and I went and introduced myself and talked for a minute and said, 'I'm here with Lou Barlow but he's too embarrassed to come over with me.' He wouldn't do it. But Elliott was like, 'Whoa, no way.' I was like, 'Do you want to meet him?' He was like, 'Yeah, of course.' And then they started talking and it was really easy and they got along—it was sort of mutual appreciation, and I think Lou invited him to open for them."

That night the three of them went out to a bar together, and Clifton remembers Smith being smitten with Joanna Bolme. When Pete Krebs and Smith started working together, Krebs was dating Smith's future girlfriend, Joanna Bolme. Throughout Smith's long, slow drift away from his old Northwestern indie gang, Bolme re-mained a constant in his life. She spent some of the mid-'90s working at the Portland club La Luna, where Smith and other Heatmiser members were often found playing pool. Eventually, she began to work as an engineer at Larry Crane's Jackpot! recording studio, and later joined The Minders as a bassist. Since

2001, she's been the bassist for ex-Pavement frontman Stephen Malkmus's Portland-based band The Jicks.

Bolme and Smith moved in together during his later years in Portland, and at one point the couple actually went so far as to move to France together, a failed experiment. Swanson remembers there being no pressing reason for the move: "I remember him and Joanna just being like they wanted to live in France. I think you hear that a lot when people are younger, 'I just want to get out of the U.S., I just don't like it here, and it's not my thing,' and I think they were both really enamored of Paris, and gave it a shot. It didn't work out very well." The couple soon moved back to Portland.

Smith and Clifton played pool, she remembers, "and we started talking and he sort of had a heart-to-heart with me about his girlfriend at the time, and how much he cared about her but he didn't believe—he was afraid she wouldn't stay with him. He was really anxious about that but really sweet about it. He just talked about her to me. I guess he just thought he was kind of a pain in the ass and that she would get fed up with him. It was more general angst. He was missing her, and he was getting uncertain about what was going to happen."

Smith's attitude toward his songwriting was a blend of ambition and self-criticism. He played an opening of Swanson's in San Francisco in 1997, and they didn't tell anybody ahead of time. They talked about how they were both looking to achieve a blend of sadness and optimism in their art. But when Swanson invited him, he spent a day and a half apologizing for wanting to do it, saying he didn't want to ruin his show and talking about how he couldn't sing.

—❧—

The last album by Heatmiser sounds less like Heatmiser than like a new indie rock band influenced by Elliott Smith. Smith's solo career had taken off to the point that Smith himself was singing less in the loud, Fugazi-like style he'd adopted for *Dead Air*. Instead, he was singing the same way he did on his solo albums. Also, there was a crucial line-up change: Brandt, who Smith later called the "most punk" of all the Heatmiser boys, was replaced by Sam Coomes, a veteran from San Francisco band The Donner Party.

The Donner Party was named after an 1846 pioneer expedition from Illinois to California that became trapped in an unusually brutal winter in the Sierra Nevada mountain range and resorted to cannibalism. The band, which formed in 1983 and recorded two albums between 1987 and 1989, has since gained some small recognition from the indie rock world for Coomes's goofy pop-folk-punk songwriting. The Donner Party rocked hard and then soft, often with a macabre sense of humor. Although The Donner Party was hardly considered a great band, Coomes's mischievous songwriting would play a major part in the bands he joined after moving to Portland.

Five years Smith's senior, Coomes was born in Sherman, Texas, and moved to California as a child. He moved to Portland from San Francisco and there formed the band Motorgoat with Janet Weiss and Brad Pedinov "circa 1990." Motorgoat released two cassettes and a single on 7-inch vinyl, and after Pedinov left, Coomes and Weiss stuck together and dubbed the stripped-down outfit Quasi. They would become Smith's touring band in the late '90s.

It's hard to distinguish Coomes's effect on Heatmiser's music from the effects of the band's having been given a large sum of money by Virgin Records, which it used to buy its own equipment and record an album in Heatmiser House. But what is certain is that the punk element of Heatmiser—in the loud, fast, distortion-soaked sense of the term—went into remission under the new circumstances. Melodies established themselves through clarity rather than pounding insistence and volume. Instead of power chords, the guitarists used finger-picking and slide techniques, and the beat deviated from the medium-fast tempo that set the tone on *Dead Air*. Most importantly, both Smith and Gust seem to have taken a hint from the success of Smith's solo records. Instead of repeating the effortful shouting that Smith tried to make his own on *Dead Air*, he sings like the Elliott Smith audiences know from his solo albums.

With the infusion of money from Virgin came the assistance of the two producers who would stay with Smith for his next three albums: Rob Schnapf and Tom Rothrock. Schnapf and Rothrock were young up-and-comers at that point, and the production of the record reflects the quiet "production" of Smith's self-titled album.

"We did it at the Heatmiser House," Schnapf says of *Mic City Sons*. "They had rented this house and filled it with equipment and started the record on their own. And I think they couldn't come to terms with one another and they needed outside help. So we recorded it up there and we mixed it at the shop. When we came in [the songs were] in varying degrees of [completion], some were pretty far along, some were barely along, some we started from scratch. It was a collaborative effort, as always. We recorded in the bottom floor of the house. The living room was where they had made the control room, and then the dining room was where the drums were cut, and the kitchen was where a lot of guitars and vocals were done, so the dining room was more dead-sounding and the living room was more live-sounding. We were separated by this 8-inch wall."

Schnapf says part of his function during the recording was to mediate between Smith's and Lash's the differing visions for the album. It had always been an unusual trait of Heatmiser's that the drummer exercised the most control over the band's recorded sound. Heatmiser's mixes had heretofore emphasized the band's beat and capacity to rock more than making the melodies clear. With the melody half of the band suddenly flexing its muscles, there was bound to be some new disagreement. "Elliott and Tony had a difference of values," says Schnapf. "I don't know this to be factual but I sort of gleaned from the situation [that] Tony had been doing it, and those records had sounded a certain way, and

[then] Elliott started spreading his wings. There just wasn't room for the two of them. [Elliott] started getting an artistic vision himself, and they were just too close to one another and they needed a third party to say 'here.'" Schnapf may not be certain that that assessment was "factual," but Smith sounded pretty sure of himself when asked about Heatmiser's transformation by *Under the Radar*: "Me and Neil kind of took over."

One of the goals with *Mic City Sons* was to achieve a more old-fashioned sound than would had been put down on any previous Heatmiser release. "With their equipment and the way we went about it we tried to make it a more analog recording, even though their equipment was digital," says Schnapf. A less punk, more ethereal feel was also abetted by Coomes's facility with slide guitar: "The harder [slide] stuff would be Sam, where finesse was required."

The irony of Heatmiser was that as soon as the band started to produce something like the music closest to Smith's soul, it collapsed. The bandmates wanted to go in separate directions, and there was no longer a workable compromise. Smith later referred to the band as a "disaster" of sorts.

Did Smith worry about being a failure in the early days? "I think," says Swanson, "in a way he was always afraid of that." But in 1996 he pieced together the album that would eliminate any possibility of a return to obscurity. *Either/Or* is in some sense the last of Smith's early Portland solo albums, characterized by stripped-down production with Smith's acoustic guitar and vocals at the center. But it's also the first of the latter-day Smith albums in that its most remarkable moments—the moments that made Smith's career, and arguably made *Either/Or* his best album— were recorded with state-of-the-art equipment at The Shop, Rob Schnapf and Tom Rothrock's state-of-the-art studio in Humboldt County, California. The instrumentation on "Between the Bars," "Angeles," and "Say Yes" might have been the same as on "Southern Belle" and "Christian Brothers" off the self-titled album, but the sound was far more delicately produced.

For one thing, there was The Shop itself, a hundred-year-old riverside barn with plenty of windows in the heart of California marijuana country, surrounded by redwoods. The facilities were luxurious. "We had a control room and we had three other spaces," says Schnapf. "We had this old console from Wally Heider Studio 4—it was the board from [Gram Parsons's] *GP* and *Grievous Angel*, and a diverse bunch of Tom Waits records—it was just a classic old board. . . . It was really good for vocals. Tom found it in the *Recycler*, it was in some guy's storage. It was the very one, the board in Wally's Studio 4."

The *Either/Or* recordings were done at The Shop in two different sessions, recalls Schnapf, both between one week and ten days long. The three songs originally recorded in The Shop—"Angeles," "Between the Bars," and "Say Yes"—were each essentially one take of Smith's singing and playing acoustic guitar at the same time, superimposed on another take of Smith's singing and playing. It's a surprisingly difficult thing to record well. "He played acoustic, sang, doubled it, another take," says Schapf. "It was really incredible. Once we got the take we would double it, and he would listen. He's doing both [takes] singularly really well and then matching them. He was out there playing acoustic guitar and singing for a while until we got a good phase relationship. He didn't seem really super loud—very controlled." In other words, the shimmering quality of the guitar sound on *Either/Or* tracks produced in The Shop—the reason it's difficult to tell if there are two guitars in play or one—is that Smith would turn in two nigh-identical live performances, note for note, voice and guitar, with the tiny differences that inevitably creep in creating a sense of depth and something similar to a subtle echo. Applying a reverb track to the sound wouldn't have produced anything nearly so delicate. The three songs were the greatest realization up to that point of Smith's potential as a musician and an innovator, and they helped make his reputation.

The only adornment to the guitar and vocals on the three songs was a keyboard track on "Angeles"—Schnapf thinks it was a Hammond B–3 organ—that Smith had put down in a mostly fruitless studio session in Hoboken, New Jersey. In addition to the three songs they recorded, Schnapf and Rothrock mixed most of the record.

"Between the Bars" on *Either/Or* is one of Smith's clearest statements of contempt for the Byronic approach to life's responsibilities taken by many rock musicians, including, on occasion, himself. The pun in the title of the song ties alcohol to prison, but the body of the song goes a step further to suggest that drunkenness is self-deceit is prison is love. "I'll kiss you again, between the bars" paints a picture of lovers on a crawl and of a jail scene. But the line leaves mysterious who is locked up and who is on the outside. Is it the narrator or his "baby" who's trapped? The first line of the second chorus could either be addressed to someone looking through the window of a cell or someone stumbling around with a bottle in a paper bag: "Drink up baby, stare at the stars." The lyrics emphasize how the comforts of love and the bottle are derived from their ability to blind the imbiber to the ambitions and other people that might trouble him. "People you've been before that you don't want around anymore/they push and shove but won't bend to your will/I'll keep them still"—that's the promise of Romeo and of Jim Beam. Smith is talking about the romance of slackness, of failure: "The potential you'll be/that you'll never see/the promises you'll only make." The narrator could easily be the bottle itself talking to its victim. To take the metaphor to its logical conclusion, the narrator could be understood as the devil, or temptation itself.

One moment in the aftermath of his own death that Smith would have liked was Beck's performance of "Ballad of Big Nothing" at an Elliott Smith memorial concert at the Henry Fonda Theater in Los Angeles. Beck's singing is louder than the voice Smith typically used in solo acoustic performances, and the chorus takes on the feeling of an anthem. "You can do what you want to, whatever you want to" sounds like it could be the rallying cry for hedonist teenagers throwing off the shackles of a restrictive upbringing. But the guitar chords undermine any such notion immediately, and the lyrics to the verse, "up all night and down every day," illustrate the problems inherent in the belief that you're free to live your life as you see fit without considering others' feelings. It's an anti-anthem, or an ironic anthem, but it's not incompatible with a morally rigorous mode of self-evaluation.

Smith had a novelist's tendency to find the ambiguities in anything. It's for that reason that he could say with fairness that the sad singer-songwriter description didn't do him justice. There's nothing wrong with being a sad singer-songwriter, but Smith's gift as a lyricist was to capture the details of a predicament, and sadness was one color in his palette. "I'm a color reporter," he sang in "Bled White," and that's exactly right. There are many songwriters who can write sad songs—for instance, the ones who beat him at the Oscars with "My Heart Will Go On." There aren't many who can describe the specifics of a condition without contorting the music to fit ungainly lines. Smith was great at doing just that.

-ᴒ-

Smith moved to New York City on May 27, 1997. Even acquaintances of his assume to this day that he lived in the East Village, because he liked to go to Max Fish and Luna Lounge, two bars that face each other on Ludlow Street in that part of town. It's easy to imagine him taking his place among the thousands of young people slouching in wool caps with tattoos protruding from under rolled-up sweatshirt sleeves. But he moved to Jersey City, which, despite its name and Garden State location, is essentially a New York suburb across the Hudson River from Wall Street.

Dorien Garry was on the cusp of turning twenty-one when Smith told her he was planning on moving to town. She knew Smith had broken up with Joanna Bolme, and that he'd decided to ditch Portland. Because Heatmiser had broken up at the same time, he was reeling from two blows. Dorien asked him if he had a place to stay and he said he didn't know what he was going to do, so she offered him a couch to crash on and joked that he should try to make it in time for her upcoming birthday. Soon after, she got a message on her machine: "My flight gets in at six that day. I'll see you at the party."

The party was at Max Fish, and Garry stood up to announce the new guest: "This is Elliott! He just moved here!" Overnight, Smith had a new base. It may not have quite been home, but it was more of a safe haven to him than just about anywhere he'd stay from then until the last year of his life.

In those days, Garry and her two roommates were always on tour with bands or putting up musicians who needed a place to crash, so it was no trouble putting up Smith. It was Smith who had trouble with the arrangement, as comfortable as he was in the Jersey City house. "About three weeks or maybe a month into it he started to speak about feeling guilty about it and in our way, which he totally wasn't. Nobody really had a problem with it and everybody was just like, 'Do what you got to do.' He was also starting to make some money for the first time in his life and he was kind of like, 'I should just get my own place.'" But New York City became more and more expensive as the dot-com boom got under way and Smith wasn't sure what he was willing to spend or where he wanted to live. After all, he was a touring musician; he wasn't home very often. Around the middle of the summer of 1997, his friends set up a new arrangement. "Ellen Stewart was his booking agent. She had friends with an apartment in Brooklyn—Shauna and Pierre—so she hooked them up with Elliott, and he sort of begrudgingly moved his stuff in there," Garry recalls.

Smith lived in two different apartments with the couple, but was never fully comfortable in either. "He loved Shauna and Pierre but there was something wrong with every apartment . . . that he lived in with them. . . . in one of them, he was convinced that the floorboards were going to fall through and he was going to wind up like Tom Hanks in *The Money Pit*. . . . The other one was in a very violent neighborhood at the time and he just couldn't deal with it and even though it's not hip and cool to live in New Jersey, my neighborhood was very quiet and safe and he had friends there, too, and there were a whole bunch of us who lived in the neighborhood at the time and there was a bar there he really liked to go to and it was more that there was always those times when it was like. 'I'll just go to your house and hang out and go home in the morning,'" Garry says.

New York City was a good place for Smith in other ways. "I think just like anything else with him he was trying to find the place to go that was just like okay. I think he liked the anonymity, that people left him alone here," says Swanson. "He never expressed that, but I think it was a nice combination here where people definitely respected him and knew who he was, and when he played a show here a lot of people would come. His biggest fan base was definitely in New York. When we all left Hampshire we all had this kind of 'meet ya in New York' sort of thing. I don't remember if Elliott was specifically part of that, but I think that whole Hampshire crew, everyone thought eventually if we could do well with what we're doing we'd end up in New York. He came for the things people always come here for, and I think he was excited to live in a place that was just big. I think he loved it because he could lose himself here pretty easily."

But Smith's life in New York City never went exactly as planned. If things had worked out differently he might have shared a loft with Swanson, which might have been a more comforting place to live. "He was in Portland and I was in San Francisco. We were both kind of nervous about moving here and we thought we'd get an apartment together," says Swanson. "He was in better shape than I was financially, so he could help with that and we thought that was a good situation. But then I went to Sweden, he moved here, and he got an apartment with Shauna and Pierre. They moved from that apartment to a bigger apartment. I moved in [to Pierre's old apartment on Bergen Street] with the idea that we would live there a little while and then find another apartment separately. So basically it turned out the idea was we'd all find a place that was big enough or he and I would find a place separately and we kind of nominally looked at a couple of loft spaces. But then he got nominated for the Academy Award and had to go, so we never really lived together."

Smith's new home was in the Brooklyn neighborhood of Park Slope. "The Slope," as it is locally known, is famous for being a hardcore bastion of Northeastern upper-middle-class liberalism, but Smith lived on its scrappier fringes. The spine of the Slope is Seventh Avenue, which runs a few blocks from the green blanket that gives the area its name. There, the organic cup of coffee has held court for decades. But Smith lived off Fifth Avenue, near the point where the neighborhood faded into the more proletarian downtown Brooklyn and Fort Greene. Now that area has joined the rest of the neighborhood in giving itself over to track lighting, but in the late '90s it was still mostly a neighborhood of blue-collar businesses.

The Atlantic Center Mall looms nearby, its giant "A" logo glowing red, white, and blue, and the phallic clock tower that dominates the downtown Brooklyn landscape looms behind that. But the streets off of Fifth Avenue lend themselves to nostalgia: near-identical row houses trailing off ad infinitum, fringed by ample trees.

Among the trains that run to and from Manhattan and Park Slope are the F train and the yellow line (the N and the R). Smith refers to both in "Bled White," the song in his oeuvre that deals most directly with his life in New York City. In the first lines of the song, there's a description of feeling out of place: "I'm a color reporter/but this city's been bled white."

While Smith lived in New York he seemed to Swanson to exhibit the same qualities that had set him apart in the first place. The spontaneity, the fondness for going to extremes, the generosity, the sense of fun, were all still intact. "We were just walking down the street, and [a man] just asked us for money or said he needed help. Later on I realized he didn't look like someone who was homeless or look like a vagrant at all. I had been in New York for a while and in San Francisco for a long time before that so admittedly I was just kind of like, 'whatever,' trying to get to this gay bar I used to make Elliott go to. And it was a time when I was trying to be protective of Elliott's time, he was already doing well for himself and it was this nice little thing that we got to go out alone in Brooklyn. And this guy kind of asked us for help. It was a very strange circumstance as I remember. Elliott kind of talked to him for a second and then couldn't really figure out what was going on but something was going on. Then we got a drink and about halfway or three-quarters or some way into the drink, the guy came into the bar and then walked back out, and I remember Elliott was like, 'I gotta deal with this guy.' Then he got up and was like, 'Are you okay?' And it was kind of amazing: He got him into this place where the guy could focus and be like, 'I'm not okay. I don't know where I am.' And I think this guy obviously had some sort of problem. I don't know if it was a schizophrenic problem and he was off medication or something, but realizing that this was a guy dressed in normal Park Slope clothes, probably forty years old, glasses, haircut, [Elliott] just zeroed in that there was something wrong. And then spent the next, probably, whatever it took, a half-hour, to call pay phones and get this guy to a hospital. Not that that's so remarkable or anything, but I wasn't on my way to do it.

"Sometimes it was frustrating to be his friend. This sounds terrible, but sometimes he would treat strangers with more respect than people he was sitting with or something; he had the utmost respect for people. If someone came up and said, 'I'm a fan of yours, I just really want to talk to you,' before they could get their first sentence out, he would immediately be like, 'What's your name? Where are you from? What do you do?' And would immediately go into 'Oh, really? You're from Brooklyn itself? Wow, that's so funny. I've never really met someone from Brooklyn. Did your grandparents come here?' [He'd] immediately try to switch the conversation to them, which was frustrating as a person who at that point barely got any time alone with him. You were used to getting time with him, and then all of a sudden he's encouraging conversation with complete strangers."

Another night, Smith practiced a form of urban camping. "I remember one night we wound up sleeping in Central Park. Me, him, and my friend Wendy, we went to this bar, to Luna Lounge, and then we went to the after-hours place, and we were kind of like, 'What should we do?' And we couldn't get into the place, or, I don't remember, we decided on the way to the place—I decided I was really missing California and kind of New Hampshire in a way, and I decided we should go to Central Park. It would be like camping, only in Central Park. And they were both like, 'Yeah! Yeah!' So then we went and got all these beers and got cigarettes and we went to Central Park and spent a long time trying to figure out the best place to camp. And we settled on this one place and basically passed out. And woke up the next day, so hung over, we had picked a really bad place in the middle of a bunch of paths, and he woke up in a really bad mood, I remember, but that was kind of him. He was really always game for that."

For all the good times he had there, New York was by Smith's own account the place he became a bad alcoholic, and moving there did constitute a move away from where his friends and family were concentrated. Being left alone meant more opportunity for rumination and also more room for erratic behavior. During this time he and Bolme got back together and broke up again at least once. Given the degree of attachment Smith showed calling Bolme on tour, this was likely a destabilizing series of events. And there were disturbing symptoms of Smith's doldrums.

"He often walked around subway tunnels when he first was here, which is not good," says Swanson. I remember a specific conversation where we both talked about New York, because we both liked it in the middle of the night, that this place was really great in the middle of the night, all the energy was still here but the people were mostly gone, but there were still people around. I remember times if he was working on music or something like that, he would just leave for a couple hours and just listen to what he'd been working on. I think it was part of—I think a lot of what he liked about here is that he could walk around by himself in the middle of the night listening to his Walkman and be part of something and not be a freak. A lot of what Elliott was worried about was being a freak. . . . When he went to buy his car, he was like, 'They're not going to let me test-drive it, they're going to think I'm a freak. I can't go in there, they're going to think I'm a freak. I can't go to nice restaurants, they're going to think I'm a freak.' I think part of it was that here [in New York] he never felt like a freak."

And people might have given Smith trouble for weird behavior in Portland—just as people do in any comparatively small town— because they were concerned he would hurt himself. One of New York City's distinguishing characteristics is that just about nobody cares if you appear to be endangering your health in public. "I think when he was walking around the subway tunnels, that was probably a pretty specifically self-destructive thing to do, because it was probably dangerous in a bunch of different ways. And I hated it when he would tell me he'd do that, it'd be like, 'You can't, you're not supposed to do that.' But it was also intriguing to me that he would do that. Like, 'What is he doing down there?'"

-ᴓ

Eventually, Smith was bought out of the Virgin contract by the music division of DreamWorks. DreamWorks SKG was a new alliance between Steven Spielberg, David Geffen, and Jeffrey Katzenberg, the former head of Disney. Geffen was walking away from the enormously important record label that bore his name. A subsidiary of that label, DGC, or David Geffen Company, had lured Nirvana away from the Seattle indie label Sub Pop and taken them big-time with *Nevermind*, the album that brought indie and alternative rock ideas to the mainstream. He'd also given Sonic Youth their first major-label record deal. But the man the trio put in charge of their new label was Lenny Waronker, and it bore his stamp even more than it bore Geffen's.

In the early '70s, Waronker had been a producer at Warner Bros. working with a number of artists similar to Smith in outlook and sound. He had mingled with the heroes of an age was to singer-songwriters what the Ming Dynasty was to vases. Randy Newman, Neil Young, and James Taylor were his circle. Young's *Harvest*, Mitchell's *Blue*, and The Grateful Dead's *Workingman's Dead* were all released by Warner Bros. during his ascendancy; back in the dawn of the hippie era, Waronker had wanted badly to sign Buffalo Springfield. These artists were songwriters who'd developed a new way of blending rock with folk after rock had climbed to the top of the pop charts in the '60s.

Not only did that make DreamWorks Records sound like a good place for Smith; the buzz was that the fledgling label was going to be a good place for just about anybody. "Everybody wanted to be on that shit," says Doughty. "I bumped into Lenny at a show, and he was like, 'Hey we missed you guys,' and I was like, 'Oh god, take me with you, please.' Hanging out with that guy was like hanging out with Desmond Tutu or something, he just had the presence of, 'I am the great benevolent figure of the music business.' [DreamWorks] was totally the place to be." The label would sign critically championed, commercially ambiguous acts like Rufus Wainwright, EELS, Rye Coalition, and Sparta, as well as hit-producing acts like Nelly Furtado, Papa Roach, Toby Keith, AFI, Saves the Day, and Alien Ant Farm.

Throughout Smith's entry into the music business, he remained, in Santen's eyes, an altruistic soul. Touring with Santen in support of *Either/Or*, he encountered an unusual audience request. "We were playing at Sudsy's in Cincinnati. It was pretty funny because there wasn't really anybody there. I had my friends from Lexington. Really, no one came to see him. This guy sat in the front row with this kid. Elliott played for twenty minutes, and this guy said, 'Play the fucking hit,' or something. And everybody heard him. And then after a while Elliott stopped and said, 'Excuse me, there's a lot of dead soldiers on your table there.' The guy had it completely covered in Rolling Rock bottles. This guy said he had six months to live and the paperwork to prove it. And he had the papers in his hand. And he wanted the 'hit'—he meant 'Speed Trials' [The first song on *Either/Or*]. He walks up to the stage, sits there, and looks at [Elliott], and hands Elliott the papers." Still on stage, Smith perused the documents, handed them back, and played the song.

There are few better examples of one of the most consistent tendencies in Smith's life, one that runs from Portland through Los Angeles: He sided with the downtrodden. Jen Chiba told the *LA Times* that Smith considered himself "a champion of the underdog." She cited his tendency to hand out large bills to the homeless, a habit his sister Ashley brought up at an Elliott Smith tribute at the 2003 *All Tomorrow's Parties* festival in LA, a festival Smith was scheduled to play before he died.

In New York, Smith developed the capacity to bar-fight on behalf of the underdog, something his Portland friends never seemed to observe. Fighting ran contrary to everything people knew of him; he presented himself as a gentle, good-humored soul. On one hand it was a sign he was drinking too much, but on the other hand his willingness to brawl was sometimes justified as a sign of courage and righteousness. "I remember one time we're at a bar and we're there with some mutual friends and we're introduced to this guy who's like a friend of a friend, and we were chatting," remembers Swanson. "And then like forty minutes, half an hour into it, this guy got into a fight. It was one guy against a group of people. It was really weird, at a bar, at Luna in the Lower East Side, I'm pretty sure. [Elliott] kind of immediately jumped into action. He was like, 'We've got to help Jez's friend,' and I was like, 'Look, we don't know that guy, he's not our friend and I don't want to get in a bar fight, and he's fighting with a bunch of people'—I'm assuming he started the fight if there's a group of people. . . . And he was kind of like, 'Well don't you think we should help him out? That's his friend,' and I was like, 'I don't think we need to get involved, you know?' And he was really like—he would kind of jump at that chance, and sometimes he'd get in a fight, which was weird, because he was a tiny guy. But then it totally turned out that this guy ended up being Jake Chapman, who's like this pretty famous artist in England, and . . . these young art students had come in and just started giving him shit, because, I don't know, that's what they do in England or something. . . . So in other words it was totally justified, we totally should've helped this guy. [Elliott would] always jump into action for 'a friend of yours is a friend of mine.'"

This side of Smith is the link between the rebellious kid in suburban Texas and the second-wave feminist he became at Hampshire, the characters that turn up in his songs and the charity causes he embraced. It's even reflected in his choices around who to let into his life as close friends and who to stay away from.

Of course, punk and indie rock had from the beginning tried to cast themselves as companions of the underdog—that's essentially where the name "punk" comes from. The same is true of folk music, and whether or not Smith approved of the label "folk-punk" for his music (he preferred to think of himself as a pop musician), there's no arguing that at the very least his first three albums drew heavily from the minimalism of punk and the acoustic guitar stylings of folk. But by the time Smith's solo recordings hit in 1994, neither punk nor folk nor indie rock could be thought of as music for the downtrodden. After *Nevermind* blew up the charts in 1991, alternative music could no longer claim the outsider status it once had, and the indie bands that came after, like Pavement or Neutral Milk Hotel, used indie as a way of making art too sophisticated for popular tastes. The days when punk bands like Black Flag and Minor Threat—bands that were simpler and more forthright than the mainstream—dominated the indie landscape were over. Indie rock had become a forum for rock that was more complicated, in every respect, than what could now be found on the radio (radio having changed to accommodate the increasing popularity of hip-hop as well as grunge). Pavement was the embodiment of all that was new about indie rock in the post-Nirvana world. Their frontman, Steven Malkmus, was a University of Virginia graduate with golden-boy cheekbones and a sunny, whimsical disposition. To listen to Pavement was to confess allegiance to a collegiate, middle-class subculture so flooded with irony that the moments of true romance that bobbed to the top were all the more remarkable. The camp poses of bands like the Make-Up and The Monorchid made for an atmosphere in which *Spin* magazine saw fit to remark that "more and more, the sort of empathic rush alt-rock once delivered with howling Marshall stacks is being conjured by boys and girls brandishing acoustic guitars. . . . It all seems to indicate that as the alt-national consensus turns to party-time ska-core, mindless pop, wordless electro-beats, swing revivalism, and other gestures of high and low irony, alt-rock's bleeding heart is still beating. Its audience may have fled the corporate doppelganger known as modern rock, but they still hunger for an empathetic connection with non-cyborg, non-smarmy wordsmiths."

The dimension this fair assessment leaves out is class. The rock world had divided into grunge or post-grunge bands that appealed to blue-collar and middle-class audiences—for instance, Alice in Chains, Pearl Jam, and Rage Against the Machine—and indie bands who sang to college kids. In his 2001 book about indie rock, *Our Band Could Be Your Life*, Michael Azerrad theorized that when it was no longer underground to be a blue-collar rock band, indie rock became more and more an activity for privileged kids hooked on Liz Phair, Pavement, and the Palace Brothers. "Perhaps to make up for the seeming elitism, such musicians placed even less of a premium on musical technique than ever. But maybe that was just a flip of the bird to the traditionally working-class emphasis on artisanal values like chops, speed, and power."

Smith's background as a child of a family of working-class musicians is evident in his musicianship. That musicianship didn't emerge clearly in Heatmiser, especially not on *Dead Air*, but it was there from an extremely early stage. Mary Lou Lord cites a song by the '60s pop band Left Banke (famous for "Don't Walk Away Renee") as a likely progenitor for Smith's style. Smith had "gone on about Left Banke" when they were discussing influences, and she identified Smith's vocal styles in the short-lived New York City pop band's only hit single besides "Don't Walk Away Renee": "Pretty Ballerina." "The vocals were very similar to Elliott's," she notes. Sure enough, the singer's mannerisms are startlingly like Smith's, and the melody and string arrangements would have fit in perfectly on *XO*. The voice sounds almost the same, half-plummy, half-nasal, slightly tremulous. The piano line is catchy but betrays a certain sadness. "It's pretty weird and kind of dark and so was Elliott," Lord told Harvard radio, which is true. Along with "Renee," "Pretty Ballerina" is about the extent of the Left Banke oeuvre, but hearing it is like a bit like discovering The Pixies after years of listening to Pixies-loving Nirvana. It's a '*that's* where he got it' moment.

In an interview for *TapeOp* magazine, Smith detailed the lengths he went to create a decent recording in high school to an aghast Larry Crane. The story reveals an early commitment to the mechanics of making music, not just the art. Smith would borrow four-track home recorders for a year at a time, he said, and stretch their capabilities. "Sometimes I would sync up two of them by cueing them up and hitting play at the same time and constantly adjust the speed on one of them to catch up with the other," Smith explained. "The cymbal went 'chhhhhhh'. . . So we'd play that and something else at the same time onto a track. We did a lot of bouncing or ping pong-ing, whatever you want to call it. We'd try not to put more than a couple of things on the same track. Everything was totally dead. We didn't have any effects at all. The next year after that, we had a real drummer and two four-tracks and we were syncing them up like I was taking about. We'd do the drums to two tracks in stereo because that was of the utmost importance, to have the drums in stereo, 'cause they could be . . . "

Smith's adult approach was grounded in an equally deep involvement in the technical side of recording music. He observed to Mary Lou Lord in a discussion for *Spin* that ". . . I can't dress up my songs so that they'll fit in on the radio, because they wouldn't be the same songs anymore—whereas your songs would be, you know? . . . Because for me, the sound of the song is the same thing as the song itself, you know? Both ways are cool, totally . . . but when I make up stuff, I can't imagine it in a lot of different settings." Smith made these remarks after the recording of *XO*, when he had expanded into songs with many layers of tricks and wall-of-sound production, courtesy of Schnapf and Rothrock, so it wasn't an avowal of loyalty to the spare sound of his first three records. It was a description of a way of looking at recording that was almost the opposite of punk rock recording, in the sense of banging out track after track in the studio as quickly as possible and trusting the tunes to break through whatever poverty of recording quality got in the way. As strong as Smith's melodies and chord changes might have been, he demanded that the production fit them, at least approximately (he had to be at least somewhat flexible about it in the early days). Later on, when *Under the Radar* magazine came to Smith's house in Echo Park for one of the last interviews of his life, he discussed his ongoing fascination with his newly purchased studio equipment, recalling how he'd mended a broken mixing board himself with a "soldering party."

Smith could get caught up in impulsive, quirky ideas about moving once he'd made the move to New York. His stay in France was not his only discarded plan to live somewhere far away. One day when they were both New Yorkers, Swanson decided he was going to move to Hawaii, and Smith was game. "It was funny because I had to broach this subject with Elliott because we were still in talks of looking for an apartment together . . . and he got really excited about the idea of moving to Hawaii. Because it was like, 'Oh, we can be in the country but you're really far away from everything.' And it was really funny because I really thought this is a drunken night thing, thinking we're going to move to Hawaii. Probably nobody remembers it because it lasted all of about five days. But I remember he played a show at Irving Plaza, and I heard him tell somebody—I remember thinking it was really weird because it was a business person—and he was like, 'I think I'm moving to Hawaii.' It was like, 'Omigod he thought about it three days later.' And then we talked about it three days later kind of seriously, and our friend was going to get us a place to stay— she knew somebody who had a house there—and I was going to fly there, and they were going to play there, and it was this whole plan, we're going to move to Hawaii. And then I came back after that tour and being in all these other cities, and I really loved it here. And then it was pretty much a non-conversation. Three months later I was like, 'Hey, I think I like New York,' and he was like, 'Yeah, me too.'"

No matter how finished with Portland Smith was, one of the toughest facts of his move to New York was its coinciding with the nearly simultaneous break-ups of Heatmiser and his relationship with Joanna Bolme. Smith said in interviews—and in still later interviews apologized for saying it—that he'd stayed in Heatmiser for the sake of his friends in the band, specifically Gust. The knowledge that in the process of becoming successful he had left his struggling friend in the lurch probably weighed on him a great deal. Worse, he had hurt Gust's reputation—albeit most likely out of reckless candor rather than malice—by insulting Heatmiser publicly. "He was always very concerned with hierarchies and the little guy," says Swanson. "Elliott was just like fiercely, fiercely upset about injustice in any form. It's almost like, he made some weird decisions sometimes and stuff, but on the surface he definitely would, after he had money, some guy would try to bum some change off him and he'd give him twenty bucks. Or like a tip at a restaurant or at a birthday party when the check comes up short, he wouldn't just make it up, he'd leave an extra hundred bucks because he wouldn't want the person to be embarrassed. That whole idea, anything he would do that would embarrass someone, cause someone else some sort of pain, was ultimately what was so upsetting to him all the time."

"The hardest thing about it was him not wanting to lose his friends," says Garry. "He spoke mostly about that and not really about the demise of the band. Sam and Neil are brothers to him."

When Smith toured with Santen in 1997, Smith seemed to be trying to pull out of Portland emotionally. In his tradition of including the names of real people in his songs, he would record the song "Amity" for *XO* after getting involved with a young, pretty woman of the same name who appears in photographs taken during his 1997 tour. In the photos, he wanders around Cambridge, Massachusetts, with her, to-go coffee cups in their hands. She has twin barrettes holding her hair back from her forehead in the schoolgirl-ish style popular among indie rockers and ravers at the time. In one photo she leans against Smith, who is smiling and has his arm around her waist, so that the bottom of her fitted sweater lifts to reveal what appears to be a tattoo around her navel. She looks young and conventionally attractive. Another photo attests to the playfulness she contributed to Smith's life. In a hotel room, Smith sits on the bed with the phone to his ear and his hair bound in tinfoil. Amity was giving him a dye job, reports Santen, who was on the tour, and the fruits of her labor are evident in the photo where Smith holds aloft a cassette, a coiffed and smiling young man with yellow streaks in his hair. Smith's expression in most of these photos makes him look unusually young.

Amity might have inspired a song, but in the wake of his break-ups with Heatmiser and Bolme, Smith's dearest wish was to find a more stable existence on his new coast. He envisioned buying an honest-to-god home for himself with the new money he was earning—for the first time in his life he was making a good living, thanks largely to Mittleman. He and Garry would drive upstate to Nyack, Woodstock, and Saugerties to look at houses where he might have enough room for his own studio and be able to take a train into the city. "He loved a lot of the neighborhoods, but he had little qualms about not wanting to have neighbors nearby," says Garry. "There was somebody who was living up in Woodstock at the time who made records who had a studio, and I mentioned it to him once when we were up there, and he was like, 'I don't want to live in the town where the other dude who makes records has a studio.'"

There was one house in particular Smith set his sights on: Big Pink, where The Band and Bob Dylan had cut legendary records. By coincidence it was actually for sale, and Smith, new to the strata of renown in which a musician has financial managers and lawyers, started to make the necessary phone calls to figure out if he could buy it. Then, says Garry, a Japanese collector swooped in and took it off the market.

But even then Smith would go and look at Big Pink, Garry remembers. "We still went up there a lot and took pictures in front of it and sat in the driveway and tried to figure out what went on in the garage. I wanted that to happen really badly because I thought it would have been good for him to get out of the city and get away from the 'I can go to a bar any time of night' accessibility of Manhattan and Brooklyn. None of those places were really suitable for having a studio or even a practice space. It was really a pain in the ass: He really didn't get to play or write nearly as much as he wanted to and it just sort of seemed like it would have been a perfect—things weren't all right then and I thought it might have been a perfect chance to get things a little bit better. He was really into it and then this need for him to be in LA just happened."

That need started with the gig that would make Smith famous: writing a song for the *Good Will Hunting* soundtrack. Portland-based director Gus Van Sant decided that he wanted Smith's music to play in the background during several crucial scenes of his most straightforward drama to date, based on a script by co-stars Ben Affleck and Matt Damon (then virtual unknowns). It was agreed Smith would contribute one original song.

It would take Smith places he didn't ever think he'd go, and it was the first of a string of commitments that rendered him temporarily homeless and then kept him in Los Angeles, a place he never chose to live. The house in upstate New York never materialized. "It's really hard when you're on tour all the time to say it's worth taking all this money I have and doing this thing, buying this thing that I'm not really going to be at. I think there was a really important need for it, but the urgency got wiped out by the fact that he was becoming really successful," says Garry. "There were people and places that he needed to be at and near."

By his friends' standards, Smith was already remarkably successful, and he was already having episodes involving drinking and melancholic reflection that left them worried. In both departments, nobody had seen anything yet.

Seven

GOOD WILL

ℰARLY ONE MORNING in the last days of 1997, Smith was in Los Angeles recording *XO* when he got a call from Margaret Mittleman informing him that "Miss Misery," the song he'd written for *Good Will Hunting*, had snagged him a nomination for an Academy Award for Best Original Song. He was up against Celine Dion for "My Heart Will Go On" from *Titanic*, and Trisha Yearwood for "How Do I Live" from *Con Air* among others. It was the proverbial single stroke that indelibly changes the course of a life. Smith didn't particularly care; an Academy Award was no big deal to him. But it was a big deal in that, for the people who don't live in one of the constellations of indie rockers scattered throughout the western world, it put Smith on the map.

Smith thought the Oscar thing was overrated on principle. "He was like, 'The Oscars are just a bunch of people deciding that someone's worth something, and it has to do with commerce and I don't know who these people are and they shouldn't be deciding and I don't know why everybody puts so much credit into it,'" says Swanson. "I remember calling him the morning I heard about it in LA. From minute one he was weirded out by the whole thing, he was never really excited, or felt like he had gotten some- where. He always looked at things analytically: 'What does this really mean? This doesn't mean anything.' But of course to the rest of the world it meant something."

The practical effects of the rest of the world's caring about the nomination were immediate and profound. "We had just started [XO] and then [the nomination] happened," says Schnapf. "It was like, 'Oh Christ,' and the next six weeks he was deluged. It was like 'Elliott who?' and then hours of press every morning." That necessitated a semi-nocturnal daily schedule for making the album: "Noon until we couldn't take it anymore," remembers Schnapf. "Usually twelve hours."

Worse, the personal consequences for Smith were huge. The most damaging rift to develop between Smith and his friends was the gap between his level of fame and theirs, as much as Smith didn't care about being famous. "He often spoke about how come he was getting all this attention when there were are all these other good bands," E. V. Day remembers. "How come his friends' bands aren't getting attention?" He felt it didn't make sense that Sam and Janet's music wasn't as popular as his. "Quasi would never get as big, get the kind of thing he was getting. And he just couldn't handle it, he felt so shitty about it. And it started all kinds of conflicts in their friendships and basically dissolved [them]. It killed the relationships, as opposed to the opposite, which I think he wanted, which was to stay friends. . . . One night when we were in this hotel on tour and Sam was staying on the bus, and he was like, 'How come I have this room and Sam's sleeping on the bus?' And I was like, 'Sam wants to be alone anyway, he did the job, he's being paid, he wants to play with you, it's okay, he's doing it. And if you asked him to come stay in this room he'd do it anyway.' And he'd be like, 'But I feel so bad he's on the bus and I'm in the hotel room.' He just couldn't deal with it. And you couldn't then also say, 'Well, you go sleep in the bus then.' There were so many conflicts like that at every turn. And it was so painful."

Pete Krebs remembers one such conflict on Valentine's Day, 1998, that nearly snuffed his friendship with Smith. "So we played this show at EJs*, and I opened up for him, and at the end of the night they were doing a Kinks cover band. He played with Neil and Sam, and Janet was on drums. They were doing 'Sunny Afternoon' or whatever. It was kind of like the Portland All-Stars playing Kinks tunes. And Elliott just had a mic, and I remember him walking around the stage like this [Krebs makes a 'raising the roof' hand gesture] singing Kinks stuff. It was really great and that was the night I heard he was going to be on the Academy Awards. And I didn't really know what to say. I was just like, 'Hey man, it's really great you're on the Academy Awards, you know? Congratulations. I really gotta go.' And he took it really wrong. I think that he thought I was mad at him. He was drunk, so I think he thought his friend was saying 'fuck you.' I didn't hear from him for a long time after that, and I think that had a lot to do with it." Krebs's congratulatory farewell was so brief because of a personal issue unrelated to Smith, but Smith took it as a rebuke. "I was really a mess that night when I heard [about the Oscars] and I had to go home. So it was really impossible for me to be genuinely happy for him, just because I was so mixed up with my own shit. I just remember him going, 'Pete, wait, man, hey, be cool,' and I was just like, 'No man, it's cool, I gotta go.' That was before things really started to go topsy-turvy, and that's when stories of Elliott just started coming."

The misunderstanding with Krebs was just a prelude to the massive discombobulation that accompanied Smith's performance at the Oscars and the scores of post-Oscar interviews in which Smith was asked how it felt to suddenly rise above his element. He generally replied that the awards ceremony was "surreal."

A little more than halfway through the 70th Academy Awards ceremony on March 23, 1998, Madonna walked onstage to introduce the last three nominees for Best Achievement in Music, Original Song (the first two nominated tunes had been performed earlier in the evening). Against a purple-and-blue backdrop, between

*A club in Portland.

symmetrical pillars, Trisha Yearwood sang "How Do I Live" from *Con Air*. Then the set turned from blue-and-purple to black, the pillars slid away, and Elliott Smith entered from stage left.

Smith wore a white suit with a maroon shirt and a darker tie. Prada, he told his friend Laura Vogel, "gave me shoes, and a belt, and a shirt, and socks. . . . I wore my own underwear." Earlier in the evening, he'd had to bend his own rules to accommodate the Academy, he later recalled; a producer had offered him anything he wanted, and then informed him a chair would be impossible. So he performed standing, expressionless, launching into "Miss Misery" with just his voice and his guitar. At the place in the studio recording where the electric guitar usually chimes in, the Academy's orchestra entered, following the chord progression with strings. After skipping from the first verse to the second bridge, there were no further edits to the song. The orchestra faithfully followed the chords, and descended into abject schmaltz only when it introduced a vaguely Celtic flute (or piccolo?) line during the final verse, an echo of a similar flute line from the movie's incidental music that seemed designed to match the shamrock logo always placed beneath the movie's title. At one point, the camera swooped in for an extreme close-up of Smith's face, and it was composed, impassive. When the song was over, he took a bow, gave the audience a tiny smile, and exited stage right.

Next, Celine Dion arrived and delivered "My Heart Will Go On," which everybody knew was going to win. Then, in a fluke moment of indie-mainstream collusion, Smith, Yearwood, and Dion walked back onstage and held hands, with Smith in the middle of the two women. They took a bow in unison, and walked off again.

When the smoke had cleared, the two middle-aged guys with beards and glasses who wrote "My Heart Will Go On" were victorious—it was the year *Titanic* won everything. When Madonna opened the envelope, she laughed: "Surprise!" Celine Dion became a huge star. On radio stations everywhere, "My Heart Will Go On" went on and on.

Elliott Smith and Neil Gust in their first house in Portland, 1991. Credit: Marc Swanson

Smith with Doug Martsch (short hair), Bill Santen (long hair), and an opening act, 1997. Courtesy of Bill Santen.

Smith poses as a deep singer-songwriter on tour with Santen, 1997. Credit: Bill Santen

Smith takes in a show with Jeff Buckley, Bolme, 1996. Credit: Ramona Clifton

Smith watches Lou Barlow's farewell-to-Boston performance, amidst '90s indie rock crowd, 1998. Credit: Ramona Clifton

Smith with Dorien Garry and Santen, on tour in Princeton, New Jersey, 1997. Credit: Courtesy of Bill Santen

Smith discovers a cassette containing Hank Williams Jr.'s "All My Rowdy Friends Have Settled Down," Cambridge, Massachusetts, 1997. Credit: Bill Santen

Smith with Glenn Kotche and Amity, 1997. Credit: Bill Santen

Amity dyes Smith's hair in a hotel room on tour, 1997. Credit: Bill Santen

Smith plays Boise, 1997. Credit: Bill Santen

Smith rests, on tour with Santen, 1997. Credit: Bill Santen

Smith plays craps with
Janet Weiss on tour in
Washington, DC.
Credit: Ramona Clifton

The tack piano at McConnell's house with Elliott Smith's bandage taped to the side (Smith sustained the injury repairing the piano), 2004. Credit: David McConnell

The basement on the hill, David McConnell's studio, 2004. Credit: David McConnell

Elliott Smith's favored guitar during the sessions at McConnell's studio and a couch he slept on, 2004. Credit: David McConnell

Dion and Smith had already had a short moment of bonding backstage. Whether Dion remembered it is anyone's guess, but Smith did. "After the Oscars," says Swanson, "we talked about Celine Dion, and I was like, 'So how was that?' He was like, 'Oh, she's so nice.' She came down to his dressing room or something, and said, 'Hey, good luck, this is probably going to be hard for you, it sounds like you haven't dealt with a large crowd like this, good luck.' And after this we'd constantly be running into people coming up and talking to him, people who didn't know him, and saying 'Oh, how's it goin', saw you on the Oscars, so, how was that?' And [they'd] make some derogatory Celine Dion comment, and every time they'd do it, I'd be like 'gasp,' and this look of rage in his eyes would come up and he'd be like, 'You know, she's a really nice person.' And they'd always recoil and be like, 'Oh, no, I'm sure she's really nice.' It was this whole idea that someone would judge someone they didn't know, even though of course he could judge people he didn't know. I thought that was a cute thing about him; he was defending Celine Dion all the time."

Celebrities didn't become a major presence in Smith's life, despite the fortunes awaiting the stars of *Good Will Hunting*. Smith was still nervous around major musicians. "There was a show he played in New York and Grandaddy was opening, and David Bowie showed up," Clifton remembers. "It got to be sort of ridiculous. He didn't actually come into the dressing room, and he may have been there because he was really interested in Grandaddy too, but I remember people coming in and saying, 'Elliott, you gotta come out,' and going out into the hallway. Bowie's a little man, but he's got that voice, and Elliott was just really modest, pleased but a little overwhelmed maybe. If he had the time to go into a corner booth and just talk, he was interested. He would be concerned about how is your life going, and your work. The most time I ever spent with him was during those first four and five years . . . during the last four years he didn't have the time anymore, but then it was more insulated. There were always people around him who would always protect him a little bit, and I would always be like, 'He knows me, I've been around for a long time, I'm not just somebody trying to get a piece of him.' But they didn't know. It was harder to spend any kind of time."

Speaking to *Under the Radar* years later, Smith would say, "After *Either/Or*, the Oscar stuff happened and that kind of derailed my train. Although it took a lot for it to fully derail." So what happened?

The lead-up to the Oscars may have constricted the recording schedule of *XO*, but there was a sudden, major upswing in popularity that was evident when Smith was on tour. "He played downstairs at the Middle East, and suddenly the place was really packed and everybody was yelling for 'Miss Misery,'" remembers Ramona Clifton. "He was like, 'Oh okay,' but the crowd sort of expanded. Within the indie scene people loved him, but then he had gathered enough people who were watching the Oscars. Suddenly he was doing all these interviews and his name was everywhere. I think he was really happy—I think he wanted people to hear his stuff, but not necessarily in that way. The *Good Will Hunting* thing happened really fast—it wasn't his album, it was a soundtrack, and it wasn't his own baby. He tried as best as he could to deal with the attention; he always looked a little bit lost with it but he never complained about it. I think he had a hard time sometimes dealing with the bigger crowds, more college kids, more people yelling."

"Miss Misery," the song that defined Smith in the eyes of Oscars viewers and headline writers, wasn't a fair representation of Smith's work if you thought it was all about depression, but it was if you considered it to be all about ambivalence. The chorus hook, "Do you miss me, Miss Misery, in the way that you say that you do?" puts in sharp relief both the narrator's emotional dependency on the woman of the title and the knowledge that she's probably not healthy for him. In her absence, the narrator looks to alcohol as a substitute: "I'll make it through the day/with some help from Johnny Walker Red" are the first lines. Later on he talks about how succumbing to "oblivion" is "easy to do," a statement that applies equally well to love and narcotics.

To E. V. Day, Smith's new life was more destructive than any of the secrets he kept bottled up had ever been. Recognition helped decimate his support system, and Smith found himself unable to scrap together a new one as sturdy as the old. "I think it was the new life," she says when asked if sadness about the past was festering and making Smith more self-destructive than he had been. "Because if you listen to the earlier albums it's all the same depth and sadness and composite characters who sound like his lovers but it's really his stepfather and twisted into these love songs, essentially. But it's composite stuff that I think he was always singing about. Even in Heatmiser he was singing about those relationships. I don't think they were the new relationships that were necessarily worse. It was the whole structure. He used to have friends, real friends. He was surrounded by some of the greatest, loving people: like Quasi, those people were really great friends of his. And Neil, and Swannie [Swanson]. He had smart, talented, no-bullshit friends who didn't do drugs. I think he missed it and I think he sabotaged it, and that was kind of one way to have control over his situation."

In a mostly unpublished May 1998 interview with Laura Vogel (a few of Smith's sentences were published in *Elle*), whose zine he'd contributed to at Hampshire, Smith expounded at length on his new prospects. For all the reports that came later that Smith was a private person, the interview shows Smith not particularly concerned with his nascent renown.

"It's a happy accident," he told Vogel. Fame, he went on, "makes some things harder, but doesn't really come close to making it not worth it. It distracts your attention all of the time. It's easier to play music if you don't constantly think about how you're perceived by people. If things go well and you get a bunch of attention for a while and [people] are asking you questions all the time, it redirects your attention to how they perceive you. . . . It's not a bad thing."

Vogel followed up by asking him if he ever wanted to "move to the mountains and just say fuck it."

"Not the mountains, but yeah," he allowed. "No, I'm pretty committed to this . . . powering through any obstacle, and it's not really an obstacle."

Vogel asked him about groupies, mentioning the ubiquity of "thrift-store PhD's" at his show at Tramps in Manhattan, "including moony-looking girls in vintage glasses frames."

"I don't know, usually after I play, I run off," replied Smith. "I don't think I really come across as a good groupie prospect. It's not like I'm going to be . . . "

Vogel: "Bringing them back to the tour bus for some blow?"

Smith: "Right. You know, having all of my security guys spec out all of the 'hot babes' from the audience. . . . Though, on this last tour I was kind of blown away by the occasional totally blunt proposition . . . and I get so into the mode of 'Oh, thanks, thanks a lot,' and someone would come up with this totally blunt proposition and I'd be like, 'Thanks, thanks.' It freaks me out, I so don't feel like that kind of guy. . . . Apparently you don't have to be handsome . . . or tall."

This had been going on before the Oscars. Not long after the release of *Either/Or*, receiving lines for Smith had been rife with aspiring groupies. One of them burst into tears in front of Santen when she saw Bolme at Smith's side.

Smith also discussed, with unusual candor, the way his family looked on his musical career. "Is your family proud of and happy for you?" Vogel asked Smith. "Yes, very proud," he said.

"Were they always supportive of your career or did they want you to become an accountant?" she pressed.

"One side of my family was not especially supportive before," replied Smith. "But now it's looking more and more like a good idea to them."

Which side, of course, Smith didn't say. But considered alongside another comment he made in one of the many interviews he did in the wake of Oscar night '98, it shows the extent to which the Oscars were an emotional boon for Smith in some ways: He said he appreciated that the ceremony gave his mother a success story she could tell her friends.

But at the same time another strain in Smith's life was starting to emerge: the increasing isolation that comes with fame and a successful performing career. Vogel asked Smith if the first person he wanted to talk to when something really good happened was Joanna. "Well, it was really funny," he said. "When I first found out that I was nominated I had to call up somebody, but I couldn't think of anybody, and it was really depressing . . . 'cause I kind of had lost track of a lot of my friends, 'cause I'm gone so much. So I called Joanna and she wasn't home, so then my list of people to call got really short."

The list of friends shrank while the legions of fans grew into an army of hundreds of thousands of literate young people. On Oscar night, Smith might not have cared, but he became a symbol of something pure and rock 'n' roll and pensive. He became something kids could associate themselves with, a quiet guy with a guitar floating in a sea of glitter. For the kids who came to his shows, who drew fan art and posted his image on the Web, he was a lighthouse in a big nothing now, the glittery monstrosity of the dance-floor music and frat metal claiming the charts. You didn't have to be an aggressive punk rocker to identify with Elliott Smith—you just had to be someone who saw herself as more thoughtful and honest and less smitten by the trappings of fame and riches than the rest of the world. Smith probably never would have wanted to represent anything in particular, much less to take sides in any dichotomy between thoughtful rock and glitzy pop, but he became a convenient rallying point for teenagers and twenty-somethings who carved out identities as Elliott Smith fans.

Eight

X O

As BILL SANTEN recalls, the pivotal moment when he lost touch with Smith was not when Smith moved from Portland to New York City but when Smith started to be surrounded by handlers. It was also the moment he saw the first of Smith's fourth album, his first for DreamWorks.

"He got a road manager, and he got his people. It wasn't where we could all hang out in his dressing room, where they'd have good food and good drinks, and it got so they'd shut the door. I was just kind of messing around. I didn't realize he had all these people guarding him. I knew he had this new record, it was *XO*, and I snagged it, and later that night I realized it was the only copy. It was the artwork copy the company had sent him to proof. I had to walk back to his hotel room and say, 'Sorry man.' He laughed about it."

A necessary evil that comes with even a small degree of fame is the process of protecting oneself from the intrusions of an overly curious public, and Smith had a small collection of people who did that for him. In addition to Mittleman's careful tending of his career, and Schnapf and Rothrock tending to his records, he had Felice Ecker, the head and co-founder of Girlie Action Media and Marketing, working as his publicist. But during the time he had this small professional group of advisors he also managed to arrange things so that he often traveled with friends. On the *XO* tour, the opening acts were Neil Gust's post-Heatmiser outfit No. 2 and Sean Croghan's band Jr. High. Marc Swanson was the tour photographer. And Janet Weiss was often around because her new band, Sleater-Kinney, was on a tour schedule that often paralleled Smith's. And while some artists crumble under the car time, sleeplessness, and heavy drinking that generally accompany the touring life, Smith had a professed fondness for being on tour and thrived under the nomadic conditions. "When we were on the *XO* tour, everyone was getting drunk every night, things were getting really rowdy at the time," says Swanson. "It was staying up all night, playing every night, and in between I would just see him switching back and forth between reading this book on quantum physics and [a book on] I think it was World War I, or, I think, a history book that was six inches thick. I could barely read *Us* magazine, and he had this endless capacity." As much as any non-commercially-minded musician can have a comfortable career in the music business, Smith had one from when he signed to Dream-Works to when he stopped touring for *Figure 8* in 2001.

The most serious source of Smith's isolation from his friends was a difference of opinion over how his struggles with self-destructive behavior ought to be handled. There was no ignoring that difference after a series of events that unfolded only a month after Smith moved to New York City, and it wound up thoroughly discussed in the CD Santen innocently swiped that day.

Dorien Garry had worked for Kim Gordon and Thurston Moore, the married couple at the center of Sonic Youth, taking care of their new baby Coco. Through Gordon and Moore she caught wind of a concert taking place in Raleigh: an anniversary party for Tannis Root, the company that made Sonic Youth's t-shirts, with performances by Mudhoney and Redd Kross as well as Sonic Youth. "Elliott was kind of in a funk, just sitting around and playing music but not much else, and it was like 'Come on, we're all going to drive down to Raleigh,'" says Garry. "And I really figured out that something was wrong when he got on the turnpike and we stopped at a restaurant and he was like, 'Is there any place to get alcohol here?' And it's like, 'On the New Jersey Turnpike? No, you're lucky if you can get a decent cup of coffee. No. Not at all. Come on, you can make a ten-hour drive without a drink.' He just wanted to be anywhere but in his own skin at that time."

On the first night of the two-night celebration, they were giving a friend a ride home from the party, and Smith had been drinking. In the North Carolina countryside, they stopped to let Garry's friend out of the car.

"It was pitch black and we were in a little cul de sac, and [Smith] just got out and started running," Garry remembers. The first to go after him was Tim Foljhan, a sometimes back-up musician for Cat Power who made his own music with the band Two Dollar Guitar. He and Smith had hit it off, and by the time Garry got to the spot in the darkness where they'd disappeared they were both off a cliff—Smith had run over the edge and Foljhan had followed him. "[Smith] landed on a tree and the branch went into his back," says Garry. "He wouldn't go to the hospital and we took him back to the hotel, and it was like, 'What the fuck is going on?' I felt responsible. It was my friend that I bring on this, everybody's fun happy road trip.

"At the show the next day he kind of said sorry he put everybody through that and bandaged up his back—the last thing he really wanted to do was to make a spectacle of himself and have everybody freaking out."

Garry wasn't sure what to do about what she'd seen. "He went on tour a few weeks after that and he called constantly and he called all through the night. I don't think I slept for six months straight all through that time. Because I was working at Girlie Action and getting up and going to work but also getting a phone call at three in the morning when he'd be having to leave a bar—this is before cell phones, so it's from a pay phone, crying."

She was coming in to work feeling like the living dead. But she believed Smith when he said he hadn't been trying to kill himself. "He just wanted to run from himself, and there was a very dark end of the road there that he didn't see, and so he fell off of it." But she was worried that Smith was going to get hurt. She had a choice between two risky courses of action: She could let people know things were getting bad and risk Smith's getting mad and cutting of their friendship, or she could keep the problem a secret and maybe lose him completely. In the end, it looked like it would be hard to maintain secrecy anyhow: "I didn't go home and share that information willingly with people, and it wasn't ever my place to tell other people what he was doing or what had happened. But *he* did that all the time. He had a humongous scar on his back from landing on a tree and he showed people and he told them what happened. And there were e-mails and phone calls that I got and I knew that he wasn't happy, and Sam and Janet were probably having a fuck of a time dealing with it [on tour]."

Garry told Mittleman and Felice Ecker, her boss at Girlie Action and Smith's national publicist, that things were "getting heavy," and soon there was an intervention where some of Smith's work advisers and friends got together and asked him to go into a treatment center. It took place in Chicago, while Smith was on tour there. Garry decided to go because Neil Gust and Joanna Bolme were going and, like them, she wanted Smith to know she'd be there for him no matter how he chose to respond.

In Chicago, the group confronted Smith and told him they wanted him to check into a rehab in Arizona. Smith cut a deal: "He was on tour with Quasi when that all went down," says Garry, "and the way that things worked out among the generals in charge and him was he had, I guess, five or six more shows that brought him back to New York. From New York on, the rest of the tour would be cancelled, but he would go to Arizona after that and he would stay out there."

The task of flying with Smith to rehab fell to Bolme. After the last shows on that tour, says Garry, "she came to New York and they left from there. They stayed with me and then they left and went out to Arizona the next day after the show at the Knitting Factory."

Bolme stuck around for a few days to make sure Smith stayed in treatment, and then she went home. But Smith didn't last very long at the clinic; he just hated the recovery culture there. "He had to go to some group-therapy thing," says Garry, "and he walked into the group and the group greeted him by making this big huge wave and going 'howdy!' And he was kind of like, 'Fuck this. Don't say 'howdy' to me like that.'"

On a Saturday afternoon soon after, Garry was hanging out with a friend up from DC, Allison Wolfe from the riot grrrl band Bratmobile. "I guess it was about four days after the Knitting Factory show, maybe a little bit more, and we had gone down to the beach in the afternoon and we came back and we were going to go meet Janet for a drink. We came back to my house and I put the key in the lock and the door was open and we came home to Elliott sitting on the couch and it was like, 'What are you doing here? You're supposed to be in Arizona.' And he was kind of like, 'It wasn't for me, it wasn't the place for me.'

"Here we are with plans to go to a bar and go meet Janet, and he's like, 'Well, I'm coming too.' We were going to the bar that he went to all the time. It was like, 'Well Janet's going to love this one, you know?' And I only say that because of the hell that she had to go through leading up to it."

But no matter how traumatic the whole rehab flight might have been for Smith's friends, Garry didn't fault him for what happened. "I never really believed that Elliott going to rehab was going to make things better. Just because a bunch of people sit there and say you've got to go to this place and do it doesn't mean you're ready to do it or it's the time to do it, and he didn't do well with authority. . . . He didn't like to be told what to do, so to be surprised in a room with a bunch of people going 'now'—it was just a fucking really stupid idea."

Swanson remembers the incident as a triumph of Smith's brains over his friends' good intentions, a case of Smith pulling the wool over the eyes of his doctors. "He basically stood up and acted right until they let him out. He could do that, even though he was obviously suicidal at the time, obviously had all these problems. He knew what to do to get himself out of there . . . after he had probably tried to break out or something. Elliott could get away with those kinds of things."

The incident resulted in a song on *XO* that was one of the most caustic Smith ever wrote: "Everybody Cares, Everybody Understands." It's in the tradition of *One Flew Over the Cuckoo's Nest* in its send-up of a mental institution's sanctimonious airs, and it drops clues to a Southwestern location with a reference to "brilliant sun." Schnapf remembers it coming out of nowhere in the studio, and its arrangement is simple, suggesting that it was written quickly, on impulse. It contains bleak references to police lying in wait and a form of exhaustion that makes you hold on to the banister. Its most devastating line comes near the end: "Stay the fuck away from things you know nothing about."

That line balances out the more tender sentiment that Smith expresses in *XO*'s "Waltz #2 (XO)": "I'm never going to know you now/but I'm going to love you anyhow." The two remarks, seemingly expressing nearly opposite sentiments, are about the same thing: how difficult it is to understand other people, no matter how much you love them. "Stay the fuck away" is addressed to people who loved Smith and thought they knew what was good for him. "I'm never going to know you" is addressed to a mother (one of the previous lines is "XO, mom") and it's a confession that she will always remain partially mysterious, unknowable. Both songs can be traced back to Smith's personal experiences, but they use those experiences to launch into a discussion of a universal condition. The two songs comprise a view of personal tragedy as something created by people's imperfect ability to understand each other. As if to make his theme clear, Smith ends the album with "I Didn't Understand," an infinitely gentle a capella number that sounds a bit like The Backstreet Boys singing a paragraph out of *Notes from Underground*. The song is about exactly what its title suggests: the narrator's failure to comprehend somebody he loves. "I waited for a bus to separate the two of us," Smith sings, and goes on to laugh at himself ruefully: "What a fucking joke." For Smith, the effort to "get" somebody else is a joke, a quixotic gesture, but also a gesture of love.

At any rate, the songs were brilliant enough that Smith's friends and associates didn't abandon him for writing them, but he was worried they'd take offense. "He didn't want me to hear these records and think that because I had been around and dealt with every little angle of [the intervention] he was writing these attacking songs and that they were directed at me. And I never felt they were and I didn't care about that anyway. It's like, 'You're a songwriter, you're a poet, you write about whatever it is you want to write about and you do a fucking great job at it and don't worry about how I feel about it, you're not hurting me at all. I loved him and I wanted him to be happy," Garry says.

Smith's friends were progressive and understanding enough to be tolerant of songs in which they appeared to play a substantial part. He'd written songs about people he loved dearly, after all, including his mother. But the flap over the intervention weakened the feelings of mutual trust between Smith and some of his friends, and that was probably the last thing he wanted. "I brought it up once," says E. V. Day, "and he was just like—part of it was the denial of being an addict, and part of it was like, 'I don't try to control other people's lives.' A group of people sort of get around you and grab you—it's sort of terrifying and I think he felt like a caged animal or something by that. And it has to do with addiction. It was very surprising to me that he never forgave his friends for doing that. He couldn't even understand why they had done such an evil thing. He thought it was evil they had done that. And that kind of disillusionment was really weird."

At the same time, he was still close with some people who'd been there in Chicago. Smith told Vogel, in their May 6, 1998, chat, that he and Joanna Bolme had reunited: "I'm going out with her again, yeah, we broke up for a year and a half."

When another interviewer asked him around this time what was important to him, he said, "My girlfriend."

Smith didn't drink to the point where it sabotaged his success. It was just a retreat from the exacting convictions he lived with, a way of forcing himself to be easier on himself. "I think his convictions were about being essentially a good person, about being fair—he was super moral," says Day. "He was so sensitive about is everyone else okay?' These are the things that preoccupied his mind, and if he was before maybe able to take care of those things, there was an overcompensation, mentally anyway, of taking care of others, protecting others, making sure everything's fair and no one gets hurt, and I think a lot of that comes from a place where you have been in a situation and you have witnessed abuse. But then there's this narcissistic thing where you feel responsible for it all. It's like a twisted psychology where he felt at this place and time that he was responsible for other people's pain. And that's the last thing in the world he would want, and I think it got worse and worse and worse, and he felt he was losing his agency and his ability. He just had this dialogue going on in his head nonstop, and the only way to stop it was to drink more and drink more and drink more and drink more. [Sometimes] he'd be drinking all day and then [there was] the show, and then he'd be drinking. It's amazing that he lived as long as he did, based on his body filtering so much beer. And he was so tiny. Not an inch to pinch.

"I think he had huge secrets that he would never reveal entirely, and [they'd] come out in little spurts in his music and show there was something there. I think he was probably so frightened that he was going to have to confront those issues, which were stuff that happened earlier. So he didn't see it as, 'Stop drinking.' I think he saw it as, 'If I stop drinking I'm going to fall apart' and confront the interior world where he had these deep, dark, black secrets."

To judge from his songs and discussions with friends, those secrets might have been his frustratingly vague memories of his childhood abuse and his inability to come to a resolution about how to relate to his family because of their vagueness. *XO* seems to arrive at its emotional climax three quarters of the way through "Waltz No. 2 (XO)," on the "XO, mom" line. It means both "I love you" and "goodbye." And that's the way the song sounds, like a love song and a farewell. The refrain of the coda, maybe Smith's most famous line, is "I'm never going to know you now/but I'm going to love you anyhow." It's the way everybody feels during the termination of a short-lived relationship, but it also fits with Smith's apparent confusion over how to look back on his Texas upbringing—the love is there, and so is the confusion.

Smith wrote a lot of the *XO* lyrics at a bar in Park Slope called O'Connor's, where he befriended a bartender named Spike Priggen. The man's name does not misrepresent the establishment. Priggen, whose real first name is Michael, no longer works at O'Connors. The owner of the bar, Pat O'Connor, said to be the third generation of his family to run the establishment, remembers Smith sitting in the second booth from the door, kitty-corner against the wall, and looking out at the room. Smith didn't say much, but O'Connor would look up occasionally and find the young man looking right at him.

At night these days, O'Connor's is the kind of Brooklyn bar that attracts young people, struggling in picturesque fashion, from Dumba and Williamsburg. But in the afternoon it's still the O'Connor's where Smith could be found in the late '90s, one customer told me. He described it as a collection of regulars back then. From the outside, O'Connor's is inconspicuous. The paint has faded on the sign in front, and the storefront has a couple small windows with neon beer signs. Inside, the bar is spacious, with a pool table in the back and a long bar that runs the length of the room. There's a Budweiser sign featuring a map of Ireland beneath the moose head, and pictures from a fishing trip Pat O'-Connor took with a regular customer are framed on the wall above the booths, near an "Irish Need Not Apply" sign. When I was there on a Wednesday afternoon in early 2004, a few months after Smith's death, a regular came in with a baby in a stroller and bought everyone in the house a round. He'd won O'Connor's annual chili contest, in which regulars eat each other's chili recipes. The maker of the winning recipe gets a free drink and everybody gets a free glass of Chilean wine. On this particular Wednesday, there was a chart on the wall documenting the votes accorded each chili entry. A jukebox full of garage rock and punk was the only sign of the bar's nocturnal transformation into a place young people hang out. In the afternoon, Pat plays Frank Sinatra and Betty Carter.

Priggen, another bartender explains, was the new bartender during Smith's stay in New York, and he led the way in O'Connor's transformation from old-school neighborhood bar to an institution that serves local regulars by day and a younger crowd at night. He introduced the jukebox full of garage rock and provoked the first trickle of youthful customers. Smith preferred the old O'Connor's.

Pierre Kraitsowitz, who with his wife Shauna Slevin was Smith's roommate in Brooklyn, comes here often. He has stubble and a shaved head—the hair on his dome is almost as short as the hair on his chin—and he's part of a group of men who work in Red Hook on the sets for off-Broadway shows. One of his more prominent memories is of Smith composing orchestral arrangements. This was a new thing for Smith. Even on the more elaborately arranged songs Smith had done in Portland—"Miss Misery" and "Cupid's Trick"—there are no string sections. It's the Brooklyn-era Smith who wrote the plunging violin parts that punctuate the end of XO.

For the strings on "Waltz No. 2 (XO)," Smith came up with a rough idea of the notes he wanted each instrument to play, but he consulted with a pro for help in finalizing the arrangements. "He had a rough idea, piano-wise," of where the notes fell, says Schnapf. "He would show the guy and then they would just go back and forth with one another. He could read but we were doing a lot of stuff and it was a lot of work."

If moving toward strings signaled a new direction for Smith—more money to make albums, two new producers, no time constraints from being in Heatmiser—it was part and parcel of a return to being the multi-instrumentalist he'd been in his junior-high "band." Piano showed up more and more on his songs. On *Either/Or*, there are keyboards on three tracks ("Pictures of Me," "Punch and Judy," and "Angeles"). On *XO*, keyboards play a central role in about three-quarters of the songs.

XO was recorded chiefly at Sunset Sound, on Sunset Boulevard. There, Studio One was the incubator for Janis Joplin's *Pearl*, *The Doors*, and *The Who By Numbers*. Studio Two was used in The Rolling Stones' *Exile on Main Street*, as well as *Led Zeppelin II* and *Led Zeppelin IV*, and Studio Four was used for Beck's *Odelay* (the last track of which, "Ramshackle," was produced by Schnapf and Rothrock), Tom Petty's *Full Moon Fever*, and numerous Prince albums. Smith didn't sit down and decide to make a louder, more elaborately orchestrated album than he had made before, but there was an understanding that that was the direction his music was taking, says Schnapf.

"The first three records kept developing more and more. And *Either/Or* could have gone more in that direction but he wasn't ready yet. And so then *Either/Or* is sort of the bridge between the first two records and *XO* as far as the development in arrangements. It just seemed like that's how we're going. I think it was unspoken. *Either/Or* could have been done that way, and we didn't go there. And now he's ready, so we do it."

In stark contrast to the recording of Smith's last album, which would take place a few years later, much of *XO* was recorded with military efficiency. "'Waltz No. 2' is the first song we recorded," says Schnapf. "And we started off with nothing in the morning, and we left with that at night. Maybe it was a day and a half. I remember saying to Elliott, 'Wow, we just won.' We kept plugging away and it kept blossoming. I mean, we started with drums and we kept going until it was that, and then weeks later we added strings. That's how a bunch of [the album] was."

Beyond the standard array of melody instruments in the singer-songwriter's palette, Smith was growing up to be a one-man band. Of all the encomiums to Smith's musicianship, few of them mention the gift that belies the folkie label he always shunned: He provided, among other things, his own rhythm.

"I am a huge fan of Elliott's drumming," e-mails Glenn Kotche, the most recent drummer for Wilco, the Chicago-based avant-country-rock band that attained its greatest heights of renown with its 2001 album *Yankee Hotel Foxtrot*. "His drumming was perfect on [his] songs. This makes sense since he wrote them and knew exactly what to do to support the songs and add to it instead of distracting from it. He played drums like a musician, putting the song first, and not like a drummer. His big-picture approach to drumming was a big lesson to me that affected the way I view drumming. He was extremely talented in so many ways that I think his drumming always got overlooked."

The attention Smith received in the wake of his Oscar nomination meant working on *XO* around press interviews, but according to Schnapf neither time nor money restraints posed a serious problem for Smith and his frugal collaborators. "We weren't worried, but we were not being wasteful in any way. We were just trying to make a good record—we were still conservative, not blowing money left and right. We weren't using the most expensive rooms. We were eating burritos for lunch and beer for dinner." In its professionalism, the album was different from anything Smith had done before; his approach was exactly what any label would want from a stripped-down indie artist making his first major-label album: speed, economy, a willingness to polish and expand his sound and catchy melodies. Even though *XO* didn't come anywhere close to going gold, its creation was so smooth and the critical response so positive that it's not surprising DreamWorks was happy with its relationship with Smith.

Smith was able to conceive of songs almost entirely in the studio. "'Tomorrow Tomorrow'—that one kind of came out nowhere," says Schnapf. "He had that guitar part. The way I remember it I gave him the high-strung guitar—you take a twelve-string guitar"—the jangly specialty guitar favored by The Byrds' Roger McGuinn, in which each string found on a normal guitar is augmented by a thinner string next to it, tuned an octave above it—"and you only put on the high [thin] strings. And you tune it the same way and all the notes are really close together now. So that whole thing is on the high-strung." Much of the rest was created through a trial-and-error process of coming up with vocal harmonies around the melody. Schnapf, Rothrock, and Smith would "send out the probe, as we would say," says Schnapf. "Explore."

"'Independence Day' we had recorded after the record was already finished, because DreamWorks needed b-sides, so we did that song and 'Happiness.' And those weren't b-sides—we said, 'Independence Day' is going on the record, and 'Happiness' we're saving for the next record." Their wishes were granted—"Independence Day" did go on *XO*, and "Happiness" became the first single on *Figure 8*. "They were both written as we finished the record, I guess in April, and early in June that happened. And we were only in the studio for three days, and we did three songs, 'Independence Day,' 'Happiness,' and an instrumental that was a b-side."

"Happiness" was distinguished in part by a drum loop Rothrock came up with—a muffled sound that was akin to a floor tom mic'd and run through a distortion pedal. It was supposed to be a click track, Schnapf remembers, a sound for Smith to keep time by while recording other instruments. But it sounded good so they kept it in the whole song.

"I Didn't Understand" underwent a swift transformation into an a capella number because of a casual remark Schnapf made that Smith took seriously. "I had been listening to a lot of Beach Boys at the time, so I knew he could do it. I was like, 'What if we did this?' 'Okay.' 'Jesus Christ!'" First they recorded one version that was more "liturgical," in Schnapf's phrase, and then they decided to redo it. Smith built up the harmonies mostly by himself. It turned out to be one of the boldest displays of Smith's formidable abilities as a singer, something he's rarely remembered for. Smith could croon; with the help of modern recording technology, he could be a one-man boy band.

Of course, most Elliott Smith songs are harder to sing well than they initially appear. While it's not fair to evaluate performers at a one-off tribute revue with the same critical standards you apply to a performer who's had time to master his material over a long time, the New York City Elliott Smith tribute concert in early 2004 was an educational experience. It showed, above all else, how difficult an Elliott Smith song is to perform.

Everyone recognizes that Smith's guitar work was intricate, but there's a particular range of expression in Smith's vocals that must be maintained if the music is to carry anything like the emotional weight it bears in Smith's own performances. In the course of the evening at the tribute—which drew so many fans that portions of the audience had to huddle together near the stage like commuters on the morning train, prompting the club to ask all customers who hadn't come expressly for the tribute to leave—it became clear that an Elliott Smith song should not, generally speaking, be delivered like a Jeff Buckley song or even a Nirvana song. Smith once said that the reason he was a pop musician rather than a folk singer was because his songs didn't have specific morals or messages. But another important respect in which Smith veers closer to '60s London than '60s Boston Commons is his deadpan delivery. While it's not without accents and trembling, Smith's singing is almost never an interpretation of the song, but the only correct execution of it. He sounds like he's singing not from his stomach but from his head, and he almost never allows himself the full force of his vocal chords. Were it not for the occasional exception that proves the rule, it would be easy to believe that Smith simply couldn't sing very loud, or high. But in a live performance of The Beatles' "I'm So Tired," at the moment where the narrator hits an emotional rock bottom and the melody hits its highest note—"I wonder should I call you, but I *know* what you would do"— Smith opened the flood gates. The note is rich and high and displays the kind of capacity other singers would be tempted to showcase at every opportunity. But a night of listening to other singers try Smith's songs shows why he kept it on a leash.

Smith's lyrics run back and forth between emotional extremes on their own. When you add even modest vocal histrionics, you fracture the complicated melody and take those extremes over the top into melodrama. Most important, you destroy the balance between sadness and resilience that is Smith's trademark. If you sing the words to "Miss Misery" like you are in the midst of the romantic turmoil he describes in that song, you cut out one of the most distinctive and least appreciated parts of Smith: the quality of "oh well, so what if I suffer?" To stray too far from the deadpan is to risk becoming a sad singer-songwriter convinced of the awesome scale of his own problems—precisely what Smith said he wasn't. At the same time, Smith isn't so modest with his vocal abilities that he sounds like he can't sing. He consistently treads a path between murmur and belt. Fall into the former and you've got a song that sounds sullen and depressing, one of Smith's least favorite adjectives to have applied to his work. Rise to the latter and you become a whiner. The occasional tremble is about all you can afford. When Smith does indulge in embellishments, he deploys them with economy. The drawn-out "s" at the end of "You should be proud I'm getting good mark*s*," in "Needle in the Hay" is barely noticeable, but once noticed it nails home the point of the tune, which Smith once described as a "fuck-you song." It's the only place in the entire song Smith deviates from the simplest possible delivery of the words, and it drives home the song's meaning more effectively than a moan. In fact, for all the talk about Smith's songs being sad, it's impossible to imagine him moaning at all. His songs are largely sad, but they're also stoical.

꒰

Mike Doughty and Smith hung out in LA when Doughty was recording what would be the last Soul Coughing album, *El Oso*, and Smith was recording parts of "Miss Misery" for the *Good Will Hunting* soundtrack. Best known for Soul Coughing's early effort *Ruby Vroom* and single "Super Bon Bon," Doughty is an unusually analytical conversationalist for a musician. "We were staying at the Magic Castle Hotel," he says, "which is like a completely weird place to be staying." The Magic Castle is a private establishment where magicians perform for each other, and the Magic Castle Hotel capitalizes on its proximity to the club. "It's basically a cheap hotel, and we were making a record with Chad Blake at the Sound Factory . . . the last record, *El Oso*. [Smith] came over, and we got stoned, and I don't really remember what we talked about. And then the next day he came into the studio. . . . I remember he's like, 'Yeah, I'm doing songs for this Gus Van Sant movie.' And I'm, 'Oh, Gus Van Sant, that's great.' It's kind of funny to think we identified it as a Gus Van Sant movie. I was like, 'Really, what's that like?' 'I don't know, it's kind of weird, there's this guy doing arrangements.'" That guy was Danny Elfman, the famous Hollywood soundtrack composer who was doing the incidental music for the *Good Will Hunting*. The arrangements would have been for the orchestral version of "Between the Bars" that appeared on the soundtrack CD. "I think he was staying at the Mondrian. He seemed relatively blasé about it."

It was during that stoned conversation and the brief recording session that followed that Doughty learned what he decided was a keystone of Smith's ability as a songwriter. "He talked about writing. He would sit at the Sky Bar at the Mondrian writing songs. He wrote songs divorced from the melody."

What was so revealing about Smith's songwriting, to Doughty, was that Smith could write lyrics for one tune, decide they didn't work, adjust them, and graft them onto a completely different song. At Sky Bar, which commands palpitation-inducing night-time views of LA's incandescent grid, or at O'Connor's—he appears to have been happy to work at whichever bar was nearby—he worked like a poet, able to keep rhythms and melodies in his head. The evidence was the combination of words and music that Doughty heard him sing the one time they got into the studio together during that trip.

"He sang a version of 'Bottle Up and Explode!': 'The record that played over and over/There's a kid on the story below.' I think he used that lyric for a different song somewhere down the line."

Doughty's right: "There's a kid on the story below" wound up as "There's a kid a floor below me" not on "Bottle Up and Explode!" but on *XO*'s first track, "Sweet Adeline."

"A lot of the songwriters I know sort of work in parallel tracks," Doughty says. "They have a music thing going on and a lyric going on and they try to match them up. He had a really great system: He would write lyrics in a certain meter. Like, nine out of ten writers, if you co-write with them or produce them and you say, 'Can we change the lyric on this verse,' they can't do it to save their lives. It's like, no that's the lyric, tried to change it, can't change it. Or they'll change little bits about it. But to wholesale pop off one lyric and pop on another is indicative of a really extraordinary level of skill and facility. To be able to have that egoless moment where you can really say, 'I'm getting rid of it.' And the thing I most remember about it is him saying, 'I went to the Sky Bar and I sat down and I wrote songs.' 'You mean you just wrote the words and then the melody later?' 'Yeah.' And you got to respect a guy whose idea of a good night out is to sit in a bar and write."

The extent of Smith's drinking was in evidence to Doughty at this time. "We gave him a beer, and I got the impression he *needed* a beer. I got the impression, it was like 'Thank you, I need this beer.' Which is a little different from, 'Oh, it's the end of the day, I think I'll have a beer.'

This was a crucial juncture in Smith's career. In the course of a couple years his label had switched from Kill Rock Stars to Virgin to DreamWorks. "I remember talking to him about 'Angeles,' and him saying, 'Yeah, that song is kind of about the music industry,'" says Doughty. "And I said, 'Yeah, I know.' He's like, 'You know?' And I sad, 'Yeah,' and I quoted back a lyric to him: 'Someone's always coming around here trailing some new kill/said I seen your picture on a hundred dollar bill.' And it's called 'Angeles.'"

For all the ambivalence about the music business evident in "Angeles," Smith didn't come off as an indie rocker cautiously dipping a toe in the world of pop. "There was some song by Chicago that he was obsessed with," says Doughty. "And it had some kind of horn-driven early stuff and some kind of '80s [stuff]. But he was like obsessed with it. It was like a ballad, some semi-obscure [thing]. I don't know, man, those were like harsh, harsh times in terms of a very steep division between cool and uncool. I actually think that probably the best song of the decade is a Back-street Boys song: "I Want It That Way." The best song. Written by a Swedish guy who didn't speak English, which kind of brings some unintentional humor to it. I think if it was like The Shams or something people would find it charming and quirky, but since it's a mega-hit people don't look at it that way. . . . The discussion about the Chicago song was interesting because he was really interested in the fact that it was considered so corny. He thought it was really great the way they did it. But there was no way you could really come out and say, 'Hey, I think this song by Chicago is really fantastic.'"

In Doughty's perception of Smith at that time, he stood in sharp contrast both in his attitude and in his music to the quintessential '90s music god, Kurt Cobain: "Kurt Cobain was essentially getting up on stage and people applauded the beautiful guy. And he did some brilliant work, but it wasn't like a fundamental difference between him and somebody that—I don't want to glibly say he was just like David Cassidy or something like that, but it was kind of like that. Certainly when he got famous there were all kinds of people just going there because he was this beautiful compelling guy. And Elliott was not that guy. And people loved him for his music. Also, I don't think he felt sorry for himself; I think Kurt Cobain felt really sorry for himself. The thing I most remember about [Elliott] is him saying, 'I went to the Sky Bar and I sat down and I wrote songs.'"

There were two Elliott Smiths around this time, just as there had been in Portland: One was exceptionally talented, hardworking, and funny, writing around the clock, knocking out great and complicated albums with business-like efficiency; the other seemed to harbor a need to hurt himself. In September 1998, Bill Santen and Glenn Kotche went with Smith to a Mekons show in Manhattan and went drinking with him afterwards.

"It was a perfect night," says Santen. "[Elliott] shows up and everything's great and we go down to Max Fish." Max Fish was at its apex of popularity amongst arty folk in the '90s, and the neon image of a giant cigarette above its door remains a glowing time-capsule reminder of New York nightlife in the pre-Bloomberg days, when the city had no important rock scene to speak of and few good small venues in which to see bands—other than The Cooler in the meatpacking district—but people were at least allowed to smoke in bars.

Smith began to drink beer and Jameson—a combination that was usually a portent of bad things to come. "He gets in line for the pool table," remembers Santen, "and we go to another bar and come back . . . This guy was kind of being a jerk, running the [pool] table, and Elliott played this guy and was up in this guy's face. I thought they were kidding around because I'd never seen him do stuff like that before. I guess Elliott hit him, and the guy was a foot taller than him, and I don't think he ever hit Elliott. Elliott knocked him down, and Glenn was holding on to this guy to keep him from jumping on Elliott, and Elliott rushes him and hits him again. This guy was a frat boy, and Elliott had fallen on a bottle, and he was bleeding. We wrapped a sweatshirt around him and ran around the back of the bar so people wouldn't kill him. There was a chain-link fence, and we were trying to get out. Security came around, and Elliott had started the fight, but they let Elliott stay—they knew who he was. He was a mess. We put him in a cab and took him home. Next thing he was crying on the way home. That was the last time we really talked that much. After that he kind of laughed about it, but he never talked about it."

Nine
———

JOGGING

IN THE LAST days of the '90s, Smith was as famous as he'd ever be. He still liked to visit Portland and show up at parties, and one night he ran into Pete Krebs. "I saw him one time after that. He showed up at a show that I played at the Laurelthirst* and it was like a Tuesday night. Nobody was there and we got to play like three or four or five games of pool in peace, and nobody came and talked to us. It was just like old times again. We would just hang out and just crack dumb jokes. We didn't talk about music or any-thing—we just made all the dumb jokes we used to make. Then he was like, 'Hey, you want to go get a drink, you want to go to Club 21?' We went there and it was just like, girls just sitting down wanting to hang out. That was really the last time we hung out, whenever that was, and after that there were just stories about El-liott in New York getting into fights, and all this crazy shit and 'Elliott, he's really not doing very well.' For a long time, Elliott was just out of my orbit."

When Krebs caught a glimpse of what had happened with Smith's ballooning name recognition, he decided it was something Smith would have hated. "I was just surfing the Web one day and I went on this Web site, a fan-club site where people had posted

———
*A Portland pub where Krebs performs regularly.

recent photos of Elliott playing live, and I was looking at the pictures. He looked like a different person. He looked like an old man; it was just shocking. I thought, 'I don't want to see this,' and then I clicked the wrong button and it was fan art, just weird obsessive pictures of Elliott people had drawn. Elliott would have appreciated that, but he would have hated that. He just would have been embarrassed by that. It just got sort of weird, so any time I saw old friends—Sam, Janet, Sean, Joanna, Neil—I'd always ask them, 'You talk to Elliott lately?' 'No, I haven't heard from him for a while.' I talked to Sam [when] they were on the road, and he said [Smith] was walking around with a plastic bag with five thousand dollars' worth of portable recording gear in a box, and he couldn't get it together enough to even play demos of his new stuff. He couldn't figure out how to make the machine work because he was so fucked up on pills or whatever. So it just got to be too much to take."

Smith's high profile was painful for Smith and his friends, but it was good for indie rock—the key word being *rock*. For a while, the new-new thing in music, from Tortoise to Pavement to Moby to Cat Power, was anti-rock: It was either electronica- or experimental music–influenced, or dissonant or loose or just weird. It was not a coincidence that after Smith became one of indie rock's best-selling artists and got swept up in a major-label hand-off, bands started to be rock bands again. Sixties-loving bands like Belle and Sebastian and Neutral Milk Hotel became increasingly popular during the late '90s, as did Rhino Records' *Nuggets* box set of '60s psychedelia. Where minimalism had once been the defining characteristic of American indie, it was being displaced by intricate, retro rock music. Phil Spector–esque violin arrangements, Keith Richards–style guitar solos, and Rolling Stones haircuts were tearing across indie land like the first blush of vintage glasses frames.

‑ə

Not long after Smith moved to LA in 2000, during the time he was recording *Figure 8*, Marc Swanson came and stayed with him for a week. As usual, the two of them had a good time, although Swanson recalls that Smith was watching a lot of run-of-the-mill TV, and that he was between girlfriends, "which was unusual for him." They played the kind of mind games familiar to any friend of Smith: "I remember we did this little game where we would write down—he liked to do this and I was doing it with him too— we'd watch TV for kind of hours on end, and then write down what people said, try to take something out of context that would change the meaning of that thing. We were watching *Cinderella* and the woman said to Cinderella, 'Life is like your pipe; you never know where you put it,' and I wound up using that for a piece later. . . . Even when he was watching TV, he was always doing something." Moreover, "he was recording *Figure 8*. The whole *XO* tour was bigger than anything else, it had sold a lot of records, and DreamWorks was excited. I don't think they were pressuring him to do that much more than that. I think he was in a really good spot. That was the first DreamWorks record. He'd gotten bought out from his contract like he wanted to, and I think Lenny Waronker was a good guy, and [Smith] told me that. He was in LA, as far as he always said temporarily, and had a nice place." But at one point during Swanson's stay the conversation turned distinctly grim.

"He wasn't doing any drugs at all, I think I would have been able to tell. He was drinking, but not even that much. I was going out every night to visit friends and he wasn't; he was at home working on stuff. He was recording every day and would come home and play stuff. But at that time we went out to lunch, and I was like, 'So really, how are things going?' And he was like, 'Not so good. . . . I don't know what I can do. I don't know what to do. It's not going well. What do you think I should do?' And we're like a week apart in age, and we seemed to be on the same kind of things with dealing with things artistically a lot of the times. I think it's one of the reasons we're close. And I had started to go to some therapy stuff and deal with stuff, and I just said flat out, 'I think you need to go to therapy, and I think you need to either go someplace where you're monitored all the time or you need to go pretty intensively, a lot.' And he totally lost his temper, and was like, 'You know, I can't believe you of all people are saying that, and you know how I feel about that.' I didn't really know that much how he felt about it. He really didn't like people telling him what to do in a certain way. Anyway, then his idea was that he should go jogging, so after that we went to the mall and bought him shoes and we went jogging instead. He knew he had to deal with some stuff, but at that time he thought getting exercise was going to help. I don't really know why."

Smith's resistance to therapy went beyond his ability to out-smart therapists and therefore sabotage the process—he was openly against the *idea* of going into therapy at this time of his life, and was looking for a physical alternative. This tendency would eventually put him in a situation potentially dangerous to his health. And this time it wouldn't be because of a self-destructive urge but a frustrated desire to rid himself of demons without approaching the problem from a psychological, intellectual, or religious perspective.

Eventually, Smith's nascent feeling of shame about his success started to rob him of his warmth; he just didn't get along with his friends anymore. He slipped further and further into an identity he hadn't wanted, a new self he would later write about wanting to destroy. E. V. Day remembers that Smith "just got so negative." He felt he had to avoid his friends because being around them became too emotionally complicated for him.

"He could not function—he just became more and more of an invalid, which I think is also pretty normal when you're being taken care of like a rock star. He never wanted to be treated like a rock star, he never wanted to be bigger than anybody else. And yet, because he couldn't deal with it, he ended up being just coddled, and that's the label's interest, is to take care of this person, get them to do the records. So I don't blame them, per se, for anything. I think it's circumstantial."

Smith had moved to Los Angeles gradually, and without any pronounced intention of doing so. His series of LA-based activities—the recording of *XO* and the original material for the *Good Will Hunting* soundtrack, the performance at the Academy Awards, the mixing of *XO*, the recording of *Figure 8*—basically constituted a move. "When the Academy Award thing happened, everything blew up: DreamWorks buying his contract, and *Good Will Hunting* was a huge movie, and all of a sudden he was pretty much in LA a lot of the time from then on," says Swanson. "They got him an apartment before that. . . . But that whole time he wasn't living anywhere, he was touring and recording, and flying around. In my mind that's when he went to LA because he wasn't near anyone for an extended period of time. He wrote *XO* [in New York] but he left right after that. . . . And then it was like, 'Well, there's the apartment, and there's the car.'"

The mainstream celebrities who lived in LA didn't hold much interest for Smith, but when he met a member of indie rock's highest circle of elder statespeople, he was worried he'd come off as a schmoozer. His modesty was still extreme, or at least conspicuous. "I was in Los Angeles for a show and he was touring there, and I had just met Exene Cervenka the night before," remembers E. V. Day. "I met her at a poetry reading out there. I'd seen her read and then I had to leave, and we'd just been introduced and she's like, 'Where are you going?' and I'm like, 'I'm going to go see Elliott Smith,' and she's like, 'I wanted to see that show.' And I said 'Well, I could probably get you in for tomorrow, but it's the acoustic set,' and she said, 'Oh, that's the one I want to see,' and she was like, 'Oh, it's at the Troubador; I could go over and get in if I wanted to, but I don't want to be like that,' so I was like, 'Oh well, I'll bring you over tomorrow.' And so I went to the show and I told Elliott, 'Do you mind if I bring

Exene?' And he couldn't respond. He was totally freaked out. And I was like, 'I don't have to bring her,' and he was like, 'Ah.' I was like, 'She just wanted to see the show, and she really likes your music.' He's like, 'Oh my god, I guess so.' So then I asked him before, too. The next night I was like, 'Are you going to freak out if I bring her back after the show?' And he just couldn't even really respond, and Swannie was like, 'Whatever, of course, she wants to meet him.' So we watched the show and it was very funny seeing it with her because it was a small space and there were all these teenage girls lined up at the front and she was making great commentary about the dewy-eyed teens who knew exactly what he was saying, could really relate. Afterwards we went [backstage] and Elliott was basically paralyzed, couldn't move, couldn't relax, couldn't really talk. And so then, after the show, it's like, 'Time to go out, where does everybody want to go?' So Exene's like, 'I know where we're going, let's go to this place called Stone Age 2000.' It's in Koreatown, and it's in a mall. You take an outdoor escalator to get there. It's a Korean dinner-party place. You go in and it's these big fake boulders and mirrored columns and big seats that go around and people drink out of pewter kegs on their table and it was just a hilarious atmosphere and so the whole band came, a ton of people came, and Exene—he wouldn't talk to her. He could not talk to her, and the other women who were playing with him were huge fans and having a great time, but he just couldn't do it.

"I think he was just too big of a fan, and I think he felt like a sheep because he was playing and he had the show and I think he always felt conflicted in a very narcissistic way about that. So after that, Exene was like, 'Why won't he talk to me? I want to play with him. We should just hang out and play music together'—not professionally, she just wanted to mix and fool around, because she's a collaborator, and loves his music, and they sing about tortured romance and love, and so she said just, 'Tell him to call me.' And I was like, 'Listen, Elliott, Exene loved the show and she thinks you're great and you're here, she's here, and she thinks it'd just be fun to play together or see if you can do something together,' and he said, 'I can't call Exene.' And I said, 'Why not? She likes you, she respects your music.' And he said, 'But she's Exene.' And I was like, 'But why can't you call her?' And he said, 'Because if I call her she'll think I want something from her.' And I was like, 'Do you expect her to call you, Elliott?' And he just didn't respond. She was approaching him and he just could not get over that. He just thought he was way too star-struck, way too big of a fan. It just didn't feel comfortable."

The irony of Smith's modesty was that he was starting to become famous enough himself that he sometimes found himself torn between fans and friends. At the very least, he didn't have much time alone with old friends anymore. "I stopped hanging out with him—I'd go to the shows, I'd see him before, and not do the whole after-thing," says Day. "Because he was always all pulled apart. It just wasn't any fun unless you could really hang out and talk. I think he felt kind of unworthy."

Smith was starting to become an island unto himself, partially as a result of his humbleness and generosity. He couldn't stand the idea that people who liked his music and wanted to hang out with him weren't going to be able to come party after his shows. Even though, as his friends pointed out, it would have been impossible for him to let in everybody who wanted to get in, and the more strangers he felt obliged to entertain, the less attention he gave people who were really close to him.

"There'd be fans coming to the after-party and maybe the bouncer would close the door and then [Elliott would] feel really bad for that person who was some groupie who couldn't come to the after-party, who he's never met before," says Day. "And he'd be like, 'I feel so bad, that's so uncool,' and it'd be like, 'Elliott, you have friends here, so what? It's just part of the deal. The whole world can't be at your after-party, and you don't want them here either. It'd just drive you crazy after a while. Your friends are here, so you gotta close the door.' He would just deflect from things that were really important to him [and focus on] anonymous people, and that's when I just knew, 'This is not making any sense.'

"And we were just like, 'fuck you,' because sometimes you'd go the shows to remind him there were people who really cared about him because you knew he was bad, and you'd make an effort to go because, sure you liked the show, but you made an effort and you knew his circumstances were a lot more limited, and he'd pull shit like that. He wasn't rock-starry about it, he was just kind of like, 'Oh, I feel so bad.' I mean that was just queer. It's like no one thinks you're a hero because of that. I think there is this dichotomy between him thinking that he's pathetic and him thinking that he should be taking care of the world in some way or taking care of everyone else's feelings. And 'everyone else' became not his friends, or people he doesn't know. But I think this happens with a lot of famous people, and I think it's this weird celebrity dysfunction."

For Smith's old friends, the consensus was that New York or Portland would have been a better place for him than LA. Part of it was the severity of the crack and heroin use that he'd eventually fall into there, and part of it was that he kept talking about how he'd like to move. "He always talked about coming back [to New York]," says Swanson. "Always talked about it. The last time I saw him here it was like they were looking for a [recording] studio, he was looking for an apartment. It was like he was never officially living in LA. He liked to make people happier, so I wouldn't be surprised if every day here he told everybody he was moving back here and every day there he told people he was never going to leave. But I do know he was always here and was enamored of it here and made friends here, and things got isolated in LA and he always talked about wanting to be here. The general consensus of the whole crowd was that it would be better if he moved here."

But the influence of old friends on Smith was waning. "I think he was conscious that it was happening, but I think that's where he started to lose it," says Day. He couldn't understand why there had to be any hierarchical relationship between him and anyone else, most of all his old friends—he couldn't accept that he was a rock star now and they weren't. "He would fixate on something they had done that was wrong"—the intervention—"and he thought that was just wrong and mean . . . and it just didn't make sense."

-ᴂ

Smith recorded *Figure 8* with Tom Rothrock and Rob Schnapf in LA, much the way they'd recorded *XO*, only with a field trip to Abbey Road Studios in London, where he fooled around on the piano on which "Penny Lane" was supposed to have been composed. The album's sound was grander, at once smoother and more rock, than anything Smith had put out before—and also less personal. There was still Smith's gimlet-eyed approach to the human psyche, with "Everything Means Nothing to Me" the darkest point in the album for its title alone. But the personal content of the lyrics, if there is some, is far more vague than on his previous records.

Take "Pretty Mary K," the album's thirteenth track. The lyrics describe a wounded soldier in an infirmary calling out for the title character. "I walk round the dock and talk to St. James," Smith sings, a reference to the blues standard "St. James Infirmary." That's a modified version of a lyric in a song also called "Pretty Mary K," recorded years earlier but never released. Where the new "Pretty Mary K" is sad but not intensely dark, the old one is one of the most personal laments in the Smith canon.

The only sounds on the old "Pretty Mary K" are acoustic guitar, Smith's voice, double-tracked, and an organ or accordion sounding out single notes that follow the chord progression. It's an unrequited-love song: The narrator talks about Pretty Mary K as a woman in some inaccessible place, "with another man." In another verse, she appears "with some little boy in blue/who can't stay away from you." It's a dilemma that comes up in a million songs, but Smith's version carries personal weight because his mother's name was Bunny Kay, and the tune ends with the narrator's vow to drown or at least somehow negate himself: "Going to walk out on the water/fill my mouth up full of sand," Smith sings. The narrator believes that he'll be with Mary K soon, "as soon as I pay." In the last refrain of the song, he vows to walk, Jesus-like, upon the water, to Mary. The reference points are Christianity, suicide, and Oedipus—not an old blues song. It's more powerful than the new "Pretty Mary K" because it more closely resembles the feeling of extraordinary intimacy Smith was able to achieve writing songs he didn't think would be released on *Roman Candle*. Most of *Figure 8*—as lovely as songs like "Junk Bond Trader" might be, and as much as Smith pushed the envelope with loud rock guitar solos and ever more orchestral production—doesn't have the same sense of secrecy his fans so adored on his other albums.

Smith toured behind *Figure 8* nearly nonstop for about a year. Myles Kennedy, Jr., a tour manager Smith met through Lou Barlow, was with him the whole time, and estimates he spent about twelve days at home the entire time. Still, Smith seemed his playful, musically expert self. It was, as Ramona Clifton remembers it, "the best sort of times. When he'd be warming up beforehand, he'd get out a little Casio he'd play. He could play Sabbath or he could bust out that music-box dancer and then switch to Mötley Crüe. He could pull anything out of a hat; you could say any Beatles song or any Kinks song."

Kennedy remembers another pre-show ritual: "It was a stupid little thing he taught me: When you've got a song stuck in your head, you just stand there going 'by *Men*non!' And every once in a while you'd see him go 'by *Men*non!' to clear his head."

"[We were in New York] and my friend Myles was tour-managing and Elliott was staying with friends in the city and he was staying in a real nice hotel suite, the Roger Smith Hotel," says Clifton. "It's like an art hotel where they put modern art everywhere and really nice suites, and he had this beautiful corner suite, and he wanted to stay with friends in the city, so he let Myles and I crash in his super-nice suite. That's how generous he was. I was living in Boston at the time, and he knew we would be crammed into some other room."

Touring was wearing on Smith, but he had become afraid of stopping. In 2000, "He wouldn't stop touring," says Day. "He'd say, 'I don't know what else to do . . . if I'm not touring I'm not making money, and so I have to tour, but I don't want to tour, and if I don't tour I'm scared because I don't know what I'm going to do.' Because he'd alienated everybody. I think he was scared that he didn't have a life anymore."

Kennedy remembers a mix of good times and trepidation on that epic ride with Smith. Over the course of at least two separate U.S. tours, all the major festivals in Europe, a sixteen-date *Rolling Stone*–sponsored run with Grandaddy, and a tour of Japan, they spent a lot of time hanging out in the back lounge of the bus, shooting the shit with a guitar tech. The band was Sam Coomes on bass, drummer Scott McPherson, who'd just left the California alt-rock band Sense Field, and two keyboardists: first Aaron Embry, an LA studio musician, and, after Embry bailed, tired of playing somebody else's stuff on the road, Shon Sullivan of the LA indie band Goldenboy. For the last shows, in Japan, Smith played solo and acoustic. For one leg of the tour, the opening band was the Portland retro-'60s rock band The Minders, with bassist Joanna Bolme. Smith and Bolme "were not a couple at that point," says Kennedy, "but they put that whole thing together." On another leg of the tour, Kennedy remembers, the opening band was the LA country-rock ensemble Whiskey Biscuit.

The *Rolling Stone*–sponsored leg, the *Rolling Stone Live* tour, gave Smith a palpable sense of how many new fans he'd acquired. Ten to fifteen minutes after every gig, starting in the fall and stretching into the winter of 2000, he was required to do a meet-and-greet with fans and corporate sponsors, with Kennedy standing by to guard him from the mob of curious and friendly people that threatened to crush him, or at least annihilate any concept of his personal space as they clamored to hug him and shake his hand and ask him to sign things. "It was everything from meeting people from Phillips Magnavox and from *Rolling Stone* to contest winners," says Kennedy. "I don't think he was somebody that enjoyed being fawned over and his fans were fairly rabid. His fans were one extreme to another, it'd be a sixteen-year-old girl or some corporate executive, so you never really knew what you were up against."

Kennedy became, in effect, a bodyguard, something it would have been absurd to imagine Smith ever having just a few years earlier. "The only person that could come up behind Elliott was me. We tried to do the meet-and-greet at a bar, where one side was protected, and I would be behind him, so nothing weird was sneaking up to him, because some of those shows were huge. People would just rush to him. After a rock concert people don't always have their heads on straight, and a lot of times fans don't know the boundaries between meeting-and-greeting and smothering somebody. People would come at him from all different ways; people wanted to hug him, people would want to ask him everything from why he wrote a certain song to 'Where'd you get that t-shirt?' I just remember helping him, and being glad I didn't have to go through what he was going through. I don't think he enjoyed those meet-and-greets in any way, shape, or form, but it was part of the contract."

On the great 2000–2001 trek, merchandise—Elliott Smith t-shirts, CDs, and the like—was handled by a Scotswoman named Valerie Deerin. In the middle of the tour, she and Smith hooked up. "On the flight to Japan, they broke up," remembers Kennedy, "and so it was me and Valerie and Elliott, and that was kind of an awkward situation, because they broke up while we were on the plane to Japan." By the time the trip was done and the three of them were back in the United States, Deerin and Smith were together again, and would stay together for roughly another year and a half.

Kennedy thinks that by the time the tour was through, Smith may have started to experiment with narcotics. But he simply wasn't with Smith enough to be absolutely sure of what he was up to all the time, and he felt quite clear that whatever drug use might be going on, it was nothing Smith couldn't control. "There was something going on, but it wasn't like, 'Stop the presses,' and a lot of the times things were going on, I could have been doing changeovers. I did a lot of the backline, a lot of the tour management. There was a lot of stuff happening that I was not hip to." What Kennedy describes sounds like the potential beginning of a problem, but not a problem in and of itself. Kennedy puts it this way: "He went to Japan," where "whatever you're doing you have to quit cold turkey, and he didn't have any collapse or breakdown happen at that point, so I would say at that point he didn't have any kind of problem."

Kennedy's stories from the tour are mostly funny memories: Smith and his band watching police helicopters hover over an English festival at which the singer of Slipknot was rumored to want to kill himself on stage (he didn't do it); Smith, Deerin, and Kennedy watching a soccer riot in Tokyo so organized that it stopped and started punctually and nobody rioted beyond the proscribed area. One of the few areas that Smith seemed less than entirely comfortable was Portland. "He was nervous anytime we'd end up in Portland," says Kennedy. "Old friends, old girlfriends. He stayed at the hotel; he laid pretty low when we were in Portland."

At this point, when Smith wasn't on the road he was living in a tiny complex of small houses known to residents of LA's Silver Lake neighborhood as the Snow White cottages. There is an urban myth that Disney built the cottages, which are set back from a residential section of Griffith Park Boulevard. They are a dark place to live by Los Angeles standards. A thick canopy of trees shades them, and they're black and white, built low to the ground, and designed to look like places the seven dwarves would have lived—cozy and spooky at the same time.

The cottage was Smith's first long-term residence in LA. He and the black-and-white dwarves' hut were not a natural couple. Day, who dated Smith for a little while early in his Los Angeles years, despite the fact that the two of them weren't living in the same city, remembers that it was "a hilarious picture, because he looked like a little grungy leprechaun, and then in that weird scale of the Tudor Disneyland landscape there was just nothing funnier. He could see the sense of humor and he would just live it with a smile. He didn't ask for this, [his handlers] just found the house for him and he just loved that it was so embarrassing. That was sort of the cartoon quality of it, he would be that cartoon character in the way he carried himself."

"God, you found my dream house," Dorien Garry told Smith when he described the place. "He was like, 'No, it costs $1800 a month, and I bang my head on the ceiling when I go upstairs.' And it was like, 'Maybe it's not easy to live in the dwarf house.' He's like, 'It's owned by Disney and built by Disney,' and it was like, 'Pretend you're a gnome, it's expensive everywhere now.' He wasn't too psyched about it."

For Day, the end of the line with Smith came during the *Figure 8* tour, on the heels of a night when the mood was flamboyant and trouble was far out of mind. It was at a show Smith played at Irving Plaza in New York. "A group of friends were joking: [We had to] liven up his show because his songs are so sad, and he just stands there, and we were just picking on him, joking around, 'You need some go-go dancers.' And he was like, 'Okay.' A bunch of people just chickened out, and me and Swannie [Marc Swanson] were just like, 'Let's do it,' because it's funny, and his sense of humor was never put into his shows. [His public persona was] so personal, and yet we felt it was so lopsided, being his friends. There was this show at Irving Plaza, and so we did it, and it was pretty fun and people loved the dancing. Just me and Swannie on either side of the stage. I wore kind of what I was wearing. Fur boots and a fur vest with a tail coming off of it. And then we came out and did it for the encore as well."

But by the time another Irving Plaza performance came around, E. V. Day had decided she couldn't take being Smith's friend anymore. She had a history of depression; her mother had committed suicide and it was unbearable to watch the things she loved about Smith slip away. "I just felt so hopeless and angry at him for not taking any action, and he would just be silent. He would come around sometimes. I was just about trying to help him. I just said, 'I can't. . . . You've got my number; you need anything you can call me.' But I said, 'I'm never going to call you again. I'm never going to see you again. I can't be around this self-destruction.'"

At that point, there wasn't a drug problem to deal with, although Smith's heavy drinking had been consistent throughout the time Day knew him. Frustratingly, Day remembers, he did carry around a bottle of anti-depressants he said he was preparing to take. "It was that he wasn't taking his medication. He was drinking pretty consistently, but it wasn't that. He performed, he wasn't a sloppy drunk, really, he was motorized on that. It was the fact that he wasn't dealing with anything. It wasn't me: It wasn't that our relationship got so torrid, I just felt the only way I could relate to him anymore was to try to take care of him, and I wasn't going to be able to do that. It was a lost cause, really. Not that I didn't have hope. But I knew that he'd already had interventions before with people. It would be like I would have to give up my career and turn into a full-time nurse or something."

But even if Smith was clearly on a downward spiral, what were the immediate reasons for his starting to use heroin? After all, his first album provides ample evidence that Smith had been thinking about every facet of heroin use for a long time. David McConnell,

Smith's production partner on his last album, *From a Basement on the Hill*, recalls Smith connecting the start of his regular heroin use to the deterioration of his relationship with Joanna Bolme. The move to LA, says McConnell, was "probably part of" the beginning of Smith's heroin problem, "but he also once told me that his girlfriend Joanna [Bolme] told him that if he ever did heroin she would leave him and that was the only way he could finally get out of the relationship . . . he was kind of fed up with the relationship. This is what he told me: He said they were fighting and she said, 'If you do heroin, I'll leave you, or become a junkie, I'll leave you'—he said that's about the time he started doing heroin. That's what he told me."

This sounds like a rationalization on Smith's part. For Bolme to come up with the ultimatum there would have most likely been some threat of an incipient habit in the first place, and Smith had recently been in plenty of emotional trouble (as he indicated in his lunch with Swanson) during a time he wasn't with Bolme. But it does indicate a certain impulse on Smith's part to distance himself from his friends and associates. If people were going to pressure him to get clean, he was going to move away from them.

In Swanson's opinion, Mittleman and the other members of the professional entourage Smith took up in the late '90s were well-intentioned and protective of Smith. The increasing alienation he felt from them after the *Figure 8* tour could easily have been a factor in his personal downward spiral. "I was suspect of those people before I knew them, but even with Lenny [Waronker], after I met these people they were like old friends, they loved him dearly. It's very hard not to love [Smith] if he put you in his sphere. They wanted the best for him, that's pretty much the consistent thing. I mean, I wanted to blame the music industry for what happened to him. I wanted to hate them for it. And increasingly there were all these surrounding groups of people around who I didn't know who didn't know me who were not very nice to me because I wasn't part of that world, or whatever.

Not that they weren't nice to me, I was just some other friend they didn't know. But then it was even grosser, finally someone would be bored enough to be like, 'So how do you know Elliott?' and I would be like, 'I know him from Hampshire.' And then it was like this whole other thing, people would add it up and go, 'Oh, he's known him for fifteen years, not a person to be rude to,' but that's the way that stuff works. I realize that now. I got really offended by it when I was younger, but now I realize they've got a job to do and part of that job is unfortunately to be nice to people that Elliott's known for a long time and not to be very nice to people that he hasn't."

Day's explanation for Smith's decline is simple: "He didn't like himself. He was turning into a person that he would hate. Which was not being some kind of misogynist jerk . . . But he turned into a person who didn't have the—I think he sort of lost the ability to fight to be the individual that he wanted to be. And I think he was just like, fuck it, just take me on the bus. He let go of something— he felt very strong about his individuality, that he had this vision in the world. I think that he just couldn't deal. And so he just would be around people that would make life easier than being the person I think he really wanted to be. Just to be a great artist. The whole time I hung out with him, he was never doing drugs, he just drank. I think that he did start doing drugs again really soon after that time. I guess I could just feel it coming on, that he was just numbing out."

Margaret Mittleman and Smith would part ways soon after his *Figure 8* tour, and shortly thereafter Smith passed into the worst period of his adulthood. "The whole after-Margaret [time] and all that stuff is all very much involved with heavy drug use: crack and whatever," says Swanson. "I don't know how many extreme drug addicts you've been friends with, but you don't really know them anymore. They turn into weird people, and I didn't talk to him much at that time, and a couple times I did talk to him and he sounded really crazy, and I was really worried. *Really* worried.

"We all knew that there was bad stuff going on. That he was not doing well. He was stubborn; he would do what he wanted. Somebody would be out in LA and someone would tell someone they saw him at a show, and we were definitely worried. Neil would go down there or Sam would go down there, and maybe they'd play. There were always trickles, someone keeping track of things and stuff like that, but you know, that's when it got really hard, that's always when it gets really hard, when somebody's doing that. I don't think anybody knew this or that, but I think we all knew something was amiss."

Ten

A BASEMENT ON THE HILL

OF ANY PERIOD in Smith's his life, Smith's last three years in Los Angeles have remained the most mysterious, since it was a time when both old friends from Portland and colleagues from the music industry lost touch with him. In Smith's own words to *Under the Radar*, he "dropped out of just about everything" for a while.

Without Margaret Mittleman and the Schnapf-Rothrock producing team, Smith became far more vulnerable to diving into situations from which he couldn't easily extricate himself. One such example is the album he named *From A Basement on the Hill*. Smith first started to record the album with Jon Brion, but after Smith and Brion decided not to work together anymore, Smith spent a long time recording the album with David McConnell, who runs the B-Girl record label and Satellite Park recording studio in Malibu. McConnell had recorded Shon Sullivan in Goldenboy, and his label was also home to Josie Cotton, singer of the '80s hit "Johnny Are You Queer?" and McConnell's cohabitant. Smith and McConnell, Smith recalled, jointly developed the term "California Frown" to describe the sound they pursued. (Smith explained "California Smile" as a music-industry term that usually connotes high highs, low lows, and extreme slickness.)

Smith ruefully recalled his preceding recording experience to *Under the Radar*: "There was even a little more than half of a record done before this new one that I just scrapped because of a blown friendship with someone that made me so depressed I didn't want to hear any of those songs. . . . He was just helping me record the songs and stuff, and then the friendship kind of fell apart all of a sudden one day." That was probably a description of Smith's falling out with Jon Brion, the producer famous for his work with Aimee Mann and Fiona Apple. Brion, who made his name with avant-garde composition and brought analog keyboards back into style, would have no doubt helped Smith make the melodious, critically acclaimed album that was expected of him. McConnell says Smith and Brion parted ways just before Smith came to him to record. In a way, the end of the working relationship with Brion wasn't so different from the end of Smith's romance with DreamWorks. Smith told McConnell that he fired Brion because Brion didn't want to put up with his drug use and the work habits that attended it.

McConnell is an amiable thirty-something with red curls and an accent that betrays a childhood spent partially in Missouri and partially in Fresno. Somehow, he or Josie Cotton seems to have come into a lot of money. McConnell is one of those doubly blessed Malibu residents who has managed to get rich enough to live on an edenic spread of land and yet remain chill enough to properly enjoy it. He's somebody who'd have a soothing influence on you if you spent a long time living and working with him; if you had a problem he'd give you friendly advice and do his best to help, but he wouldn't throttle you over it.

McConnell's Satellite Park studio is in his house, which sits in the hills above the Pacific Coast Highway (PCH). The spot is just east of the Malibu bluffs, which, together with the beach on the other side of PCH, constitute one of the most tranquil landscapes confronting the American driver. The place is on the opposite side of the greater Los Angeles area from Silver Lake, where Smith was living, and it is economically and aesthetically on a different continent from LA's east side, let alone Portland. This was indie recording in the sense that it was a studio with no major-label affiliation, but it was also upscale, a far cry from the kind of environment many people in Silver Lake or Portland envisioned as the source of anything truly indie rock.

To get to McConnell's place, you snake up a series of back roads, finally arriving at a rectangular metal gate. When it opens you can see mist-teased hills from the driveway. There is a bounding, flawless green lawn and the house sits squarely upon one of the hills. A black BMW SUV was parked in front the day I visited.

The décor is relatively unobtrusive on the top floor, where McConnell recorded many tracks with Smith, running cords up from the recording devices on the bottom floor. The bottom floor consists of McConnell's bedroom, the guest bedroom where Smith lived during his recording sessions there, and a bathroom off of Smith's chamber. A wall separates McConnell's bed from a mass of vintage recording equipment set up on racks. Across from the equipment is a Chamberlain organ, a favorite keyboard of Smith's. There is wall-to-wall leopard-print carpeting, and '50s Chinese kitsch art on the walls. In the bedroom that once housed Smith, there is a giant Warholian portrait of Mao. The huge windows look out on exquisite Californian natural bliss, with nary a woodshed in sight. This is a place the Rolling Stones would have recorded.

Smith came to a decision quickly about McConnell's facilities. "Elliott was looking around for a studio, and asking around, for somebody to record with and work with, and Shon [Sullivan] recommended me," McConnell says. "He and Valerie were calling me to set up a time and come up here and look at the place, and see if he wanted to work with me up here. So one day he said, 'Can I come up tonight at look at the studio around ten?' He was in Big Bear, so they were going to drive down from Big Bear and check it out. So ten o'clock rolled around and they didn't show up. And it was like twelve o'clock and I was getting tired, almost ready to go to sleep, and then finally after a few more phone calls they said they were almost here. It was like 2:00 a.m., and they finally got here around 3:00 a.m., maybe even later. And Elliott was basically in my driveway and he hopped out of the car, and I said, 'Come on in.' He looked at the gear that I have and the mics and stuff and the instruments and whatnot and he just liked the vibe of the place so he said, 'Great, let's start, right now.' So basically he had all his instruments in his car. Generally when you do these things it's like, 'Okay, great, so next Tuesday let's start,' but it was like, 'Okay, great, can we start?' And I was like, 'Uh, sure, I guess so, if you want. I guess we could start.' So all of a sudden, he and his girlfriend and a friend of theirs all just started loading in all this stuff: clothes, and guitars, and all this equipment and books and sleeping bags.

"He basically just moved in, in the course of like thirty minutes, that night, right on the spot. It all happened within an hour, him looking around and deciding he wanted to work here. I guess I passed his little interview. He was real into the vintage old gear and Beatles techniques of recording, so I guess I passed that test. Within an hour he was like, 'Let's go,' so I guess he didn't have to think about it too long. And that began the first six weeks of recordings."

During those six weeks, starting in the last week of April 2001, Smith lived at McConnell's house; Valerie Deerin was a part-time resident. The *Figure 8* tour had only recently concluded and there was still nothing irregular about the schedule on which Smith was approaching the new album. The one disaster so far had been the split with Jon Brion. There was still every reason to believe the album could be ready for release in 2002, two years being the standard amount of time between albums for an artist on a major label.

But there were hints of trouble brewing. Weeks earlier, Smith had had another run-in with a flawed intervention, this time in a meeting with DreamWorks, according to McConnell. Smith apparently told McConnell that the "intervention was a meeting at DreamWorks with Lenny and Luke." But the meeting didn't end with Smith in a clinic; it ended with Smith storming off, refusing help, full of resentment. "I think that helped pave the way for him to be moving away from DreamWorks," says McConnell. "I think that started him on his path to get off the label." It was a path that wouldn't lead to a formal split from DreamWorks, but to an agreement that Smith's album-in-progress would be released on an indie label. That didn't stop Smith from candidly expressing a desire to get off of DreamWorks to numerous friends—Swanson and McConnell among them—throughout the next few years. Lenny Waronker's ship looked like the best the major-label world had to offer, and in Smith's eyes it wasn't all that appealing.

Smith's work habits during the McConnell recordings were exceptionally grueling—it was hard to keep up with someone whose state of mind was as medically pumped-up as Smith turned out to be. And Smith was dead set on making a great album at full speed, for the most part spurning rest. McConnell says he and Smith "pretty much worked around the clock. I would take cat-naps constantly because I wasn't able to stay up. I didn't have help. So I pretty much stayed up as long as I could with catnaps and then I would crash every three days or something. [I crashed] for ten or twelve hours every three days, whereas he would crash every five days. A lot of that was because he didn't want to go to sleep without finishing each song; he wanted to complete each song before he got into bed. The whole song: Drums, guitars, bass, keyboards, vocals, everything, he wanted it all done, and then he'd go to bed and have me mix."

Smith had always been the kind of songwriter who explored the most idiosyncratic parts of himself. That process involved a risk: If you spend day after day reaching into the innermost darkness of your own psyche, aided by whatever substances you think will help you get there, you might not find it easy to return to a state that other people would call normal. In Portland and New York he'd walked the streets and subway tunnels at night, and sat on church steps talking to god. In LA, he holed up behind a gate in the hills and drove himself downward, into himself and into a form of madness, with legal and illegal drugs and hard work. In doing so he built the foundation of a great album, at the cost of his ability to function out in the rest of the world.

"He'd end up either passing out on the floor here," says McConnell, indicating the leopard-print carpet, "or falling asleep up on the couch. He'd be trying to stay awake, so there was a lot of that for the first six-week period." In the end, the creative results were incomplete, as excellent as the songs might have been. Because of the breakneck schedule Smith imposed on himself, McConnell says, "basically what happened is it didn't get finished."

Smith's defense of such behavior was an aesthete's defense: "We talked a lot about 'we're not going to do that, that's what normal people do,'" says McConnell. "That was a big thing for him, to take the artistic road instead of the high road or whatever. It's definitely, 'I'm going to do my record and I'm going to do as many drugs as I want, because art is not about being sober and it's not about being some society figure, it's about art.' And he's right, you know?"

E. V. Day sees this as a sure sign of Smith's not thinking like his former, wiser self—the one his closest friends had known and loved for years. "A lot of artists do that, they take drugs in order to make music—and I don't really think he needed it. I don't think he needed it at all. I think he needed it to deal with the people and his conflicts with the relationships, which do come into the music. I think he could have gone a separate way and not have turned to drugs. I think that was a cop-out. That's what I mean about him turning into a person he didn't want to be. I don't think it was like, 'I'm going to make better music because I'm going to do drugs.' That's just an addict talking."

This was the beginning of making an album, but it was also the beginning of a descent into a psychological crisis. The recording of Smith's wildest, most independently created album since *Either/Or*, if not his wildest ever, went hand in hand with a series of personal break-ups and crises. Mittleman and Smith seemed to have ended their professional relationship weeks before Smith came to McConnell's studio, McConnell recalls. Mittleman and Smith "communicated once or twice" on banal matters, and then she was out of the picture.

Schnapf may have been linked to Mittleman, but Smith's differences with Schnapf seemed to McConnell to be creative, while Smith's differences with Mittleman seemed more personal. "He complained a lot about Rob, [but] kind of more about his production than him as a person. Whereas with Margaret he complained about her as a person—'Oh she really pisses me off.' It seemed like he had falling-outs with people all the time. It was really weird. It was almost like he sought out relationships on purpose so that he could have a falling out."

Smith knew exactly how he wanted the post-Schnapf album to sound. "He wanted to get away from his last two albums," says McConnell. "He was proud of the albums, he liked them, but he felt like they were a little too polished for what he wanted to portray. For his next album he would say things like, 'Oh, listen to *Fun House,* by the Stooges, that's not polished, that's one of the best albums ever made. Listen to the Saints.' Or whatever, 'Listen to the Beatles; the Beatles aren't polished, their guitars are out of tune, they sing out of pitch every now and then, and it's okay, it sounds great. That's good, let's do that.' And I think that's why he hired me: He knew I had studied the sounds of the Beatles, and how they got them, and I think that's what he wanted, and he would refer constantly to The White Album and stuff like that. And I think he was going to pretty much emulate The White Album in many respects. At one point, he was talking about having thirty tracks. He definitely did have thirty tracks, a preliminary set list of thirty tracks. Basically he really liked the era of his second and third albums [*Elliott Smith* and *Either/Or*]. He really liked that style of recording because it was more raw than the DreamWorks records."

In many ways, the creation of an unpolished record was a more exacting process than the creation of a polished one. "Basically we'd be sitting here recording, and if anything ever sounded too polished, we'd fucking redo it. 'That's not right, let's redo it to make it sound more human, less robotic,' [he'd say]. And even to the extent of detuning the guitars slightly. On most of the songs we ended up doing that, we were kind of forced to do that. One guitar would be sharp, one guitar would be flat—just a little bit, just enough that they could be distinct. We used lots of strange mic techniques. We did a lot of bouncing, like The Beatles did. You might start off with the drums on six or seven tracks, but bounce them down to one or two tracks.

"The idea was to slowly degrade the sound. But in a way that we liked, in a way that was unique. We didn't want to degrade it and have it be like, 'Oh yeah, it sounds like every other lo-fi band.' Instead we wanted it to have a lo-fi sound that was something that somebody couldn't duplicate right off the bat. So we spent a lot of time doing that, which is also why the record took a lot of time that first year. It was just because of a lot of meticulous deconstruction of the songs. The song might start off [with him] playing acoustic guitar and singing, and sure enough it sounded like a pretty standard song. By the time we got the rest of the instruments on there, it's like a whole different song, a whole different world, in a very extreme range. It was deconstruction of the song. We would always use the less obvious approach. If it was like, 'Oh, for this next guitar track we should use this mic on that amp,' instead we'd go, 'Okay, if that's what it should be let's not do that. Let's do this other mic, this other guitar.'

"He would say things like, 'Whatever happens to me, don't let anybody clean this up. Don't let them put it through Pro Tools. Make sure it's released like this.' In fact, we did a lot of mixes together, and he would say, 'If anything happens to me, make sure these are the mixes that end up on the album. Don't let anybody else remix them.' He would even threaten to erase the masters, so that they had to use those mixes. And I stopped him. There was a number of times he tried to erase the master tapes, because he liked the mixes that we had and he knew that if the label got a hold of it they would try to clean it up. And so I would stop him from erasing the masters." Of course, whether DreamWorks would have actually remixed them is anybody's guess.

To McConnell it didn't seem like DreamWorks was hostile to what Smith was doing, only surprised. "We had meetings with Lenny Waronker and Luke Wood where we'd play them some of the songs. [Waronker] looked really tripped out by it. . . . I think he was probably thinking, 'Oh my god, this is most crazy drug album I've heard in fifteen years.' It was kind of like that. I think he felt almost like he was going back to the '60s listening to this album. . . . Lenny seemed very supportive of Elliott. He seemed concerned, he also seemed afraid of Elliott too, kind of scared of him, intimidated by him. . . . It wasn't like he was saying, 'This is unreleasable.' It was more like he was saying, 'This is really fucking trippy.'"

Smith's complaints about DreamWorks were of the kind very commonly voiced by artists about their labels, but they were adamant. "He wasn't happy with DreamWorks at any time that I knew him," says McConnell. "The whole time he was very unhappy with DreamWorks. He felt like they had let him down, they hadn't promoted him correctly, they had spent all this money in the wrong way. They had spent a fortune on promoting his records, but it wasn't, to him, how that money should be spent.

"He also felt that creatively they didn't know what the fuck they were talking about. He was going to do the next record on his own with whoever he wants, and not make it polished, you know? That's basically when he took this record into his own hands, and decided he was going to fight to get off Dream-Works, and a lot of the time he would just sit there and obsess about it, just talk about—'Oh, those fuckers . . . '—you know, there was a lot of that. Just basically, he would talk about people as if they were going to fuck him over, a lot of animosity toward DreamWorks."

When I mentioned to McConnell that Marc Swanson says Waronker felt Smith was capable of doing a lot of his own production, he said, "That's cool of Lenny to have said that. I wish Elliott could have heard that. Because he felt that way."

It becomes clear from McConnell's stories that during this period Smith was just as fastidious about protecting the independence of his music as he was about protecting the independence of his brain. The annoyance he expressed when Swanson suggested a rigorous dose of therapy was a lot like the suspicion he expressed of anyone's efforts to fiddle with his new music. In both cases, his fear was of becoming normal, of some form of propriety impinging on his freedom to create and think whatever he wanted.

Even so, he knew he had a problem on his hands. He tried to get rid of it and he tried to hide it. "He was very into quitting drugs," says McConnell. "I don't think he liked being on drugs, and I don't think he liked people knowing he was on drugs, necessarily. He was always lying to people about it. It was almost humorous to me. It was almost kind of a joke, 'Yeah, I know. I've been straight for two weeks. I'm doing great.' And then after he'd say something like that to his manager or whoever, he'd come inside and smoke some heroin and some crack. It was kind of a joke after a while—'Oh yeah, guess who's sober?'"

For a few days during this time when he was heavily addicted, according to Dorien Garry, Smith spent time with Fugazi's Ian MacKaye in Washington, DC, talking about his problems. He hoped MacKaye, famous in the punk rock world for espousing sobriety, might show him a way out of his dependencies.

Smith also tried to solve the problem through unconventional treatments. Los Angeles, of course, is to alternative therapy what Florence is to Renaissance art. Smith had a man he called his "brain boss," McConnell says, showing me a note Smith left on a piece of tape that once labeled the different tracks on a mixing board. The note says "psych appt. 2 pm" and indicates that whatever Smith was working on was still unfinished. McConnell also showed me a prescription pill bottle for Steven Paul Smith, left over from Smith's stay at the house. The prescription is for

Klonopin, an anti-anxiety medication known for its potential to create dependency. Smith at one point posed for a photograph, McConnell says, next to a pyramid of his prescription medicine bottles. McConnell remembers there being about ten different prescriptions. Smith also received visits from a man affiliated with the Malibu-based Telesis Foundation, says McConnell. Telesis uses some of the same 12-step meetings Smith seemed to reject in Arizona.

"I just knew he really had absolutely the ability to kill himself. From college I think it was really bad," E. V. Day told me in an interview. But the moment I came to grips with what Smith was going through during the last few years of his life came when McConnell showed me two pieces of black construction paper filled with dense, neat handwriting in silver marker. The rows are even and the entire space of both pages is filled. This, McConnell explains, was a document Smith made of one of his dreams during that time. He suggested to McConnell that he frame it in order to preserve it.

The two-page note begins with Smith musing over if he were able to physically assault himself, he would choose to do it; segues into a vow to stop buying cocaine; and eventually finds Smith reaching the conclusion that he must choose between drugs and relationships. Then Smith writes, "Must separate drug use from escaping my past and/or stupid 'I don't remember what happened.'" It's hard to be sure what Smith is referring to by "stupid 'I don't remember what happened,'" but since he's on the subject of "escaping" his "past," it seems possible Smith was bringing up his uncertainty about whether or not he was sexually abused as a boy. Smith's preoccupation with what he couldn't remember had to stop being a reason to take narcotics. He had to find a more lasting way of putting his past behind him. The note concludes with a reflection that maybe the reason Smith is on anti-schizophrenia medication is because of how conflicted he feels, which is followed by a remembrance of a dream in which a huge ship was stretched and split apart, apparently a reflection of his own divided state of mind, topped off with an image of Smith digging at his own brain with a fork.

The fact that the note veers far from standard personal-essay structure shouldn't in and of itself be seen as a sign that Smith was in a troubled state when he wrote it; when asked in an interview magazine if he'd ever write a novel, Smith said no, and explained that the kind of writing that came naturally to him was the kind of free-associative liner notes one finds on Dylan albums. The silver-on-black note at McConnell's house is squarely in that tradition.

That said, it's a rueful, vaguely suicidal series of reflections. Smith copiously reminded his listeners in interviews that his songs weren't diary entries; here we have what *is* essentially a diary entry, and it's grimmer than the grimmest of his songs. The vision of the ship stretched to the breaking point mirrors the vision of a Smith divided between an old self and a new one, the former threatening violence to the latter. What this section of the note has in common with the first part is its implication that the past must be confronted. Otherwise, it will creep up to kill him from behind. The whole note is roundly anti-drug, in its way, from the vow not to buy coke to the observation that there must be a reckoning between narcotics and love.

At this time, Smith was striking out at himself, albeit in a quieter fashion than the above ruminations might suggest. McConnell kept finding Smith had drugged himself into oblivion in places that were easy to find, "with the intention of killing himself. Which I didn't know until much later. He would be like, 'Dude you know the other day when you found me on the floor asleep for twenty-six hours? Well, I took twelve Klonopin and I drank a bottle of scotch.' I'd be like, 'Fuck, Elliott, why didn't you tell me?' 'Well, I just couldn't stand it.' So he tried to kill himself a number of times here, but he was always in a place where I would find him and wake him up and be like, 'Hey dude, what's going on?'" McConnell says Smith would inform him of his suicidal intent "after the fact."

"That first one he'd be like, 'Hey, don't tell anybody—if you do, it's going to get worse, I will for sure kill myself.' But I would take it up with his girlfriend, and be like, 'Hey, Elliott tried to do this, would you please take the appropriate measures to remedy this situation?' I couldn't call the police."

But Valerie, like just about everybody who knew Smith, found Smith difficult to control. "Valerie's reaction was basically, 'I don't know what to do,'" says McConnell. "God, she was so up and down. One minute she'd be real smiley and happy and passive—'Oh, that's just Elliott'—the next minute she'd be in tears—'I don't know what to do about him, he's going to end up killing himself and there's nothing I can do.' He later told me, 'Hey, I tried to kill myself at your house at least ten times and it didn't work.' His statement about drugs was that he was invincible when it came to drugs, that he couldn't OD. And he might have been right."

It was hard to figure out how to react to Smith's drug problems at this time. On the one hand, he didn't like it when somebody intervened, as DreamWorks and Mittleman did. McConnell remembers Smith saying of Mittleman, "She tried to clean me up. Tried to get me on the bandwagon." To which Smith's response, McConnell says, "was basically like, 'Fuck that, I'm an artist.' I don't know, obviously Margaret would know more about it. But he definitely was resentful. She was on his shit list, let me put it that way, whereas maybe Rob [Schnapf] wasn't really on his shit list." The difference between declining to continue a professional relationship (as he did with Schnapf) and ending a professional relationship on a note of rancor seemed to depend on whether there had been some kind of attempt to get Smith off drugs. At the same time, McConnell, who showed Smith more deference in this area, couldn't get Smith to finish his album in anything like a timely fashion, let alone take care of himself.

And Smith's eating problems during the recording of the record were almost as bad as his drug problems. McConnell got the sense that crack was one reason Smith didn't eat right, but not the whole reason. "I think it was partially just him, he just didn't feel good when he ate. He just didn't like the way food made him feel. You know when you eat and feel tired? He hated that feeling. And what he would do was he would eat ice cream late at night, he loved ice cream. We would go to the grocery store and buy two hundred, three hundred dollars' worth of ice cream, stick it in the freezer, and it'd be every kind of ice cream you can imagine. But he wouldn't eat real food. He'd eat nutritional bars now and then.

"One day I forced him to go with me to a restaurant, because he didn't like going to a restaurant. So I took him down to a sushi restaurant, one of my favorite ones, down the street. I took him in there, but not against his will. He sat in the car. I said, 'I'm going to go in and eat, you don't have to go with me, but you know where to find me, I'll be in there eating if you want to come in.' And he said, 'No, I'm not ready to eat food, I'm not going in your restaurant. No way.' So I said, 'All right, well I'll be back.'

"So I had him in my car and I knew that he either had to sit in the car and wait for me or he'd have to come in. So I went in and I ate. Then after fifteen minutes he caved and he came in and sat down next to me and he had a bowl of soup. That was like— his girlfriend and everybody was shocked—'Oh my god, you got him to eat.' It was one of those things, you know? I kind of planned it, planned it all out, that he would, because I knew he'd eventually come in, and just out of curiosity he'd want to see what was going on. So he did. He had a bowl of miso soup, he ate about half of it. And he was like, 'Mmm, that's actually pretty good. Not bad!'"

Basement on the Hill had become an exercise in self-depriva-tion, a search for rock bottom. This becomes plain when you lis-ten to the music. McConnell played me three tracks from *Base-ment on the Hill*; they all court chaos without abandoning prettiness. "Shooting Star" in particular is orchestrated to sound like something falling apart. The verse-chorus-verse structure is framed by guitar solos that compete for attention in the rough mix, and at the end the song gives itself over to them, with the drums leaving behind their regular snare on the two and four to join in the clamor.

The mix of the album that will end up being released is being worked on by Schnapf and Joanne Bolme as I write. "Passing Feeling" is more contained than "Shooting Star," but still grittier and more flamboyant than the music on Smith's other albums.

The piano that McConnell transformed into a tack piano, changing its sound to create ghostly reverberations, sits near the entrance to his home, and there's a bandage taped to it with some of Smith's dried blood still on it. Smith had cut his hand fixing up the instrument, and affixed the bandage to it afterwards as a humorous reminder of the battle he'd fought with it. The sound of the tack piano, like the guitars on "Shooting Star," suggests entropy, the breakdown of order, flirtations with madness. In other words, the album aims for the same effects the darkest tunes on *The White Album* aimed for. This is Elliott Smith making his own "Glass Onion" and "Helter Skelter."

Sometimes, the Smith-McConnell sessions slid into the creative bacchanalia associated with late '60s rock and with California in general. About once a week, McConnell would join Smith in some form of drug use—usually it was coke (they mixed "Shooting Star" coked up, late one night) or inexpensive black tar heroin, both of which Smith could procure easily in downtown Los Angeles, but occasionally speed, which Smith found harder to come by. The songs are infused with the melancholy of somebody pursuing a version of rock and roll long abandoned by the people who first came up with it: the sun-kissed California of The Byrds and The Doors and *Harvest*-era Neil Young, a place and time and approach to music that aimed to express of states of mind that had never been adequately expressed before. It was a place and time before glam rock increased the distance between rock stars and fans and punk rock eliminated it, when musicians tinkering on beautiful secluded real estate in Malibu could feel isolated without feeling guilty about it. A discarded dream of the '60s haunts *From a Basement on the Hill*. Those rough early sessions, with the drugs, the reverence for *The White Album,* and the rejection of anything like a regular work routine, produced music that was melodious but lawless. Smith felt he had to put himself through a maddening process to make the songs he wanted to make, and he was probably right.

It didn't last. Like some of his brilliant '60s progenitors, Smith started to lose it. "He felt like DreamWorks was following him for a while," says McConnell, "that they were spying on him. There was one point he even thought the CIA was watching him. He was always seeing white vans everywhere."

Smith—and maybe the drugs—even made McConnell wonder what was going on. "He talked like a crazy guy on drugs, and a crazy paranoiac. But it's funny because I'd watch him, and actually he had a point. There were white vans everywhere following him. It was really bizarre. I was like, 'No, this guy's cuckoo,' but then I'd go in the car with him and for like three days we'd be driving around, and he'd be like, 'Look, dude, it's a fucking white van.' It was really strange. There was one point we went to go get a prescription pill one night, and this white van followed us to the fucking drugstore. We got out of the car, went into the drugstore, and these two guys got out of the white van and went into the drugstore and were watching us inside the drugstore. It was really bizarre. It could have been one of those crazy things, where maybe he was right and maybe DreamWorks wanted to get bad dirt on him, but in all probability he was just paranoid."

Smith's behavior got to be heartbreaking. "There were times he would come up to this house, up the hill," says McConnell, pointing through the window at the soft green gumdrop hills. "Valerie would drive him as far as Los Flores Canyon right here, [and] he'd make her stop right down there, see where that car is driving? He'd make her stop right there, and then he'd come up the hill through the bushes. He'd walk through the bushes, sneak through, 'cause he didn't want the CIA to see where he was going. And then he'd come up and tap on the door." McConnell whispers: "'Hey, it's Elliott, let me in quick before they see me.' And then Valerie would pull in the front gate. I'd be like, 'Fuck dude, where'd you come from?' And he'd be like, 'I just came up through there.'"

Smith's appearance during the LA years changed rapidly. Sometimes he looked as if he were in the midst of physical trauma, and sometimes he looked fine. But the moment when alarm bells went off about Smith's health among his audience was the Sunset Junction Music Festival on August 18, 2001.

Sunset Junction is one of the two hearts of Silver Lake (the other is a district adjacent to the Silver Lake reservoir, where the club Spaceland sits). It's just east of where Hollywood Boulevard shakes off its scuzzy Hollywood odor, turns southeast, and merges with Sunset Boulevard. Immediately after the two boulevards meet, Solutions, the audio-supplies store with the black-and-red swirls that made the backdrop for the *Figure 8* cover photo, emerges on the right. The stage where Smith performed on August 18 lay shortly west of that point. He came on solo with his acoustic guitar and proceeded to launch into a set that onlookers found painful, even as fans continued to sing his praises afterwards. His hair was bound into two braids, Willie Nelson–style.

One fan's account of that show, posted on the fan site www.sweetadeline.net goes like this:

Shooting Star
  Let's Get Lost
  Somebody's Baby
  Say Yes—stopped the song right before "crooked spin can't come to rest" cause he couldn't remember it
  Alameda—stopped this one early too
  Son of Sam—did the first 2 verses and the bridge fine, but didn't try the last verse. . . it was still good though
  Pretty (Ugly Before)
  A Passing Feeling
  Division Day
  Needle in the Hay—abandoned right around the second verse

Angeles—beautiful, the crowd helped out a little bit on the words

Between the Bars—also beautiful, didn't need our help this time

Southern Belle—didn't even make it to the words before he stopped, he just couldn't get the guitar part down

Last Call—sang "last call, sick of it all" then stopped and laughed and said that's all he could remember

Blackjack Davey—a Woody Guthrie cover, was very cool

Happiness—didn't get very far here either, may have sang the first few words

The Biggest Lie—did this one pretty good, it was very pretty regardless, I loved it. Then he said thanks and that was it, walked over to the girl taping him (his girlfriend I believe?), talked to her for a second, came back and sat down, said, "just had to talk to my coach," and carried on with more songs

Thirteen—Big Star cover song, heartbreaking as usual

Clementine—got thru around the first verse before he had to quit

Independence Day—couldn't get the guitar part right so he abandoned it

See You Later—played this one very well

Then he left the stage, the lady in charge of the stage got us to help bring him back out for "one more song," and he obliged

Everything's Okay [not the actual song title]—he got thru most of this song but couldn't remember the end I guess, so he had to quit it there

Needle in the Hay—he asked if he'd already tried "Needle in the Hay" and stopped, and the crowd said yes, so he said he'd do it right this time. And he did, and it was great. Then he said he'd do it better next time.

His fans might have been willing to quietly put up with the weirdness—"It's been a while since Elliott played in front of any-one," someone else writing on the site remarked sympathetically—but alarm bells went off around the music world. If people had wondered before if Smith was just singing about drugs without doing them, which was in fact the case at some points, they now couldn't help but wonder if he'd been doing them the whole time. The way people looked at him as a musician and songwriter started to change.

The effect on Smith's reputation was particularly acute because his sets had so recently been near-perfect. From Portland to Stockholm his hallmark had been competence. It had been the clean page on which his lyrics and melodies could be understood in all their subtlety.

Part of the problem during this time was that Smith—notwithstanding any falling-outs he might have had with old colleagues—just wasn't particularly good at correspondence. People who might have rushed to his aid had lost track of how to reach him. "Elliott was a person who lived very much in the moment," says Swanson. "When you were there you were everything. When you were gone I think you could feel pretty insecure about how he was always terrible about staying in touch. Always. Even before anything happened, I remember calling him three or four times threatening, 'I'm going to punch you next time I see you,' and he would always call me being like, 'Okay, sorry.' But he was always so sweet, every time I would see him he'd start babbling right away about how he meant to call, and thought about it a million times."

Swanson had once given Smith a bracelet. "He'd often bring up that bracelet, to let me know he thought of it every day," he says. His annoyance with Smith for losing touch would "melt away so quickly because he was always so sweet and would bring up this very personal thing. It was nice, because after that when I hadn't heard from him in a few months I would see a picture of a show and there would be the bracelet. And he made that known, that's what it was, but he couldn't, no matter what, he couldn't [keep in touch]. And I don't think I ever really took it that personally, which I think made it more okay for me than other people."

Smith was somebody who quickly attracted new friends, a likely reason why the move to LA stretched from temporary to permanent. Smith would eventually express frustration that he felt stuck there because of relationships that were important to him. "There was a sense that people wanted to take care of him, wanted to help him." Swanson says. "There was a general sense that no one understood him, but then he would connect to people really easily so people could think *they* really understood him. Increasingly, that's what made you more insecure as his friend, because you would think you were *the one* and then all of a sudden it was somebody else and you read it in a magazine. After [hearing] his music it was kind of undeniable why people wanted to be friends with him: He was a genius, and people like to be close to geniuses if possible. And even if they don't think he's a genius they're willing to be close to someone who's a celebrity."

But Smith was still discriminating in his choice of friends: "I think even celebrities wanted to be close to him and he would blow them off. He never had any sort of care of whether there was someone he should know, or anything like that, it was whether he connected with someone and whether they were nice."

McConnell came up with a plan to protect Smith from some of the effects of his problems. He met with mixed results, but it was a decision that profoundly affected the making of the album. "After about six months of working together, maybe it was less than that, we started buying equipment for his studio, and there's a whole story about why he bought his studio—basically he was spending a lot of his money very quickly on things that weren't going to be around, things that he was consuming. Drugs, alcohol, prescription drugs. Frivolous things: ice cream, just because he wanted to come home and eat the flavors. . . . He was just spending so much money, and I would even get messages on the machine from his financial manager. She'd be like, 'Hey, I'm calling for Elliott, I'm real worried about his balance.' He was spending thousands of dollars a week. Anyway, I sat him down on the couch, and I said, 'Look, man, what do you think about buying your own studio? You could have all the gear you would want at your fingertips, and all the gear I have here at your fingertips. [It's] kind of an investment, but [it's] also so that you can have all the cool stuff that you love.' And after talking for about two hours, he was like, 'Yeah, let's do it.' So my whole plan was to save him from financial ruin. Basically, I just wanted him to have something as an investment, so that if he did hit rock bottom—he was on the street, homeless, all that shit—at least he would have $100,000 worth of equipment. And we bought particular pieces, carefully chose the pieces. We chose the ones that would escalate in value—the ones that he liked, but also vintage pieces that would go up in value. It was quite an investment. Pretty much the next day we started looking for gear. That's when we found his studio."

That studio was near a vast stretch of car dealerships on Van Nuys Boulevard, in the heart of the San Fernando Valley. Part of the storefront-sized Valley Center Studios complex, the entrance was next to a dumpster, adjacent to the rear parking lot. Outside, heavy-metal guitar solos were often clearly audible. There was nothing secluded or '60s or glamorous about it. For a long time, it was a far less productive place for Smith than McConnell's house had been.

"We did some work there [at the new studio], just trying to get the studio set up, and we quickly learned that all the gear was so old. We kept coming back here, eventually. That was when he decided, 'I want to name the record after your place. That's the only place the music can continuously get done, is here.' . . . But somehow he thought the record was coming from the energy of this place or something. He'd be talking about the sound of the crickets here late at night, he would record the crickets. He'd take mics outside—they're really frogs down by the creek, but they sound like crickets—trippy things like that, and he also just felt safe here, just private, felt kind of like it was an escape from, you know, a lot of the . . . he had some paranoia about people following him and stuff like that. But he also just liked being alone. He just liked that he could come here inside the gate, and be here. He would wander around the property with his headphones on listening to the mixes, on the trails and stuff, he really got off on that."

But no matter how much affection he had for the hillside basement, and no matter how productive he was there, Smith stuck to the plan of building his own studio.

"Elliott decided to buy all of his gear—he had cool old gear and we bought all of it. And we bought separate pieces that we were looking for, specific things, you know, stuff like The Beatles used, bought him a new board, a cool old Trident board, which are rare. One of them was in Trident Studios where The Beatles recorded a couple tracks on the later albums; when they didn't want to be at Abbey Road they'd go to Trident, they did a few songs over there. He wanted that board because he knew there were only thirteen made and The Beatles had worked on it.

"So anyway, we did some work there, just trying to get the studio set up, and we quickly learned that all the gear was so old . . . the board was so messed up that it had to be rebuilt, basically, by a technician. Well, months and months passed of technicians coming in and trying to work on the board, and some of them were dishonest, and these techs were messing up stuff more than fixing them, which was very frustrating for him."

Smith would try being his own tech sometimes, and while he would later tell *Under the Radar* proudly that he had fixed his mixing board by having a "soldering party" inside it, the combination of drugs and faulty equipment slowed the creation of the album to a crawl as Smith began to engage in the obsessive manual labor typical of somebody who's been taking too many drugs and getting too little sleep. The freedom and wildness that Smith had hoped to attain by taking whatever substances he wanted and being as particular and dictatorial about his sound as he wanted had turned into a trap. It was the kind of trap he'd described in "Between the Bars" and in "Angeles," the kind that uses license and comfort as bait to imprison you.

During this tortured recording period, Marc Swanson and Lenny Waronker wound up discussing Smith at a chance meeting at Diner, a Williamsburg restaurant so centrally located with regard to the New York art scene that a gallery in Sweden once constructed a replica of it, flying out creative-looking Williamsburg residents as part of the package. Slender waiters with dyed floppy hair write the names of the specials in pencil on the paper tablecloths. Waronker remarked that Smith was probably capable of doing a lot of his own recording. Swanson was feeling the distance drug addiction creates between old friends, "waiting for [Elliott] to come back. . . . [Lenny] said to me, 'I think he needed less production,'" says Swanson, "which I don't think anybody else was telling Elliott. I had just assumed he wanted to produce himself and they wouldn't let him."

Back in California, Smith's self-recording was going slowly. "I think he would kind of be . . . just tweaking on stuff, not in the way of speed tweaking, he would be like trying to fix his guitar amp, and he might be on a drug run staying up," says McConnell, "maybe doing coke or whatever he'd have to do to keep him up, and the prescription medicine he was taking would keep him up too. But he'd be up and just kind of like, 'just trying to fold my cables.' He would have bought a new piece of gear that he'd got real cheap off eBay, and sit there trying to fix it, and he didn't really know what he was doing. He'd have a concept of how it worked, but he wouldn't really know, he'd be bitching about it, like, 'God damn it. I can't get that fucking thing to work, aggh.' He'd get real frustrated, pulling on his hair and stuff.

"But it also reminded me very much of Thomas Edison or something in his lab, not sleeping. Yeah, a lot of it was drug-induced, but there were also periods when he wasn't on drugs, when he'd be totally . . . It's kind of interesting—one point I'd like to make regarding this—he'd be sober sometimes, and sometimes he'd be pretty drugged out, and what was interesting to me was that, when he was sober I was always expecting him to be like a different person . . . see things different. His body language and his talking were very clear and very present like a sober person is. But his ideas and the things he was saying, and his concepts, were all the same as when he was fucked up. Which was fascinating to me, because I know when I'm fucked up I'm saying things and thinking things differently from when I'm sober, but for him it was, even though he was acting sober when he was sober, the words were the same, and his ideas were exactly the same. When he was sober, he wouldn't tweak as much. But he'd still have the same opinion, of music, of life, of people."

By this point, Smith was only occasionally able to successfully commit some music to tape. "This happens to a lot of people when they record. Almost everyone I've ever worked with can get caught in this rut, but for him it really spiraled out of control," says McConnell. "You get a lot of work done, so that you feel like you've got it under control, but then maybe you take some time off from it, and it's just really difficult to get back to work, to get back into the flow of finishing the album, and there would be like weeks going by where he would kind of be in the studio without getting a whole lot done. It'd be weird because he'd call me over there, and I'd get over there, and two days would go by, without any music getting done, and I'd be like, 'Look Elliott, I'm going home, call me when you're ready to work, when you're ready to get some shit down.' I wouldn't hear from him for like a week, and then like a week later he still doesn't have any work done. Sometimes I'd kind of force him to work, I'd call him up and I'd be like, 'Dude, we're starting tomorrow at one o'clock. Be there. This is what we're going to do, we're going to lay down guitars first and then start on vocals.' And then I'd get two or three good days out of him, when I'd force him to work. But left to his own devices he didn't get a lot done, especially when he was in his own studio, because I think he felt like he wasn't having to pay by the hour. He'd just kind of cruise along."

Smith was working on an album that deftly used a grain of chaos to create an original feel, but far too much chaos had worked its way into his life. The studio in Van Nuys was a mess of non-functional equipment; his bank account was draining; and his live shows, a surefire way to replenish funds and maintain his reputation, were falling apart. The Sunset Junction experience wasn't an isolated incident.

On May 2, 2002, Smith shared a bill with Wilco at the Rivera Theatre in Chicago, Wilco's hometown. By this time the American indie crowd had heard the stories of Smith's shambolic Sunset Junction performance, and the Rivera show confirmed their worst suspicions. Smith explained at the show that he'd fallen asleep on his arm on a plane and couldn't feel his fingers; it's hard to imagine the flawlessly tight musician Smith had been in 1998 offering that kind of excuse. "I felt like I'd walked into my house to find Robert Downey, Jr., sleeping on my chaise lounge," wrote the indie rock Web site *Glorious Noise* of Smith's performance that night. Andrew Morgan, then an unknown young musician living in Chicago, with no connection to Smith, remembers the show as "sad and brutal to watch." After Smith's death, the site *Pop Matters* published the saddest recollection of that night: "He didn't even seem to know where he was: 'I love Portland,' he announced, apropos of nothing."

Morgan would get to know Smith soon afterwards, when he was in the middle of giving up the punishing lifestyle he'd stumbled into while recording *Basement on the Hill*. In August 2002, Smith checked into the Neurotransmitter Restoration Center in Beverly Hills, an addiction-treatment clinic run on principles developed by Dr. William Hitt. This was the second of Smith's two stays there, Smith told Morgan. Smith described his treatment to *Under the Radar* as being hooked up to an IV that delivered saline solution and amino acids, which, he said, "kick all the shit out of your nerve receptors. The different proteins in the amino acids eventually sort of rebuild the damaged neuro-receptors." He talked about the center like a convert: "I was coming off of a lot of psych meds and other things. I was even on an antipsychotic, although I'm not psychotic. It was really difficult, but also something to get the word out about because it doesn't cost as much as it does to keep someone in a twenty-eight-day rehab. It's usually a ten-day process, but for me it took a lot longer. I think most people just go there for a week. . . . But nobody seems to know about it. There's been like 15,000 people treated with it, and its success rate is 80 percent versus 10 percent for the normal twenty-eight-day twelve-step."

Smith's description matches official Neurotransmitter Restoration Center language. The center's Web site credits the NRC with treating thousands of people, and in a short documentary a man who's supposed to be Dr. Hitt portrays his technique this way: "Within a few days, three or four days, we'll have the craving for drugs James [the client depicted in the film] has used totally obliterated. We feel our success rate is probably close to 80 percent. The treatment feels almost like the substances they're using." The film shows a client being hooked up to an IV in non-descript chambers that will look familiar to anyone who's been in a typical family doctor's office. It also shows Hitt preparing medicine for eventual use on a client. Different amino acids, he explains, are effective for curing addiction to different substances, so each client gets a different cocktail, depending on her or his type of abuse.

The clinic Smith appreciated so much was run by a man who'd been found in a Houston court to have misled his patients, in violation with state and federal laws. Court papers show that Dr. William Hitt, credited with developing the process the Neurotransmitter Restoration Center uses to treat addiction, lied in Texas about being a doctor.

The clinic's Web site broadcast impressively ambitious descriptions of his credentials. The rap sheet on Dr. Hitt would be an inspiration to any screenwriter looking to deliver the next *Chinatown*. The Center's Web site states, "Dr. Hitt has been honored with numerous awards as a scientist and physician, including the Van Leeuwenhoek Award of France for excellence in microscopy and the Ely Lily Award for his discovery of a new system of microplasma." There may be an Ely Lily Award, but Eli Lilly and

Company, the multinational pharmaceutical corporation that introduced Prozac, bestows no such honor. There may be a Van Leeuwenhoek Award of France, but the Leeuwenhoek Medal, bestowed by the Royal Netherlands Academy of Arts and Sciences, is one of the highest honors in microbiology. Dating back to 1877, it is given to a scientist once every ten years, and the winners include Louis Pasteur. They don't include Hitt.

It was in 1987 that a Houston judge shut down three clinics operated by Hitt and forbade them to treat allergies and AIDS symptoms by injecting patients with urine, according to court records; the assistant attorney general said she sought the injunction because she felt the treatment was dangerous. The court ruled that Hitt misrepresented the effectiveness of the treatment and misrepresented his own qualifications. Hitt was not a medical doctor or a PhD, and he claimed both titles. He was found to have violated Texas laws a handful of ways. Among them was "selling, or offering for sale, a 'new drug' as defined by the Texas Food and Drug Act and by the Federal Food, Drug, and Cosmetic Act (Title 21 U.S.C. 301 et seq.) without having applied to or acquired approval from the Federal Food and Drug Administration." Another was "engaging in false advertising by making false and misleading representations as to the safety and effectiveness of the treatment offered." The most pertinent to Smith's situation: "representing that Mr. Hitt is professionally qualified to diagnose and treat human patients when he is not" and "failing to disclose that claims made concerning the treatment were false, unsubstantiated, and undocumented, with the intent to induce consumers to enter into a transaction into which they would not have entered had the information been disclosed."

In Texas, the court enjoined Hitt and the companies affiliated with him, Allergy Control Group and Vita Scale, from (among other things) "representing expressly or impliedly that Defendant Hitt is a doctor, that he holds a PhD or any other graduate or post-graduate degree which he does not hold or that said degree is from a particular institution when such is not the case, that he is a licensed physician or that he is qualified or certified to treat any illness or disease." The state hit him up for twenty thousand dollars, eighteen thousand of which covered its legal fees.

Presumably the reason no article about Smith contains this information is because Smith was unaware of Hitt's background, at least for a while, and didn't feel the need to go public with it if he ever found out. He tried Hitt's treatment after a few attempts to get clean through other rehabs. As *Under the Radar* put it, after noting that the center wasn't FDA-approved, Smith apparently gave the place a whirl as a last resort and felt it helped him in ways that other places didn't.

Given Hitt's legal history, it's unclear what kind of treatment Smith actually received. If he got an IV drip that he thought helped purge his addictions, what exactly was in that IV? Given that the Texas judgment was quite clear on the point that Hitt misled his patients about the content of his treatments, and that Hitt's signature is on the judgment testifying to his own acceptance of the judgment, it's hard to feel confident that the drip going into Smith really contained the custom blend of amino acids it was supposed to. Smith told *Under the Radar* that he required a much longer stretch of treatment than most people who went to the clinic, that he received an unusually large amount of it.

The clinics shuttered by the State of Texas purported to treat AIDS with filtered urine, which has nothing to do with what the Neurotransmitter Restoration Center purports to do: help addicts. But treating addicts was one of the numerous functions of a Hitt clinic in Tijuana that was searched by local health authorities before the eyes of an NPR reporter in 2001 and that closed that year after the inspectors discovered code violations. According to NPR, the inspectors found mucus samples and "tubs of unknown medicine." They also said that Hitt wasn't licensed to practice experimental therapies. As of this writing, there was still a Web site online for a William Hitt Center in Tijuana, with links to a hotel that advertises itself as housing many patients of the center. The place where Hitt's clinic used to sit in a Beverly Hills office building is now empty, but the Neurotransmitter Restoration Center's name is still on the directory in the lobby. It's in one of the most expensive areas for commercial real estate in Los Angeles.

This isn't the first report on Hitt's past—Pamela Sterling wrote about it in a *New Zealand Listener* article. The Associated Press covered the closing of Hitt's Houston clinics, and, as noted above, National Public Radio covered a raid on his Tijuana clinic by local health officials.

Still, Smith had undergone an apparent change for the good. "He told me he didn't need heroin anymore," says Morgan. "I was there in the transition period between the well-documented problems that were going on and during his rehabilitation at the institute. Paranoia? For sure. But it wasn't constant."

The cause for the changes in Smith may have been psychological rather than medical, but the changes were real. It's possible his change was due to something else that happened around the same time he went in for his final week-long stay at the center: He and Deerin split up and he moved in with a friend he had once dated, an art therapist named Jennifer Chiba. A slender Asian or half-Asian woman with friends in the LA music scene, Chiba had known Smith for about three years—they'd both performed bit parts in the same low-budget movie *Southlander*, made shortly after Smith moved to LA in 1999. He'd played a roadie; she'd played a pretty girl at a pool party.

"Granted, I wasn't with him 24–7, and I was in no position to interrogate him," says Morgan, "[but] what I'll say in general is things were really fucking bad prior to the rehabilitation institute, when he was moving out of the Snow White castle, or whatever you want to call it. Then—into the institute and then over to Jen's—dramatic changes. Russ Pollard* would be like, 'I can't believe it. I haven't seen Elliott looking this good in so long.' He was a new person, and he was groggy and irritable and, yeah, paranoid, but then he was funny and warm and vital . . . still frail from

---

*Smith's bass player on tour.

the treatment, which was very radical. It was a rebirth—it was all about reclaiming his greatness and his identity and everything. Yeah, obviously he was still suffering some problems but he was doing better and everyone was taking note."

Smith's own descriptions of his post-treatment state jibe with Morgan's. The hardest part, he told *Under the Radar*, was lacking the strength to even reach for a glass of water.

By that point, moving out of the Snow White cottage was probably deeply therapeutic in and of itself. Before Smith went to live with Chiba, who then became his girlfriend, he lived for a week at his studio, sleeping on a love seat, Morgan recalls. "The cottage was just Grimm brothers, it was weird. Why would you live there? It was right by the street . . . It had some notice, 'Steven Paul Steven, aka Elliott Smith, blah blah blah,' something like 'leave me alone,'" says Morgan. "It's charming and fairy tale. But the problem with the cottage was inside it was just a fucking mess. It had lots of cool stuff—there was tons of recording gear, and there was a piano there and some guitars, some artwork he'd done—but it was like Tasmanian Devil there. It was crap everywhere; it was like they were having a yard sale inside. You'd come over to see him and he'd be like, 'Sorry guys, this place is such a mess,' and it was funny because it'd recently been cleaned."

While Chiba eventually became Smith's girlfriend, in the weeks after his Neurotransmitter Restoration Center treatment, Smith was in need of care more than romance. He may have become healthier in some ways after his rehab treatment, but his strength was gone.

"Initially he was very weak [after his treatment]," says Morgan. "He was briefly at the [Snow White] cottage house and I was constantly checking on him to make sure he was all right, because he was so terrible about taking care of himself. Even when he was living in the studio beforehand, it'd be like, when you ate you'd naturally be like, 'You want something to eat?'" And Smith wouldn't eat. So Morgan started to try to monitor his diet a little. "I'd be like, 'Elliott, I'm going to the grocery store. Do you want some water or a sandwich?' And he'd be like, 'Oh yeah, turkey sandwich.' Then I'd go over there with my friend and maybe his sister would come and we'd show up with a week's supply of water and all kinds of stuff, just because watching him sit up to talk to you at this point right afterwards, it'd be like watching your grandfather sit up. He was totally post-treatment. He was totally getting better and still had an IV or some kind of, I don't know, home treatment. One thing that was clear is that he was dehydrated. He wouldn't eat a lot or drink a lot—but you'd give it to him and he'd be like, 'Thanks, thanks, man.'"

Oddly enough, Chiba and Smith developed a serious relationship under these conditions. He moved into her house on Lemoyne Street in Echo Park, and the Smith who was determined to churn out a masterpiece at great personal cost had downshifted. For a while, getting healthy was going to edge into his list of priorities.

Smith's relationship with Deerin tapered off gradually. "She was still in the Snow White cottage for a day or two and then he drove her to the airport, and she'd call the studio every day and check up on Elliott and stuff like that, and he just kept saying he couldn't bear to break up with someone again," Morgan remembers. "He just constantly kept saying, 'I don't want to hurt anyone,' and was concerned with other people's feelings where he was neglecting his own sometimes. It really shook him up that he had to go through a break-up." Smith didn't always take Deerin's calls: "She never talked to Elliott. She talked to me a couple times on the phone. He was never there or 'wasn't there,'" says Morgan.

One lasting product of Smith's relationship with Deerin was the foundation they created together. The Elliott Smith Foundation for Abused Children was devoted to raising money for exposing abused children to the arts, and Smith talked about it with pride to journalists and friends. It was the fruit of thinking he'd been doing for some time: "He started this foundation for abused children, and there was always this idea flowing around of abuse, but he didn't talk about it much," is how Swanson puts it. He declines to answer the question of whether Smith considered himself to have been abused.

Whether or not there was any correlation between Smith's break-up with Valerie Deerin, his going into rehab at the Neurotransmitter Restoration Center, and his decision to rekindle bonds with old friends, he did follow through on his professed desire to reconnect with people. In January 2003, Smith went to New York and played at the Bowery Ballroom and Lit, a small club in the East Village, with The Jon Spencer Blues Explosion. "He was here for five days and we definitely talked every day and he called and stuff and I almost fell over," says Swanson. "He was being more pro-active about staying in touch."

One of Smith's songs from this time seemed generally concerned with reconciliation. "Flowers for Charlie" could be directed at least partly at Smith's stepfather Charles Welch. "I'm not a good GI Joe," Smith sings, "because I always hang low." It works as an appeal to a conventional father figure from a rebellious kid, offering hope for a solution. The narrator both wants to get over caring about "Charlie's" disapproval and wants to put an end to hostilities. Toward the end, he says, "You don't have to hide." That would make sense as a remark either toward Charles Welch or toward Smith himself. Of course, other interpretations are feasible—Smith might have been thinking about mending some of the bridges he'd burned recently with friends. "Charlie" could carry the meaning it had in the Vietnam War, for example, of "enemy soldier," which would tie into the "GI Joe" reference and the theme of forging a non-aggression pact. But it wasn't as if Smith's old friends could simply take up with him where they'd left off. His old self wasn't really there, says Swanson. "You could see like spots of it, but no. He was pretty out of it."

When Smith reached out to Morgan in the summer of 2002 Morgan represented new blood, a new colleague happy to keep Smith company and urge him on as he recorded. They'd met because a college friend of Morgan's worked at a music store where Smith went to buy studio gear. His friend told Smith he ought to meet Morgan, who like Smith was a Beatles freak. "Elliott brought it up again," says Morgan, "and said, 'You should come over to the studio.'" Soon, Morgan was using Smith's facilities to record his debut album free of charge, and for the six weeks he recorded there, providing Smith with a new confidante.

Smith and Morgan bonded quickly, Morgan says. "We'd stay up all night talking about everything from The Beatles to non-Euclidian geometry to physics to women and love—we had this personality flash, just really hit it off."

Smith's studio was part of a complex of studios called Valley Center Studios, and Smith was toying with what to name it. It was labeled Studio One, so Smith joked about making it Studio One and Only or Studio Lonely before he finally christened it New Monkey.

The dominant mood for Morgan was the exhilaration of getting a break and working with an idol, but to Morgan it seemed that for Smith the mood was one of re-entrenchment. "When I met him he was in this massive give-up-or-fight place in his life." He didn't want to be seen, Morgan says, as a semi-retired Brian Wilson figure who once made great music. "Smith's thinking was, 'I don't want [music] to be what I used to do. I want this to be what I'm doing.'"

The comparatively upbeat new mindset was accompanied by a taste for assertive, catchy rock. "He was listening to music from way back, and he went through a huge Brit pop phase," says Morgan. "'Telegram Sam' by T-Rex. We all thought it was a big dumb rock song, but he loved it. He was changing his messages on the phone. One was him singing 'Hey Now' by Oasis, and we'd be sneering like Liam, and he started playing 'Supersonic' [by Oasis] at shows." Morgan and Smith were both Beatles maniacs, and talked about them at all hours, but Smith's listening tastes were turning toward the Beatles rivals. "There were no Beatles albums around, but there were tons of Stones albums and Velvet Underground albums everywhere. . . . He never spoke in terms of, 'I want to do this from The Beatles, do this to it.' He was going through a big dumb rock phase, listening to T-Rex, loving Oasis. Not just early Stones, melodic Beatles-y Stones, but late '60s/early '70s boring, barroom Stones, in my mind. *Sticky Fingers*, *Exile on Main Street*. He had the rock out. He was looking for drum sounds, electric guitar sounds. I think he was expanding his sonic palette, his textures; he was mining for materials."

The White Album still exerted force over Smith, and he clung to the idea of *From a Basement on the Hill* being a double album with thirty tracks. But the songs he started to make up were changing along with the way he wrote and recorded them. Smith's way of treating himself had become gentler, his thinking less aggressive and confrontational and more regretful, introspective. If "Shooting Star" was the banner song of the six weeks Smith spent living at McConnell's house in Malibu, the song that best signified Smith's new existence was "Memory Lane."

"Shooting Star" had been a bitter song that disavowed connection to the "you" it addressed in its lyrics and declared the emotional independence of the narrator in its wild music. In McConnell's recollection, the lyrics carried a specific meaning for Smith. "His favorite line was 'Your love is sad, shooting star.' He'd talk about that, he'd sit there and he'd tell me, 'Can you imagine, someone's love is sad?' You know? That was about an ex-girlfriend. He never said who."

"Memory Lane" was the opposite, a gentle, folky lament built around Smith's finger-picking. It's unclear in the final version, but the way Smith tried recording it reflected a theme of regret. "One of the most sad yet beautiful nights," says Morgan, "was when Elliott was in a real bad state, and it was me and him and he was playing my dad's twelve-string, and I [was helping to] start and stop a tape machine, and he was recording 'Memory Lane,' this brilliant amazing new song. He was in a real bad state but he thought he'd record it; he wanted to document the state he was in.

His voice sounded ragged. He thought maybe it'd be cool having—in my words—a Johnny Cash performance."

⁂

The house on Lemoyne Street where Smith lived with Chiba for the last fourteen months of his life stands halfway up a long hill from the basin where Sunset Boulevard becomes the exhaust-coated spine of Echo Park. At the bottom of the hill is a neighborhood that appears almost entirely Latino, with the exception of a couple hipster boutiques and the Brite Spot, an old burger joint now gentrified. As you climb past block after block of small houses with children and dogs playing in lawns, Hispanic blue-collar gradually gives some ground to young middle-class. One block contains a yard decorated with a sign informing passersby that the house is guarded by a "pit bull with AIDS." The barking of a wide variety of breeds provides the soundtrack for the climb. A few blocks later the sounds have faded and an old car sports a Jim Morrison bumper sticker. Flowers twist around tastefully distressed latticework. A glance down the hill affords a vague, blue-gray tableau of downtown skyscrapers. Between the houses you can see the opposite hill, which is barnacled with houses like the ones on this street as well as a square brown apartment complex covered with cramped balconies. Erratically cut grass and palm trees fill the dells. This is a place where cool LA and poor LA dissolve into each other.

The house itself has one story exposed to the street, the bulk dropping out of sight down a hill. It's not altogether unlike a Hampshire College mod. On the left side is a door and a path leading away from the street. Whether or not privacy is what attracted Smith to the property, it certainly allows for seclusion. And like so many other aspects of Smith's life it teeters between toughness and hipness. Any way you look at it, it's not the kind of structure one envisions as a den for an LA rock star of the old school.

Chiba was a friend of Smith's when he moved in with her, but not yet a girlfriend. Smith was courting her, says Morgan, and would try to figure out what songs he should learn to play for her on the guitar. When Morgan suggested "Race to the Prize," the first song off the Flaming Lips album *The Soft Bulletin*, it was a eureka moment.

After Smith died, Chiba told the *LA Times* that Smith once told her that reading Kafka's short story "A Hunger Artist" would help her understand him. "A Hunger Artist" is the story of a man for whom fasting is a passion and a vocation. He sits in a cage for up to forty days at a time without food. For the people who come to see him the fasting is an impressive ordeal, but for the hunger artist it's a necessity. He fasts under squalid conditions, and after the crowds lose interest and nobody is paying attention he fasts beyond the forty-day maximum. He's discovered near death. He never liked any food, he explains, and wouldn't have fasted if he'd had food, but still clearly remains attached to and engaged in his fasting.

On the surface, this might seem to undermine Smith's refrain that he was wrongfully understood to be a depressed guy, because the hunger artist was doomed and misunderstood, and his art consisted of self-destruction. The story isn't so much about suffering as it is about the mindset of an artist, of somebody obsessed with some form of work. For Smith, probing the dim corners of human experience with music was a calling. But it was a calling that made people think he was constantly in pain.

Moving into the last year of his life, Smith wasn't nearly as downcast as one might suspect—he was mostly ambitious. Smith was too self-deprecating to say he was starting or participating in a movement. But he talked to Morgan as if the two of them had a mission to accomplish. "He spoke in terms of, 'We are going to do these things, we are going to write songs with content, inspired by books that subject matter–wise are different from pop songs. Utilize the pop format, but infuse it with more substantial ideas, and manipulate the form in pop by adding intriguing, even polemical content. Acquire rules so you can break them, build up and deconstruct art, and play with the form.'"

At the same time as he was forging ahead with his modest musical revolution, gathering fresh troops and equipment to help him along, Smith was also testing his own limitations, in a sad, wised-up way. Some of the topics Morgan remembers discussing with Smith long into the night in the summer of 2002 were distinctly brainy: Both of them had studied philosophy in college, and the subject matter included non-Euclidian geometry and Epicureanism. Chiba, who became closer to Smith during this time, would later recall to the *LA Times* that Smith was thoroughly amused by, and would read aloud from, a book that detailed what a nuisance the number zero is in mathematics. Part of this, Morgan believes, was that Smith was drawn to intellectual extremes. He was a radical in that he loved to inspect the roots of systems of thought. "He was always writing down books for me to read. . . . I think he was very interested in making the impossible possible. He was interested in unified theories, and these huge revelatory, there's-a-bend-here-it-doesn't-work [thoughts]." While he'd broken from the most radical feminist positions he'd taken at Hampshire, "he was not afraid of extremes in his life. If there were a theory that the world would collapse on itself, he'd be into it."

But there was another motivator behind the studiousness, Morgan believes: "Part of it was proving to himself that his brain still worked. The year before this rebirth when he got back with Jen, it was like, 'Let's see how much damage I've done.'" Before his descent into drug addiction in Los Angeles, he'd produced an acclaimed solo album once every two years and toured behind each one, despite the fact that when he was making the first three of those five albums he'd also been writing, rehearsing, recording, and touring as a frontman in Heatmiser and working enough hours at odd jobs to stay afloat financially. Now it was two years after *Figure 8* had come out and he was nowhere near finishing the follow-up.

The Smith Morgan knew during that time was still a prolific songwriter. "Elliott said he's always had thirty or forty songs around, and it baffled him how Neil [Gust] would make time to write a song. Elliott was a channel, a conduit, he'd have a ridiculous amount of stuff. His curiosity was really provoked by his method and Neil's method, and he could never imagine going, 'Okay, I'm going to sit down and write a song now.'"

Morgan found himself astonished by "the rate at which Elliott learned covers. And he was still covering 'Long, Long, Long,'" says Morgan, referring to the Beatles song by George Harrison. The reason? "Because it was about staying around, is why."

"Long, Long, Long" might be interpreted as being sung from the perspective of a ghost. At the end Harrison makes some sepulchral moaning noises against a creaking noise that sounds like a coffin opening, and his delivery throughout is ethereal, wistful. But the lyrics are about redemption. "Now I'm so happy I've found you," Harrison sings, and the bridge is directly about the past: "So many tears I was searching/So many tears I was wasting." It is a ballad about trying to get rid of self-imposed suffering and returning to a place where you can relate to other people.

Smith was actually performing for an audience again. He never orchestrated any kind of comeback fanfare for the show he played at The Echo in Los Angeles that fall, and he probably wouldn't have wanted people to think of it as a comeback because he didn't want them to feel as if he had ever gone away. But he played for the first time since his recovery that summer on October 1. "It was the night I left LA, and we were sitting backstage, and he was nervous," Morgan remembers. "He was nervous about going back because of the trials and tribulations."

Smith had returned to playing out not much more than three months after his last Neurotransmitter Restoration Center visit. Things may have been on an upswing, but Smith still wanted to finish the album and release it without the label he was signed to. "Elliott wanted flat out of DreamWorks, he didn't want anything to do with them," says Morgan. It's not surprising that Smith might have found the DreamWorks relationship frustrating, given the inherent tension between an artist who sells more copies of an album than he's ever sold before (about 200,000 in the case of *XO*, compared to 100,000 each for the two Kill Rock Stars records) but not nearly enough for an average major label to turn a profit. By the turn of the century, a major record label generally needed to sell around a million copies of an album to make a significant profit on its investment. The hope for any major-label album was that it would at least go gold, selling 500,000 copies domestically. DreamWorks, while it saw Smith as a great artist, not a cash cow, could conceivably have encouraged him to figure out how to move toward gold on the next album.

And Smith had never liked anyone telling him how to adjust his music. In Heatmiser he'd blanched at how his songs had been changed when passed through the "filter" of his bandmates' musical contributions. He lamented to Morgan that the piano part that was added to "Baby Britain" immediately "dialed up The Beatles," and felt he'd let it get away from him. He referred to Schnapf and Rothrock as his "quote, 'producers,'" making quotation marks of his fingers.

Smith was determined to make the album in his own studio now, despite the time he'd put in with David McConnell in Malibu and, to a much lesser extent, at two other studios: Cherokee and Sound Factory. But the decision to achieve a new kind of independence was accompanied by a desire to reach out to figures from his not-so-distant past. "He was rediscovering Heatmiser, and we would sit around with Jen just blaring Heatmiser. And I'd be like, 'Man, it's your early Beatles period.' This light bulb went off—he was like, 'Thanks, man.' He realized he'd improved, but looked back on it with fondness. It was this last kind of rebirth in his life, and he was reconnecting with people he'd cut off, and so it was commentary about Tony or Sam and stuff, and we'd also listen to tons of unreleased Elliott Smith songs, and he'd be like, 'This is okay,' and 'Turn it off,' or 'I just don't know.'

"He was very much the absent-minded professor," Morgan says. "Not only would he lose lyrics to songs, but master tapes would disappear. He poured out songs. There were so many he would get bored of or forget or misplace. When he was in a creative streak, it'd be like, pow, song." The gift was supplemented with work ethic: "When he first went to LA his neighbors would complain about hearing the same piano part over and over; he'd work really hard and really diligently to finish [the song]." The absent-minded professor/staunch independent combination could be a dangerous one—it's hard to see it as purely coincidence that his bad period took place after he broke with Margaret Mittleman, his manager.

This makes one of the songs Smith wrote late in life seem like a reckoning with this aspect of himself. In "A Distorted Reality Is Now a Necessity to Be Free," the first verse starts with "I'm floating in a black balloon," an efficient way to paint a picture of somebody in a state of unhappy isolation that has as its compensation a sense of freedom. The narrator goes on to assert in the chorus that "I'm sorry that you're chained to the ground," and "no big brother is going to bring me down." Elsewhere in the song he talks about the ways emotional dependencies can be mutually destructive: "You drive people like you drive a car/until you don't know where you are." The guitar that comes in at the end is both triumphant and downbeat, a combination of the guitar in Prince's "Darling Nikki" and George Harrison's darker moments.

Smith had approached this territory before. In "St. Ides Heaven," on the self-titled record, he'd spoken of a moon that "won't come down for anyone." The character he talks about in the verse is someone you'd probably want to come down, given the way he's staying aloft, "high on amphetamines" and walking around late at night drinking. This is the paradox he puts to the listener in both songs: What I'm doing is self-destructive and perhaps beyond my control, but you have no right to think you understand me well enough to intervene in a helpful way.

It's no wonder some kinds of rehab wouldn't work for Smith. When explaining to *Under the Radar* why he went to the Neurotransmitter Restoration Center, he said he tried more conventional programs but couldn't honestly take the first step. If you consider that the first step in Alcoholics Anonymous and other twelve-step programs is acknowledging a higher power than oneself, it becomes easy to understand why Smith would have rejected their help. He didn't like to trade intellectual independence for psychological health. The appeal of the Neurotransmitter Restoration Center must have lain partially in the fact that it advertised an entirely physical cure. You hooked up to an IV; nobody tried to get you to concede a philosophical point. It left him physically feeble and intellectually whole.

Even if the implementation of this outlook in Smith's personal life could be problematic, it did help produce good music. The sound on "A Distorted Reality Is Now a Necessity to Be Free" is almost as important and distinctive as the music. Any trace of the sheen that separated *XO* and *Figure 8* from his earlier albums is gone. Each instrument's tone is robust, gritty, and clear. It's as if a contemporary rock band, having absorbed the influences of the past thirty-five years, traveled back in time to the studio where *Rubber Soul* or *Beatles for Sale* was recorded and used the same sound equipment. Far more than the parts of *Figure 8* that were recorded at Abbey Road Studios, "A Distorted Reality" sounds like something manufactured in the '60s.

Months after Morgan had worked on his album at New Monkey, he spoke to Chiba on the phone and she told him the studio was finally up and running. It seemed conceivable that if Smith wanted to, he could now have the album out in 2003. Of course, as Morgan recalls, Smith at this time in his life was meticulous enough to spend an entire day perfecting a song's drum sound.

Morgan's presence in Smith's life had had a practical function as well as an emotional one. Smith had blown through enough of his touring money that while he never asked Morgan to help pay rent on the studio or chip in for use of the equipment, Morgan did, at Smith's request, pay an electricity bill. Smith could have made money playing out whenever he wanted, but it's hard to imagine someone in such a fragile state hitting the road for a national tour. And he had an album to put out.

Smith told Morgan he wanted the studio to be a place where "good bands" who were "nice people" could come to record for free or at least for cheap. Blake Sennett, a member of the LA rock band Rilo Kiley, was one of those musicians. He was embarking on his first album for his new band, The Elected. In addition to providing his own songs and bands, Sennett provided his own producer: Mike Mogis, the man behind the sound of Saddle Creek Records. Rilo Kiley was on Saddle Creek and benefited from the signature clarity that Mogis bestowed on records by their labelmates The Faint, Cursive, and Bright Eyes. The completion of New Monkey as a functioning studio may well have rested largely on Mogis's shoulders.

There was a violent disruption amidst what looked like gradual progress. On November 25, 2002, Smith and Chiba went to see Beck and The Flaming Lips play at the Universal Amphitheatre, in Universal City, just north of Hollywood. According to *Under the Radar*, security "assaulted and arrested Smith without probable cause." The officer who arrested Smith injured Smith's back, the magazine says, and as a result Smith was forced to start taking pain pills, which worried him and Chiba because of his history of addiction. The officer's report described Smith interfering with the arrest of a violent concertgoer.

McConnell remembers the event like this: Smith saw a cop dealing with some kids outside the Amphitheatre in what he thought was an abusive manner, and after Smith and the officer exchanged words, they started to wrestle. "Elliott put up a great, great fight. This guy was twice his size, you know, this cop. He was really giving him a run for his money. Finally the cop sprayed him with pepper spray and took him down, and they cuffed him." Elliott was still kicking and shouting, McConnell remembers, as they pulled him into a car. "That was the last time I saw him in person. [After that] there were messages, like, 'Hey, I want to finish the album.'"

According to court records from the Beverly Hills County Clerk's office, which handles Universal City cases, Smith, Chiba, and the concertgoer were arrested that night by the LA Sheriff's Department. Each was charged with unlawfully obstructing a peace officer. Smith didn't attend the arraignment on January 27, 2003; a lawyer, Ed Rucker, represented him. Rucker again represented an absent Smith and filed a not-guilty plea on his behalf at a court date on March 4, 2003, in Beverly Hills. After representing Smith at a series of court dates throughout the spring, Rucker was granted disclosure of peace officer personnel records. In the end, Smith came into court on July 3, 2003. He pled no contest to disturbing the peace, as opposed to the original charge of unlawfully obstructing a peace officer. He was asked to perform eighty hours of community service and pay a fine of $150, showing proof of his completed service by January 5, 2004. He remained on his own recognizance—that is, out of jail—throughout the trial process documented in the clerk's records. It looks like an unremarkable plea bargain. Chiba was also represented by a private attorney, and the charge against her was dismissed. The concertgoer, who used a public defender, made the same no-contest plea as Smith to the disturbing-the-peace charge. A probation and sentencing hearing for Smith was set for July 6, 2004. How Smith's sentence might have differed from the service and fine described in the record is unclear.

Meanwhile, rumors swirled around LA that the cops had roughed up teenagers unnecessarily and asked Smith to get out of the way, then arrested him when he refused. On April 26, 2003, six months before Smith's death, www.sweetadeline.net posted news messages that Smith had cancelled shows because he had "suffered a severe injury in November which has progressively gotten worse." He'd gone on with shows "despite chronic pain and subsequent treatment issues," the site explained. "He recently had an adverse reaction to new medication prescribed to him and he is now undergoing different treatment for this injury. At this time he is hesitant to reschedule or schedule any shows until he feels confident that the treatment is healing him and that it will enable him to play shows." He was back to playing shows again by May 3, when he played Austin's Steamboat at a benefit for Gwyn Allen Owens, a local musician and schoolteacher.

The Web site and *Under the Radar* both provided contact information for Rucker and asked witnesses to come forth. That seems like the gesture of folks confident of his innocence.

Smith probably pled no contest because he didn't want to risk going to jail. The incident haunted him in early 2003, even when he was far away from LA in New York for some of the handful of shows he played there in the last year of his life. "I saw him when he was here for that Jon Spencer [Blues Explosion] show," says Clifton. "It was right at the time he didn't know what was going to happen and I think that day or the next day his lawyer had to go into court and represent him, so it was really on his mind, and he was very, very worried about what would happen. But he said they were outside and saw a kid being belligerent or something and saw the cops pushing him around and really attacking this kid when he didn't deserve it, and kind of brutalizing him. And he said that he stood there and purposely watched to witness it, because they wanted to witness it and they planned to report it. The cops noticed that he was doing it and were like, 'What the hell are you doing?' and when he responded they somehow pulled him into it. He said [he and Chiba] ended up getting pepper-sprayed and arrested that night. But when he was talking about it he didn't know what was going to happen and he was very frightened and he was very worried he was going into jail. And he was saying he didn't think he could stand it there, and he was really scared about what could happen to him then, and what he might have to do to protect himself while he was in jail. He was really worried about that. Because he knew that he's not a typical guy to end up in jail and he was worried about the sort of people he'd encounter there, and I think he'd become kind of paranoid about what might happen and was thinking about really awful stuff happening to him if he was put in jail, and he couldn't stand it. So at the time he was saying if he could get through that and win this case then he hoped to leave LA. He was really pissed off at LA at that point. He felt that the cops were criminals and it was an inhumane kind of place. He was really ranting, he was really upset about it, and [Chiba] was trying to reassure him but she was also really scared because she was involved too."

In the meantime, Smith was still moving in a more experimental, instrumental direction with his music than he'd ever gone before. "When I talked to him in February, he was pretty foggy—it was hard to kind of get to stuff," says Swanson. "But he told me about these soundscapes he was making that sounded pretty great. It's that kind of stuff we talked about that seemed so esoteric, but I remember in that conversation it kind of brought focus: There it was, *he* was there. I was talking about doing this project, this installation, and I was trying to build it up and almost understand and then break it down again and build it up again, and he said, 'That's one of the things I'm trying to do with these soundscapes.' I think Elliott was always trying to do a lot of things with his music, and it often would be like, 'That's great, that's what I'm trying to do.' A lot of times I'd be really struggling with something and there wasn't a lot of people I could talk about it with and I would talk about it with him and he would get it exactly. And that was really important."

Ramona Clifton remembers a Smith from that time who seemed both to be surviving and still not fully restored. Smith performed at Maxwell's and at the botched Field Day festival, which was supposed to take place in a field in Long Island but had to switch to Giants Stadium at the last minute because of local resistance. "I didn't talk to him that day because it was a big-stadium crappy show. I saw him at Northsix, the last show, I think—he did four or five shows in the course of five or six days—and I saw him then. At the Maxwell's show we talked some, we went downstairs, and he told me he was doing pretty good, he said he was clean. He was drinking a lot; he was not his perky self. He was still very sweet. Kim Deal was around that night. He had some really good friends there, and then the last night I saw him was the Northsix show. I think that was all in June. He looked really exhausted, and I felt kind of bad. Jen helped get me into that show, and afterwards I said hello to him and there was a bunch of people and I think there was some good old friends he was talking with and he just looked so exhausted, he just looked totally wiped out. That was the last night, and he had spent the whole time in New York playing shows and seeing so many people, and he was just full, it was like, 'I can't talk to a single 'nother person, I'm going back inside, good bye.' I was always sad that that was that. It was kind of a bad note to end on; nothing bad happened, but he just looked so exhausted, and I don't really know how he was doing. When I said, 'Hey, how you doing?' He said, 'Oh, pretty good. Not on narcotics.' But he didn't see the same. There was kind of a distance. Sort of a spark missing or something."

Smith's earlier New York visit had left Dorien Garry irritated with the Blues Explosion and their coterie. Smith's health was so fragile, it seemed wrong that the band should party around him as if they didn't know his history. And their two days of shows turned into an ongoing party, with the Explosion's posse swelling to include Russell Simmons, she remembers. "I hung out with Elliott after the shows but I didn't like what was going on. When he lived in New York he didn't really hang out so much with the New York rocker people. He actually kind of made fun of them when he'd see them at Max Fish and stuff, and then somewhere down the line they became embracing of him, and he of them. But he didn't really seem like himself and he didn't seem like he was necessarily sober. I'm sure that the Blues Explosion people knew more than anybody that he was not always okay. And I sort of think you have a responsibility, morally, toward somebody if you do really care about them. When Elliott came to town it wasn't my idea to go to a bar, it was like, 'Let's go to a movie or go get some food or go get some tea or something, I don't want to sit in a bar and sit with you and be an enabler,' for lack of a better stupid term for it. Everybody was going out to the bar after the show and buying drinks and shot after shot and it was like, 'Fuck them for thinking this was a good idea, you're supposed to be getting your shit together. You've been trying to get your shit together and everybody knows you've been down some rough roads, and fuck the people who live some stupid rock and roll party lifestyle and think that it's okay.' I know that's maybe just what their lives are like but if you really care about somebody then you sort of leave your own shit behind for a couple of days when they're here and have some real fun with them instead of doing shots of whiskey in some shitty bar in the East Village."

But when Smith came to New York that June—the last time he would ever play New York—for Garry it was a quiet, pleasant occasion and he and Garry mostly goofed around, barely drinking at all. He was still intent on moving back to New York, as he'd been consistently the whole last year of his life. "I was like, 'Do you want to live in Manhattan?' And he was like, 'I don't know.' I was like, 'Do you want to live in Brooklyn?' And he was like, 'Oh, I don't know . . . maybe I'll move to Jersey City.'" He and Garry were cracking jokes again—"I was like, 'In that case I'm moving to LA.'"

Morgan kept in touch with Smith via Jennifer Chiba, and he recalls talking to her on the phone shortly before Smith's death. "Aside from the police incident it'd be, 'Oh yeah, the studio's finally in order.' Or right before last October: 'Elliott is so healthy, Elliott is doing so great, he's getting done and he's so healthy.' It leapt out of Jen's voice. So aside from that police incident, it was always like, songs are getting done, studio's in better order, Elliott's healthy, great stuff.

"Two weeks before it happened, that's when she was like, 'Elliott's doing great, he's so happy. We just went and saw Supergrass and that's Elliott's favorite band. We loved them, we left before Radiohead.' I was like, 'You left before Radiohead?' . . . Anyway, it sounded like he was really sticking to rehabilitating himself, just being good to himself. I was so happy he was . . . restored to form. . . . That's why I felt so fine about leaving. I didn't check in that often anymore, and I heard that just two weeks before from Jen: 'Yeah, Elliott's great, his new record's done,' and for me as a fan it was like, 'Oh my god.'"

Chiba had a band, Happy Ending, that had been readying its first release. Smith had invited himself to help produce it, remembers Morgan. "I don't know if he was actually doing it, but was talking like, 'C'mon, let me mix your record.'"

Happy Ending was a distinctly un–Elliott Smith kind of production. Rene Risque, a satirical rock act who shared a bill with Happy Ending at the Derby in Los Angeles, remembers "that Elliott Smith was at the show we played with them, and that they were all squeezed into what appeared to be tiny vinyl go-go dresses."

Sean Worrell, the head of Organart, an English indie label that purported to be working with Happy Ending on their release, later told *The Guardian* that Smith's involvement in the record was creating problems because of his tendency to mix and remix until he was perfectly satisfied, and that a member of the band had stolen the tape reels from Smith. After Smith's death, he said, the record was shelved. He added that the band's Web site had to be taken down because of death threats directed at Chiba.

Two weeks before October 21, Sam Coomes and Janet Weiss toured through Los Angeles as Quasi, accompanied by Marc Swanson. Swanson got Smith's number from Ashley Welch, but never found the time to call him. He never managed to make contact with Smith again.

Garry visited Smith and Chiba three times in LA between the Northsix show and Smith's death on October 21, and found a Smith looking toward the future—and making room for domesticity. Smith wanted to start a family and Chiba did too, Garry recalls. "They definitely wanted to have children. It was something they both talked to me about. In my first year of knowing him, we had this really funny conversation about having kids, because I took care of kids off and on, and he was like, 'If I have a kid it'll be the most important thing ever, and I want to have a kid but it'll be the thing that makes me want to kick my ass into shape more than anything else, ever.' And it was like, 'Well, yeah, you don't have a choice, because when you have a kid it's yours forever,' and I remember we both laughed and were like, 'We can't have kids.' He wanted to have kids and that was something they were both trying to do. I think that was what a lot of the cleaning up and trying to be healthy was about and I know the last time he spoke to me about just quitting smoking it was kind of like, 'I'd rather have a baby knowing that I wasn't smoking while I was having a baby.' That was a big one."

In business matters, Smith was returning to the ethic of early '90ss indie rock. He wanted a label like Dischord or Kill Rock Stars or K to release his record. "He was getting really interested in the mentality and punk and indie and DIY ethics of ten years ago," says Garry. "He wanted to be on a label he could call up and be like, 'hey,' instead of, 'I'll have my manager call this person in this department and see what's going on in my life.' He was becoming really super-obsessed with Built to Spill and Fugazi again, and I know he admired Ian [MacKaye, of Fugazi] and Doug [Martsch, of Built to Spill] like crazy. It was like, 'Wow, this is just so ten years ago. But fucking go for it man.' Those guys know how to do it and they're honest and they're sincere and they're successful in their own hearts. He wanted that thing that guys like that had, which is, 'I'm just going to do this my way and I'm going to do it for me.'" It was a return to the puritanical Smith. The independent-minded, anti-commercial, mildly ascetic code of behavior that Martsch and MacKaye represented was the kind of thing Smith needed—the strict feminist philosophy he'd adopted at Hampshire was also an ethical code. His flight into fame and real money had been accompanied by desperate and self-destructive behavior. The change of attitude didn't save Smith, but he spent his last days in some degree of contentment.

-⊘-

According to the coroner's report, this is what happened on the day of Smith's death: In response to a 911 call placed by Chiba at 12:18 p.m. on October 21, 2003, an ambulance came and found Smith, still alive, lying on the floor with two stab wounds in the chest from a kitchen knife. They took him to the hospital at the University of Southern California, a short drive to the south, near downtown LA, where he died an hour later, despite a successful emergency surgery in which some of the perforations in his heart were mended. The investigation that followed ruled the death an apparent suicide. But the autopsy report left room for the possibility of homicide for three reasons: the absence of hesitation wounds on Smith's body (stabbing suicides typically hurt themselves non-fatally before they deliver the serious wounds, out of uncertainty); the fact that Smith was stabbed through his clothing, also out of keeping with the typical details of a suicide by stabbing; and what the report describes as Chiba's initial refusal to speak to the police. The report mentions no evidence of breaking and entering or participation of a third party. It describes Chiba's testimony that she was in the bathroom at the time of the stabbing and emerged only after hearing a scream to find Smith walking with a knife protruding from his chest. Speaking to the *Los Angeles Times* after Smith's death, Chiba said that during the days leading up to October 21 Smith's general happiness was undercut by "traumatic memories from childhood" as well as "biochemical imbalances . . . due to the gradual discontinuation of psychotropic medications." Her story matches Garry's recollection of Smith's comments about cleaning himself of all dependencies, great and small. Garry remembers Smith and Chiba getting into health food and taking pains to be clean, in the ordinary sense of the word, by taking baths. It's sad to think of the simplicity of the life Smith envisioned for himself after *From a Basement on the Hill*: raising kids somewhere in the New York area, just another liberal creative professional in his thirties, coming back from tour to push a stroller alongside the organic-baby-food shelf at Whole Foods.

There are other feasible reasons Smith might have killed himself besides traumatic memories, if his death was indeed a suicide. "I think he had such conviction about quality and music and art, and I feel he gave up what his gift was," speculates E. V. Day. "And I think he emotionally couldn't face that he was losing it—he couldn't deal with it—and I think he just decided to drown himself. And so the thing is, unfortunately, I always expected he would overdose on something and be kind of passive like that. So the fact that he stabbed himself—it's like he got the final word. He got to say, 'No, I mean it. I am choosing to do this. I really mean it. I really feel this much. I am so broken-hearted in this life, I am so broken hearted.' It's like the artist who's just too sensitive. And that sensitivity can be heroic the way that vulnerability can be strength. He decided to go out like that to prove it. He wore his heart on his sleeve. He's so sensitive no one understands."

Robin Peringer, who befriended Smith in the summer of '94 and started to recognize his greatness watching him compose "Some Song" on tour, became Smith's drummer at shows during the last year of his life. Now he's Chiba's roomate. He remembers hanging out with Smith either one or two days before he died, talking on his porch. Smith talked about marrying Chiba and having children, and expressed a desire to move somewhere less expensive than Los Angeles, where he could buy a nice house. Peringer reminded him this would be expensive. "Why does everything have to be about money?" Smith lamented—they weren't playing as many west coast shows as they would have liked, Peringer says, because club owners were concerned about Smith's history with performances. But Smith, while concerned about what he might have done to his brain with drugs, was still upbeat about releasing a double album's worth of songs, says Peringer, possibly putting out a single album, touring for six months, and then putting out another. He had enough material, Peringer estimates. A couple songs Peringer remembers Smith recording in this last phase of his life were called "Suicide Machine" and "Abused"—those titles aren't listed on the album coming out this fall.

There was a memorial service in Portland, and a tribute concert featuring Beck, Bright Eyes, and Beth Orton at the Henry Fonda Theater in Los Angeles.

Smith's friends have continued to hang out together since his death. Garry had Chiba over for Thanksgiving in Jersey City, continuing a tradition she'd started with Smith seven years before of celebrating the holiday with friends instead of going home to their families. The first Thanksgiving dinner they'd shared, Smith had invited his half-sister Ashley to eat with them and Garry had been touched at how affectionate an older brother he'd been. She upheld the tradition through the years at her place.

"He and Jennifer had been talking about coming out. I'd been in LA about a month before he died and it was like, 'Okay, see you at Thanksgiving.'" Chiba and some of Smith's New York friends came over and Garry found it made her feel better.

There's something deeply Elliott Smith about Thanksgiving with friends. If we assume Smith committed suicide, then the story of Smith's life reveals someone who needed camaraderie, and who lost his way, never to recover his old self, when the artificial warmth of narcotics replaced real friendship. If we assume Smith was murdered, the story, oddly, changes only a little—it would be the story of someone who lost his old friends, picked up bad habits and fell in with the wrong company. Either way, Smith ultimately looks like a brilliant man in dire need of guidance. He needed guidance to pursue his calling, he needed guidance to let the public see his best work, and he needed guidance to survive. Unsure of how to come to terms with a childhood that remained painful and mysterious to him, he needed friends even more than most people do.

EPILOGUE

Even toward the very end, Smith held on to his nervousness about snatching attention from anyone. "His last idea, which is sad," says Swanson, came in 2003: Smith suggested that at a show of Swanson's in 2003, he could "play music from behind a curtain in the gallery, so that no one would know that he was [Elliott Smith]. It was kind of this nonsensical attempt to be like, 'I want to play your show but I don't want to take away from'. . . It's really sweet when I think about it now, but at the time I was like, 'You're going to play behind a curtain?' and he was like, 'Yeah, I think that's a good idea.'"

That reminds me so much of the guy I saw on stage in Portland in 1999 that it breaks my heart. He played as if he *was* behind a curtain, and each member of the audience seemed to indulge the illusion that she was the only soul behind it with him. The picture of Smith behind a curtain also reminds me of the Smith that recorded *Roman Candle* in a Portland basement, alone with his art and with no public to embrace him and tell him what a genius he was.

The Smith I want most to memorialize is the one who played Pete Krebs a tape he'd made in his bedroom on a scaffold in a Portland construction site. It was a Smith who could do heavy physical labor and endure work he hated and finish a collection of astonishing songs with one piece of recording equipment, then play them live before a tiny crowd. Or the Smith that cleared out a portion of the cluttered basement below JJ Gonson's house on Southeast Taylor Street to work over his songs without any intention of releasing them to the public.

By accident, that Smith was eroded, by the coddling and isolation that become a financial necessity in the music business and then, suddenly, by serious drug habits. But while it lasted, that version of Smith epitomized a work ethic, a code not unlike a religion, a relentless self-criticism, a need to get something done, that I perceived in some of the friends of his I interviewed. It would be stupid and elitist to expect every musician to think this way, but it's a good thing a few of them do. I believe some of that discipline might have come back to Smith toward the end, as his studio finally came together and albums started to slide out of it.

Dear friends of Smith's who might have been his staunchest defenders are absent from this book because they don't generally talk to the press about him and they wouldn't make an exception for me. This isn't surprising, because while as a college kid I moped around Portland talking about how influential they were, I never met Portlanders Neil Gust, Joanna Bolme, Janet Weiss, and Sam Coomes. They're the collaborators who knew Smith most intimately for the longest amount of time, and I hope someday they talk to someone in depth about Smith's life. The same applies to Smith's family. If one of those four musicians or any member of Smith's clan decides to talk one day, I bet it'll change the way people look at his story. That would be a palliative to much of the posthumous press about Smith, in which reporters were obliged to use quotes from people who barely knew him and people who wouldn't give their names.

Because I can't talk to Smith's family, I don't know how they handled the curatorial task of figuring out what music should wind up on *From a Basement on the Hill* and tying up whatever loose ends Smith might have left. This book should find its way into the hands of its first readers at the same time as Smith's posthumous album, released by the indie label ANTI- Records, which has put out CDs by Nick Cave and Tom Waits. At the end of this project, the words that ring loudest in my ears belong to David McConnell, who admired Smith's father, Gary, but worried about the task that confronted Smith's loved ones: "Gary and I, I think, saw eye to eye about what should be released. I think what I really appreciate about Gary is that he is—he has enough insight to understand that what Elliott did when he was on drugs was very artistic and very much—it is really strong, artistic music. I think partially because Gary is familiar with the music of the '60s, and he's also just a very smart guy." The risk, McConnnell felt, was that other family members working on the record might want Smith "to be represented in the best light." He compares the task to Van Gogh's family trying to finish a painting: "'Oh, let's make this sky look a little more real. That flower's a little too big, let's clean that flower up a little,' you know what I mean?" It is a re- markable situation: Smith wrote his share of family songs, and then the people he wrote about were forced to try and be objec- tive about his work.

The track list for the record includes both songs Smith worked on with McConnell and at least one song, "Memory Lane," that Andrew Morgan remembers Smith developing in the second half of 2002, as well as one that sounds like the kind of soundscape Swanson and McConnell talked about with Smith. As of my writ- ing this, the list goes "Coast to Coast," "Let's Get Lost," "Pretty (Ugly Before)," "Don't Go Down," "Strung Out Again," "Fond Farewell," "King's Crossing," "Ostriches and Chirping," "Twi- light," "A Passing Feeling," "Last Hour," "Shooting Star," "Memory Lane," "Little One," "A Distorted Reality is Now a Necessity to be Free." The song McConnell recalls Smith saying he wanted to lead the album at the time they were working to- gether, "Shooting Star," comes near the end.

I wouldn't fault Smith's family for any decisions they make in finishing the album. Smith recorded different versions of many songs, and it would be a weird, necessarily speculative task trying to reconstruct his intentions. There's no way the album that's released this fall, mixed by Rob Schnapf and Joanna Bolme, could ever be exactly the one Smith intended to produce. That said, I hope *From a Basement on the Hill* was mixed and cut in the spirit in which Smith approached *Roman Candle* in the basement in Portland. I want listening to the last Elliott Smith album to be as voyeuristic an experience as listening to the first. I want to feel that shock of recognition that comes with listening to a really good Elliott Smith song for the first time.

AFTERWORD

While I was writing this book, I dreamt many nights that a specter of Elliott Smith was floating toward me with hands braced to strangle me or perpetrate some other act of violence the real Elliott Smith would never have considered. His family hovered in a blur behind him. Sometimes he ate part of my head. He always seemed vaguely displeased.

During the day, Elliott Smith was my charge. I was a shrink or a father or a priest. It was my job to find out what ailed him, what sustained him. Once I was asleep, Smith assumed the paternal role, challenging me, threatening to swallow me up. Can you handle this? he seemed to ask. Are you doing right by my name?

The first biography of Smith, this book is carefully researched but fairly modest in scope. I would have liked it to be thicker, to have written it on a more lenient schedule. Looking at the critical response, I'm prone to wonder if some of the harsher assessments have a point: This book contains a lot of detective work, but it amounts to something like a large, well-organized case file, the results of an investigation, not a you-are-there, all-access, blow-by-blow journey through a life. Nobody had printed much about Smith's personal affairs before I wrote this book, and what had been published often reduced Smith to a simple character he felt he was not. This book waves a flashlight methodically through the dark. It doesn't light up every corner of the house.

Part of the reason this book contains so much sleuthing is that an informal rule of secrecy prevailed among many people who knew Elliott Smith. Shortly after the LA coroner's report surfaced on The Smoking Gun, a Web site that publishes official documents that expose the lives of celebrities, *Blender* magazine printed a report on Smith's last days. Smith's family in Portland wasn't crazy about the *Blender* piece—one friend of Smith who consented to be interviewed in it told me he'd received a hurt phone call, and another quoted extensively by the *Blender* writer canceled the interview we'd scheduled, explaining that Smith's family disapproved of the article and that he'd been burned by reporters enough already. In this kind of atmosphere, with word spreading quickly among Smith's friends, interviews were hard to score. The only reason I was able to write this book at all was because the family and friends who kept quiet eventually gave permission to others to speak to me, and for this I'm in their debt. My most important sources made it clear they had checked with others before they spoke with me. A small group of people could have talked amongst themselves and effectively shut this book down without much effort, and despite the awfulness of what they were going through they didn't.

That's why certain critics confuse me. Dear indie rock scholar who writes for a Web site, a weekly newspaper, or the reviews sections in Amazon.com: When did Elliott Smith write you a memo containing a list of his *real* friends? The most frustrating remark about this book (which got reviews all over the spectrum) went something like this: "Nugent failed to gain access to Smith's close friends, cobbling together interviews with obscure acquaintances and old magazine articles."

There were friends of Elliott Smith I would have loved to speak to who wouldn't speak to me. I would have given a limb to speak to his family. But about half the people close to him did talk. Every source in my book was named and described in relation to my subject. Among them were JJ Gonson, his live-in girlfriend at the time he recorded his first record and Heatmiser's manager;

Rob Schnapf, the producer on the majority of his records; Marc Swanson, one of his closest friends from his early twenties on; Dorien Garry, one of his best friends during the last seven years of his life; Shannon Wight, the high school girlfriend who gave him the name Elliott; and another close friend, whom he dated, the artist E. V. Day. Part of the reason some of these friends appealed to Smith as confidants was that they weren't musicians, but certain reviewers assumed that Smith's real inner circle must have been composed of only Neil Gust, Sam Coomes, Joanna Bolme, and Janet Weiss. Though these people were undeniably important to him, he fell out of touch with all of them for extended periods of time. There were other people who knew him well.

It's understandable that people with some tie to the indie rock world could get a skewed impression of Smith's social network through the grapevine: Everybody who knew Smith seems to have a different map of who his real friends were and where they lived. LA people tend to think Smith had good friends in town; a substantial portion of Portland and New York people thinks some of the LA friends were bad news and that the Elliott Smith who lived in LA after the *Figure 8* tour was not the "real Elliott." I spent half a year, full-time, obtaining and weighing different accounts to try to establish who the real Elliott Smith was; I'm baffled when other writers seem to think they've got the problem licked after looking into it for a few weeks or a few days.

Half a year is not four years, and I hope someday somebody does get to write a brick-sized book about Smith—not an easy assignment to get, given that, though Smith is tremendously admired, his records sold hundreds of thousands of copies in the United States, not millions. I hope this book serves as a good starting point.

That said, I made one really stupid mistake writing it. I misinterpreted Elliott Smith's friend Dorien Garry when she told me Russell Simins—the drummer for Jon Spencer Blues Explosion—was hanging out at a gathering with Elliott Smith. I knew JSBX had a drummer named Russell Simins. I knew it seemed weird for the hip-hop impresario Russell Simmons to be hanging out with scruffy New York rocker Siren Festival types. I don't know why it didn't occur to me in time to check with Garry. I like to think it was inconsequential, only four words or so, corrected in subsequent editions. It's embarrassing anyway. Dorien, Russell, and Russell—I'm sorry.

—Ð

I started to think about *Elliott Smith and the Big Nothing* very shortly after Smith died. His death at that point was considered a simple case of suicide. The kind of book I wanted to write seemed relatively simple to execute: a respectful study of a life and career that was about Smith's music more than anything else. When I started it, three months after Smith's death, the economics were on my side: The people who were going to buy the book were Elliott Smith fans, and they, presumably a thoughtful collection of people, wanted reporting about how his music came into the world and analysis of what that music was about. It would be half biography and half rock criticism.

Then the LA coroner's office issued its provocative report opening the possibility that Smith had been murdered, and my position became awkward. My publisher still needed a book that could hit bookstores at either the same time as Smith's posthumous album or the first anniversary of his death. I was determined to make sure it was the former, because pegging the book to the anniversary seemed to suggest the book was concerned chiefly with Smith's horrible end, and I felt people disposed to read a biography of an indie rock musician, most of all Smith's fans, would find this distinctly unattractive. In the end the album was released at the same time as the anniversary, so the story stuck in the press that the anniversary was the guiding principle behind our schedule. More important, the new scenario presented a new quandary: how to write a book that deals in some fashion with the mystery of Smith's death and also deals with his life as a life rather than as a car wreck. I decided to err on the side of exploring Smith's productive hours rather than his demise. Many of the issues that plagued Smith toward the end were of a surprisingly conventional celebrity dysfunction variety. He was a very smart man, but fame messed him up. The issues at play in Smith's music—family, addictive feelings of all kinds—were richer territory.

I'm still not sure if there's a right way to write a book about someone who's recently died young. There's a scene in *Fanny and Alexander* where Alexander, one of the child heroes, is punished by an evil cleric. Cane, castor oil, or cellar? the disciplinarian asks. Writing this book could be a little like that. From the December morning I started to seek out interviews to the afternoon in July when I signed off on page proofs, I anticipated the critical response with dread. Like Alexander, I had the luxury of a choice. I could write a mercilessly investigative book, so that people would call me a sleazehound, or I could leave the darkest, most personal secrets alone, and henceforth be known as an inept reporter. It was unlikely that literary indie rockers, known for their inflammatory writs, were going to give it an easy pass. I knew this because I was one of them, and if I'd have read about an upcoming Elliott Smith biography I might have immediately fired off several pitch letters and hoped for a chance to skewer it.

I was ambivalent about how much testimony regarding Smith's personal secrets I should print, and at the last minute I swept a small mound of dirt from the manuscript. *Spin* promptly published an article about Smith's death containing the details of what everyone said Smith told them about his childhood traumas. Is my book morally superior to the *Spin* piece? Did *Spin* find itself in a whirlwind epistolary romance with a litigation firm? I don't know. But the result is that this is a relatively gentle book, and so far there have been no threatening legal actions. It wasn't gentle enough for the reviewer who found it uncomfortably "invasive," and it was too gentle for the one who stated that I had "no crucial interviews." Several months earlier this latter writer, a friend of a friend, had put me in touch with David McConnell, who broke down in a vivid and careful way the processes by which parts of *Basement* were recorded, pointed out where on the floor of his home studio Smith had nearly killed himself with alcohol and pills, and showed me Smith's prescription bottles. I kept that stuff in.

-Ω-

New information on Smith's death? Though some friends of Smith have professed to some kind of certainty about his fate, I don't believe that they know anything. They haven't submitted any evidence. Generally speaking, those who suspect foul play are concentrated in Portland and New York, and those who are satisfied that Smith killed himself live in Los Angeles (the latter group was quoted extensively in *Spin*'s "exclusive"; the former, presumably more tight-lipped, was not). A year after I turned in this book, nothing about Smith's death is any clearer to me than when I finished it.

There is a police report that came into my hands too late to include in the hardcover printings of this book—a Los Angeles County Sheriff's Office account of what happened between its officers and Elliott Smith outside the Universal Amphitheatre in December 2002. It begins when cops arrest a young man with a Biohazard tattoo on his lower leg who has a ticket for one seat but insists on sitting in another. When they drag him out of the amphitheatre, he starts kicking and screaming. A crowd watches, and out of that crowd walks Elliott Smith. The security officers and county sheriff are on the ground, wrestling with their suspect, when Smith comes up to reprimand them for what he seems to take as police brutality: "That's not right," he says, and when an officer tells him to get back, he argues; the officer repeats the command to no avail. Eventually it becomes a physical struggle and the cops pepper spray Smith, cuff him, and carry him off. Jennifer Chiba, they report, finds them on their way to the police car and tells them he doesn't know what he's doing and she can explain. In the months that follow, the courts dismiss a charge against Chiba of obstruction and resisting a peace officer, but Smith dies while still on trial for allegedly disturbing the peace.

-∅-

In the end, I don't think anyone will care about the tribulations of Smith's last years as much as they'll care about his persistent influence. When I finished this book a year ago, Smith's lingering presence in new records was appreciable but subtle. Now it's more obvious. The first time I heard Joanna Newsom's record, there was an immediate rush of familiarity. In "The Book of Right On," she sings, "Do you want to run with my pack? / Do you want a ride on my back?" What an Elliott Smith couplet. It invites the same ambivalence as a line from "Between the Bars"; both songs can be read as the imagined siren calls of monstrous lovers, invitations to hook up with somebody or something you probably shouldn't hook up with. First I noticed the similarity. Then I thought: God, I wish he could've heard this. I wanted the specter to return, and to give his impressions of the latest Devendra Banhart record.

Readers can judge how close this book gets to its subject. How close *I* got, talking to Smith's friends eye to eye for hours at a time and smoking their cigarettes, loitering in the neighborhoods where he grew up—that's a different matter. I hope I was able to give his fans some piece of my experience and convert a few casual listeners. That hope enables me to persuade myself, as I go to sleep, that I shouldn't be haunted.

INDEX